The Red River Trails

THE RED RIVER TRAILS

Oxcart Routes between
St. Paul and the Selkirk Settlement
1820–1870

Rhoda R. Gilman
Carolyn Gilman
Deborah M. Stultz

MINNESOTA HISTORICAL SOCIETY PRESS

www.mnhs.org/mhspress

Manufactured in the United States of America

10 9 8 7 6 5

♾ The paper used in this publication meets the minimum requirements of the American National Standard for Information Sciences–Permanence for Printed Library Materials, ANSI Z39.48–1984.

Cover and title page photographs: Red River oxcarts at Third and Washington streets in St. Paul, about 1858–59 (James E. Martin); front-cover background: *Map of the Territory of Minnesota Exhibiting the Route of the Expedition to the Red River of the North in the Summer of 1849,* by John Pope (detail)—Minnesota Historical Society collections

International Standard Book Number 0-87351-133-6

Library of Congress Cataloging-in-Publication Data

Gilman, Rhoda R.
    The Red River trails.
    (Publications of the Minnesota Historical Society)
     Bibliography: p.
    Includes index.
    1. Red River Settlement.
    2. Fur trade—Red River Valley (Red River of the North)—History.
    3. Red River Valley (Red River of the North)—History.
    4. Trails—Red River Valley (Red River of the North)—History.
    I. Gilman, Carolyn, 1954– joint author.
    II. Stultz, Deborah M., 1948– joint author.
    III. Title.
    IV. Series: Minnesota Historical Society. Publications.
    F1063.G54   971.27′4′01   78-11045

PREFACE

THE RED RIVER TRAILS have provided one of the most intriguing, colorful, and hotly debated chapters in Minnesota's history. Although scholars have dealt thoroughly with the economic and political implications of the trade that moved over the routes, the rutted paths themselves have always been something of a conundrum. They crossed, for the most part, a level, open, and well-watered country, and they were not confined by geography to fixed — and therefore easily traceable — routes. The trails tended to vary from season to season and year to year according to accessibility, weather, and the cart drivers' personal preferences. And while travelers were occasionally imperiled by Indian attacks, the trails were never the object of fierce and sustained warfare. Although traffic was suspended for a time following the Dakota War of 1862, the hazards of travel between St. Paul and the Red River Settlement at Fort Garry near present-day Winnipeg were never comparable to those encountered on more western routes like the Oregon or Bozeman trails. Little has been written, therefore, about how the Red River cart paths developed and exactly where they went. Perhaps it is for this reason that they have never taken their rightful place in American history and folklore beside the other great trails that contributed to the opening of the West.

Although the trade that had grown up over the Red River trails in the years between 1820 and 1870 was a major factor in the planning and building of railroads through the area, the steel rails followed in few places the old cart routes. Travel and freighting over the trails themselves came to a final close in 1872 with the opening of the Northern Pacific to Moorhead. They continued to be used locally, and in a few places the public right of way was maintained and eventually developed into a country road. But for the most part farmers plowed up the rutted paths (with notable difficulty where years of use had packed them hard), and they were replaced by new roads running along the grid of township and section lines laid down by surveyors.

The surveyors with their notebooks, chains, and transits moved into the Red River Valley before the last dust from the oxcarts had settled. Some of them recorded meticulously where the trails crossed section and township lines; others ignored the meandering tracks. In many cases these were merely identified as "wagon road" or "trail," or the nearest destinations were noted, as, for example, "road from Sauk Centre to Alexandria." Nevertheless, without the fragmentary record contained in the original survey maps and notes, there would be little chance of knowing today even approximately where the Red River trails went.

Another fortunate circumstance was the interest taken in the trails by the Minnesota archaeologist and historian Alfred J. Hill. Trained as an engineer, Hill first became aware of the trails and their importance when he worked for the United States Corps of Topographical Engineers in the 1850s. Throughout his long life as an obscure civil servant and a distinguished amateur historian, Hill devoted himself with exceptional vision to preserving a record of the ancient, undisturbed land surface that was being obliterated by the farmer's plow and the lumberman's ax. His best known achievement was the monumental Northwestern Archaeological Survey, but he also copied and preserved many early maps, talked with men who had traveled the trails, and noted with a geographer's thoroughness many of their landmarks, river crossings, and campsites.

Hill's papers were preserved by the Minnesota Historical Society and furnished the principal basis for later essays on the trails published by Grace Lee Nute, Willoughby M. Babcock, and others. No major study was undertaken, however, until the 1930s when the Historical Society launched a state-wide historic resources survey under the auspices of the Works Progress Administration. This project included tracing the Red River trails and recording their routes on township maps. The WPA based its work for the most part on the original survey maps, but careful examination shows that there must have been many other sources of information also. Much of it was apparently supplied by local people in the counties through which the trails were known to have passed. Unfortunately the project was never really completed. Few records were kept of the research other than the maps themselves, which the present study has shown to be faulty in many instances.

Another wave of interest in the Red River trails accompanied the celebration of Minnesota's statehood centennial in 1958. On this occasion Delmar Hagen of Gatzke in Marshall County re-enacted the long oxcart trek, leaving Pembina, North Dakota, on July 10 and arriving in St. Paul on August 23. His route followed as closely as possible the northern section of the Woods Trail, the link which joined the Middle Trail near Fergus Falls and the stage road (also called sometimes the upper Middle Trail) from there to St. Cloud. In the same year a pamphlet on the history of the oxcart traffic was written by E. Neil Mattson of Warren.

The two decades that have passed since that time have seen further obliteration of the old routes by highway construction — notably the building of Interstate 94, which follows the Middle Trail between Fergus Falls and St. Cloud more closely than any previous major highway. They have also seen, however, increasing public interest in local history and in the marking and preserving of significant sites. At last, in 1975, the Minnesota legislature appropriated $25,000, supplemented in 1977 by another $10,000, to finance research on the state's historic trails.

The task was assigned to the Minnesota Historical Society, and as supervisor of research, I was given responsibility for the project in September, 1975. Burton Cannon, who helped to launch the work as my research assistant, was succeeded in May, 1976, by Deborah Stultz. Other assignments and more urgent deadlines kept me away from the Red River trails for nearly a year while Debbie Stultz assumed responsibility for the long chore of examining the original survey records both in Minnesota and North Dakota and combing the archives of early railroads, the reports of military expeditions, the records of the United States Topographical Engineers, and the papers of early traders and settlers. She also visited nearly all of the counties through which the trails passed, talked with innumerable local historians, studied county manuscripts and maps, climbed through barbed wire fences, and — like her intrepid predecessors on the trails — survived the hazards of sunburn, mosquitoes, wood ticks, and poison ivy.

In July, 1977, Carolyn Gilman joined the project as editor, writer, and map maker, also adding further research in newspaper and manuscript sources. While all three authors contributed to the text throughout the book, the first chapter, which outlines the over-all history and development of the trails, is largely my own work, and the chapters on the individual sections were written mainly by Carolyn Gilman. She also drafted and corrected the maps from which finished art work was done by several artists associated with Guild House, Inc., of Minneapolis. Carolyn subsequently wrote an article, "Perceptions of the Prairies: Cultural Contrasts on the Red River Trails," published in the Fall, 1978, issue of *Minnesota History*.

The chief difficulty in putting the story together was not a lack of information, but the extremely scattered and fragmentary nature of the sources. This is reflected in the length of many of the footnotes. Unwieldy though some of these are, we feel strongly about preserving a complete record of our sources. Not only have we suffered from the failure of some previous researchers to do so, we also know that a part of the task remains to be accomplished. It is our hope that county and local historians will pick up the trails where we by necessity have left off and will trace them in greater detail over the actual ground that they traversed.

Some of these people have long since made a beginning, and their work contributed significantly to our own research. It would be impossible to name all of them, but the following lists those to whom we owe a special debt.

Associates of local and county historical societies include Pat Schwappach, Leslie Randelf Gillund, and Helen Potter, Anoka County; Frank Long and Otto Zeck, Becker County; Mrs. Alberta Anderson, Errol Anderson, and Magdalene Sparrow, Big Stone County; Leota Kellett, Paul Klammer, and Mary Jo Read, Brown County; Mrs. Clarence Ostlie and Roy Wallien, Chippewa County; Frances Miller, Dakota County; William M. Goetzinger, Grant County; Keith Rosengren, Kittson County; Mrs. Charles Buer, Lac qui Parle County; Jan Warner and Raleigh Meyer, Morrison County; Fred E. Wetherill, Nicollet County; Herman Natwick and Lenora Johnson, Norman County; Sharon Hintgen, Otter Tail County; George Walter, East Otter Tail; Bruno Jurchen and Albany Capistran, Polk County; Olive Barsness and Norton Schensted, Pope County; Harry M. Willcox and Sylvester Neudecker, Redwood County; Harold L. Fisher, Royalton; Elaine Anderson, Sherburne County; Peter L. Card, Jr., Staples; Patricia Morreim and Ruth Knevel, Stearns County; Mildred Torgerson, Swift County; Frank A. Delsing, Todd County; Marie Kieserling, Traverse County; Carl W. S. Peltoniemi, Wadena County; Oscar J. Karlgaard, Wilkin County; Zula D. Aakre, Yellow Medicine County.

Assistance provided by other institutions came from Ann Rathke, Larry Remele, Nick G. Franke, and Frank

Vyzralek, State Historical Society of North Dakota, Bismarck; John E. Bye, North Dakota Institute for Regional Studies, North Dakota State University, Fargo; Edward C. Oetting, Orin G. Libby Manuscript Collection, University of North Dakota, Grand Forks; Father Louis Pfaller, OSB, Assumption Abby, Richardton, North Dakota; Elizabeth Blight, Provincial Archives of Manitoba, Winnipeg; Richard J. Jackson, Betty Campbell, Richard F. Pahr, Dave Johnson, and William A. McKenzie, Burlington Northern Inc., St. Paul; and Margaret MacFarlane, Murphy's Landing: A Minnesota Valley Restoration, Shakopee.

Thanks are also due Duane P. Swanson and John M. Wickre of the Society's Division of Archives and Manuscripts; Susan W. Meyer of the Society's map library; Barbara Johnstone, Selkirk, Manitoba; J. H. Sylvestre, Crookston; Lawrence Revier, Ed Zalusky, Horace Agnew, Delmer Urvig, and Mrs. Merton Maus, Mahnomen; Glanville Smith, Cold Spring; M. J. Daly, Perham; Irene Delsing, Osakis; Joseph H. Stoetzel, Carlos; Edwin Johnson, Benson; Carl A. Zapffe, Pete Humphrey, and Catherine Ebert, Brainerd; Frank Svoboda, Olivia; Mrs. Owen Anderson, Echo; Goodwin Roise, Henning; and E. Neil Mattson, Warren. South Dakotans who shared information were Fred Trende, Rosholt; Herman Chilson, Webster; and Oliver Swenumson, Sisseton.

ST. PAUL, MINNESOTA   *Rhoda R. Gilman*
JANUARY 2, 1979

CONTENTS

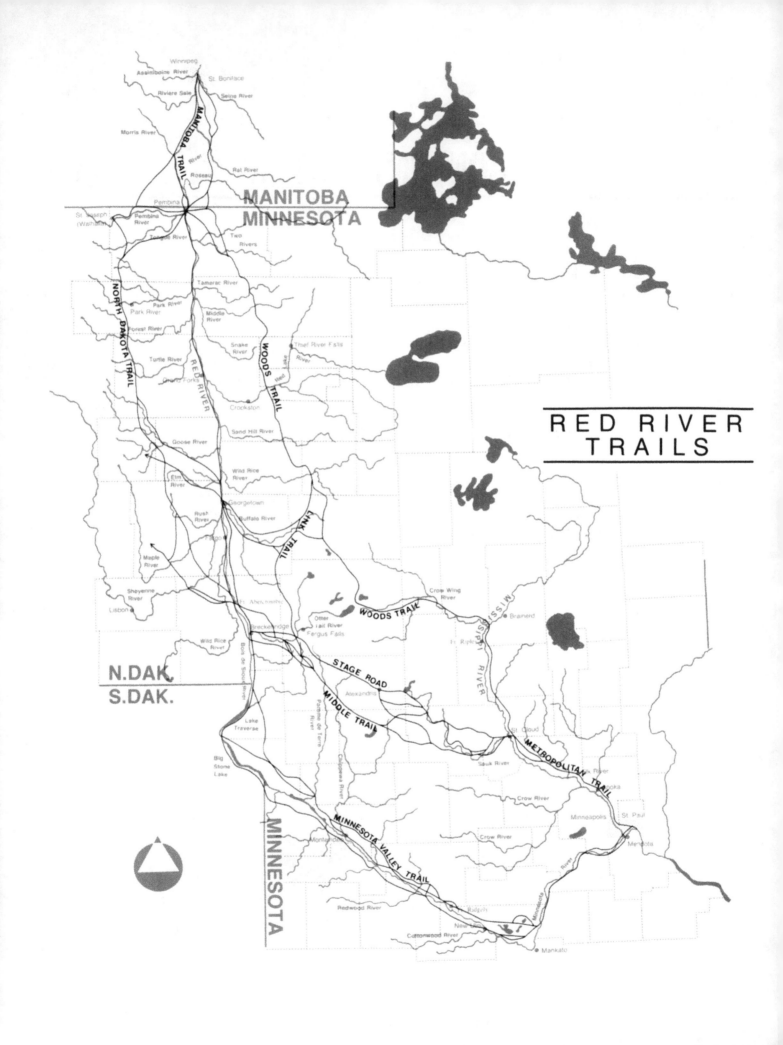

RED RIVER TRAILS

1 ~ THE HISTORY OF THE TRAILS

IN LATE DECEMBER of the year 1817, Thomas Douglas, Fifth Earl of Selkirk, stopped briefly in Baltimore, Maryland, on his way from the Mississippi Valley to Montreal. The Scottish peer was nearing the end of a journey that had taken him from the colony he had founded on the Red River of the North in what is now Manitoba to the eastern United States. He had business to conduct with a suspicious and hostile United States government. From Baltimore on December 22 he addressed a letter to Secretary of State John Quincy Adams pleading that American restrictions be lifted on the passage of trade through the more than 500 miles of unmapped Indian territory he himself had just crossed in what is now the upper Midwest.

"I have had occasion to observe," Lord Selkirk wrote, "the great facilities which nature offers, for a commercial intercourse between the country which I propose to establish, & the American settlements in the Missouri & Illinois Territories; from whence our people might draw their supplies of many articles, by way of the Mississipi, & River St. Peters [*Minnesota River*], with greater facility than from Canada or from Europe. This traffic, tho' it might be of small account at first, would increase with the progress of our Settlements, creating a growing demand for many articles of American produce."[1]

In this prediction, as in many things, the visionary earl was far ahead of other men. The route he had traveled spanned the continental divide between the drainage basins of Hudson Bay and the Gulf of Mexico. After following the Red River of the North from its mouth at Lake Winnipeg to its source in Lake Traverse on what is now the Minnesota-South Dakota border, he had crossed three miles of low, swampy valley to Big Stone Lake, whose outlet was the Minnesota (then called St. Peter's) River, which flowed southeast to the Mississippi. His path skirted the eastern edge of the Great Plains throughout its length. Only a few miles to the east lay the pine forests that still shrouded in mystery the exact source of the Mississippi, and on the west, sometimes out of sight and sometimes dominating the horizon, was a line of grassy hills that marked the first step in the thousand-mile climb to the Rocky Mountains.

The land was flat and open; wood and water along the route were plentiful. Yet before the earl established his colony in the country he called "Assiniboia" scarcely any travelers had followed the route he took. From the east white men bound for the Red River had to cross the length of Lake Superior as well as a difficult chain of portages, rivers, and lakes. From the north the Red connected via various waterways with Hudson Bay. From the south the broad highway of the upper Mississippi led to the Minnesota Valley.

A prairie camping scene with Red River carts

The easy link from the Minnesota to the upper Red River was known only to a few venturesome traders and to the Indian people of the region. For them the area represented a frontier between opposing tribes and cultures — between the Dakota or Sioux of the plains and the Ojibway or Chippewa of the northern forests.

Selkirk's prophecy was nevertheless accurate. In time, various well-established land routes joining the Mississippi and Red rivers would achieve a commercial and political importance comparable to that of the Santa Fe Trail connecting the Mississippi and the Rio Grande. The traffic that creaked over them in wooden carts drawn by oxen did much to build the city of St. Paul, and the economic ties the routes fostered threatened for a brief time to overturn British control of all western Canada. That the oxcart routes known as the Red River trails have been less noticed by history than their southern counterpart is due to a quirk of destiny: American expansion in the south was ultimately successful; in the north it was not.

For early British fur traders no less than for Native Americans, the valleys of the Minnesota and Red rivers were a borderland. After the formation of the Canadian trading monopoly known as the North West Company in the 1780s, independent operators were largely barred from the country reached by way of Lake Superior. This included not only the Canadian northwest, but the rich fur region around the headwaters of the Mississippi. Ruthless competition forced latecomers to the trade and others outside the ranks of the Nor'westers to move southward. The supply point for these independent traders was Michilimackinac at the junction of Lakes Huron and Michigan, and their headquarters in the Indian country from the 1780s to the 1820s was the settlement of Prairie du Chien at the mouth of the Wisconsin River. From there they pushed up the valleys of the Mississippi, Minnesota, and Des Moines rivers and westward to the plains of the upper Missouri.[2]

These traders formed no great combine comparable to the North West Company, but they made a number of short-lived attempts to organize the competition. The dominant figure in these efforts was Robert Dickson, a tall, ruddy Scotsman with flaming hair and a temper to match. He traded with the Dakota Indians of the Minnesota Valley and married the sister of Waneta, a leading chief of the tribal division known as Yanktonai. About 1800 Dickson built a post at Lake Traverse, where he not only traded across the plains to the west, but pressed upon the borders of the North West Company's preserve to the east and north.[3]

The purchase of Louisiana Territory by the United States and the subsequent exclusion of Canadian traders from it, together with the War of 1812, in which Dickson took an active part, ruined his business. In the meantime, however, he had become an agent for Lord Selkirk, who was already known in eastern Canada as a philanthropist and the founder of two colonies in Ontario and on Prince Edward Island for the settlement of Scottish peasants dispossessed of their farms by the rise of large-scale commercial sheep-raising in the Highlands. The earl sought to establish a third agricultural colony in the Red River Valley. To do so he obtained a huge grant of land from the Hudson's Bay Company, in which he owned a controlling interest.

Selkirk's plan for an agricultural settlement on the Red River posed a direct challenge to the wilderness empire of the North West Company — a fact that may have helped engage Dickson's interest. In the summer of 1812 the first small band of farmers arrived at what is now the site of Winnipeg, and for three years the colony clung to survival in hunger and isolation. War raged to the south; the traders of the North West Company surrounded the interlopers with a cold wall of hostility; and the annual contact with Britain by ship through Hudson Bay brought only a trickle of support and a few additional colonists.[4]

In April, 1814, while war continued in the Mississippi Valley, the earl sent a request to Dickson to secure "a parcel of cattle at the Ouisconsin" and have them driven across the plains to the beleaguered colony. Nothing could be done until peace arrived, but in the summer of 1815 a contract was let to a pair of Missouri drovers named Dick Carr and Lewis Musick, who undertook to convey a small herd of cattle up the Des Moines River Valley and down the Red to the Selkirk Settlement. According to tradition, the livestock arrived safely, the two men returning by way of the Mississippi. The fate of the cattle is unknown, for that summer the settlers on the Red River were dispersed and their farms were burned by agents of the North West Company.[5]

By the time news of this setback reached Selkirk, another contingent of settlers was already embarked for Hudson Bay. Selkirk himself set out by way of eastern Canada to re-establish his colony. Leaving Montreal with an armed force in the spring of 1816, he had reached Sault Ste. Marie at the eastern end of Lake Superior when he was informed that a party of the newly arrived colonists had been attacked and

Thomas Douglas, Earl of Selkirk

and the Selkirk Settlement on the Red River. In January, 1817, Joseph Rolette of Prairie du Chien wrote to Selkirk offering to deliver more cattle from Missouri at $100 a head, but apparently his price was too high. A year and a half later Michael Dousman, a competitor of Rolette, contracted to supply 200 head of cattle at a somewhat lower figure.[6]

In the meantime, Selkirk himself had pushed west to the Red River in the summer of 1817. There Dickson joined him, and they traveled south together with a small party of men and carts to the height of land between Lakes Traverse and Big Stone. The international boundary was still uncertain; British and United States treaty commissioners were even then negotiating to arrive at a revision of the impossible line created in the treaty of 1783 on the basis of faulty geography. There seemed to be a strong chance that the boundary might be fixed at this watershed, for Britain had always claimed ownership of the Red River drainage basin. Duncan Graham, acting as agent for the Hudson's Bay Company, had traded with the Dakota on the upper Red River the year before and planned to winter in 1817–18 on the Sheyenne River in present-day North Dakota. Dickson was also prepared now to reopen trade in his old territory, armed with a United States license made out to his half-Dakota son, William, and supplied with goods by merchants at Green Bay in what is now Wisconsin. Dickson suggested to Selkirk an arrangement whereby he would remain an independent trader but obtain his supplies and sell his furs in partnership with the Hudson's Bay Company. The earl was impressed by the trader's knowledge of the country between the Red River and the Mississippi, by his influence with the Dakota, and by the advantages to the colony of open communications with the Mississippi Valley. He agreed to Dickson's plan at once. The Hudson's Bay Company's officers remained cool, however, and their opposition was strengthened the next year when the boundary was proclaimed to be at the 49th parallel, placing Dickson's post as well as the entire upper Red River Valley in United States territory.[7]

Before Selkirk continued the journey that took him ultimately to Baltimore, he and Dickson negotiated with the Dakota for buffalo meat and horses to supply the colony, and after promises had been given, Selkirk went on by canoe down the Minnesota and Mississippi rivers. Dickson spent the winter trading at Big Stone Lake in company with Joseph Renville. In April he left the business in Renville's hands and started for Prairie du Chien, but near the mouth of

massacred by followers of the Nor'westers. Proceeding to Fort William, the fur company's headquarters on the north shore of Lake Superior at Thunder Bay, the earl arrested its leaders and established himself in charge for the winter.

During the months that followed, Selkirk sought diligently to strengthen his ties and those of the Hudson's Bay Company with independent traders in American territory. Like him, they were entrenched rivals of the North West Company; those who had not yet shifted their allegiance to the United States welcomed the chance to ally themselves with the energetic peer and his British firm. Dickson was their leader, and with him or independently came Mississippi Valley traders like Duncan Graham, William Stitt, Joseph Renville, Peter Powell, Amable Grignon, Charles Brisbois, and Henry M. Fisher. Others who remained firmly rooted south of the international border were also keenly interested in developing business contacts with the Hudson's Bay Company the St. Croix River he met a United States Indian agent who arrested him for traveling without a passport and took him to St. Louis. There he was released and allowed to travel to eastern Canada, where he conferred with Selkirk and spent the following winter spinning dreams of an additional settlement in the Red River Valley. Making it a reality involved persuading the Menominee Indians and several other tribes to move there along with more traders from Green Bay and Prairie du Chien. Dickson also envisioned, no doubt, the prospect of increasing trade with the Mississippi Valley.[8]

Fate, however, ruled against these dreams. Grasshopper plagues visited the Red River Valley in 1818 and 1819, destroying the colony's crops and putting an end to immediate hopes for new migration there. Lord Selkirk's health was failing, and his death early in 1820 removed all support for Dickson within the Hudson's Bay Company. Moreover the United States government had been watching the movements of Dickson and Selkirk with interest. The suspicion that their activity cloaked a scheme to continue British control of the fur trade in United States territory added impetus to the urgings of Secretary of War John C. Calhoun that a line of American military posts was needed along the northwestern frontier. Accordingly in 1819 a detachment of the United States Fifth Infantry began construction of a fort at the mouth of the Minnesota River. Protests were also registered against the continuing operation of Hudson's Bay Company traders at the headwaters of the Red River.

In 1818 and again in 1819 Renville and Graham traded near Lake Traverse. Whether from mismanagement or because of stiff competition from American traders who swarmed into the area, the returns were dismal. In 1820 Graham was dropped and management was turned over to a clerk named John Palmer Bourke. The spring of 1820 saw Dickson once more at Prairie du Chien, accompanied by Graham and William Laidlaw, the manager of the Selkirk Colony's experimental farm. Graham and Laidlaw were on a mission to buy grain, for the voracious grasshoppers had left the settlers without enough seed to sow new crops. The men traveled from the Red River Settlement on snowshoes in the hope of returning by planting time.[9]

Loading three Mackinac boats with wheat, oats, a few peas, and some chickens, all purchased from Rolette, they embarked on April 15 and headed back up the Mississippi and Minnesota rivers. Water levels were high in the early spring, and they were able to reach Big Stone Lake by boat. From there they

dragged and floated the craft across the marshy divide to Lake Traverse. It may have been the first and last time that the entire journey was made by boat.[10]

Meanwhile, back at Prairie du Chien both Rolette and Dousman were studying the potential Red River trade with speculative eyes. Dousman's 1819 contract to deliver cattle to the settlement was as yet unfulfilled. A herd collected at Prairie du Chien had perished there during the winter of 1820. Late in 1821 others were driven as far as Lake Traverse, where they were wintered, but once more the losses were great, and the contract remained substantially unmet. Early in 1822 Dousman himself arrived in the Red River Settlement with small supplies of pork, flour, liquor, and tobacco. He sought contracts to furnish more of these items and again promised to make good on the cattle.[11]

Rolette was more successful. Acting purely on speculation, he dispatched a herd to the Red River Colony in the fall of 1821 under the care of a resourceful young employee named Alexis Bailly. Bailly managed to get the animals through, and Rolette's cattle were bought up by the settlers at prices that became a legend. Encouraged, Rolette played with the idea of contracting to send further supplies from the Mississippi Valley. By then, however, he had become an agent for the American Fur Company, and the company's management frowned on the risky traffic. Several more droves of cattle apparently reached the Red River Settlement from Missouri in 1822 and 1823. One of these was sold by Lewis Musick, who had brought the first herd in 1815, and who seems to have followed his old route up the Des Moines Valley. Involved in the same enterprise was a Dickson — probably the trader's son, William.[12]

Robert Dickson himself set the stage for another major development in the traffic between the Mississippi Valley and the Red River. The year 1821 had seen the demise of the North West Company, which was absorbed by the Hudson's Bay Company, its stronger British rival. It was a time of change, disruption, and — for some — new opportunities in the border fur trade. In December of that year several men left the Red River Settlement with cattle driver Bailly when he returned to Prairie du Chien. Among them were Laidlaw, the farmer, and Kenneth McKenzie, a young trader who faced dismissal by the Hudson's Bay Company for unruly conduct. At Lake Traverse the two men conferred with Dickson and Renville, who still operated there as independents in defiance of American authority. The four put together the beginnings of a new trading partnership.[13]

Renville was the only one with any claim to United States citizenship. He had been born on the Mississippi, although he had served with the British forces during the War of 1812. Laidlaw and McKenzie, joined by Dickson and Daniel Lamont, another Canadian, went on to Prairie du Chien, where they persuaded the Indian agent that Renville was loyal to the United States and procured a trading license in his name. The new partners then proceeded to St. Louis, where they acquired additional American associates. Among them was William P. Tilton, who became the formal head of the firm. Dickson, Laidlaw, and McKenzie next went east, perhaps in search of suppliers and investors, but also to clear away the thicket of official hostility. In this they were partially successful, for Dickson persuaded Secretary of War Calhoun of his usefulness in Indian affairs and secured a passport to travel on the upper Mississippi and Minnesota rivers. He had little time to follow up these moves, however, before death claimed him in the summer of 1823. The turbulent but energetic McKenzie assumed leadership of the new enterprise which became known as the Columbia Fur Company.[14]

During the next five years the post at Lake Traverse served as anchor point for the new company, much as it had for Dickson a quarter-century earlier. Sitting astride the height of land, the partners pushed their business north to Devils Lake in present North Dakota and west to the Mandan country, where McKenzie had previously traded for the Hudson's Bay Company. In the Minnesota Valley they gave brisk competition to Rolette and the American Fur Company, and on the James River and the upper Missouri they threatened the interests of the powerful St. Louis firm of Bernard Pratte and Company. Before it was at last absorbed by the expanding empire of American Fur in 1827, the Columbia Fur Company left its mark on the history of the region by developing well-marked trails between the Mississippi and the Red rivers.[15]

The Columbia Fur Company opened four posts in the Minnesota Valley — at the river's mouth near Fort Snelling, at the Little Rapids (now Carver), at Traverse des Sioux (near present-day St. Peter), and at Lac qui Parle. To supplement the undependable water route up the Minnesota River and hasten the movement of its goods and furs, the company introduced two-wheeled wooden carts drawn by horses or oxen. The carts could move easily across the open plains, avoiding the delays caused by shallow water

and rapids on the upper Minnesota. From Lake Traverse and Lac qui Parle the carts regularly traveled as far east as Traverse des Sioux, the lowest point on the river which could be reached without cutting a road through woods. That post therefore became the customary depot and transfer point for goods bound westward and for furs headed down the Mississippi.[16]

Although the company was apparently the first to use such carts in the Minnesota Valley, they had long been a familiar sight on the banks of the lower Red River and on the level grasslands of Manitoba and the Dakotas. The Red River carts were similar to the two-wheeled charettes used throughout French Canada, and their design was undoubtedly carried west either by early French traders or by employees of the North West Company. In the Red River Valley the carts had been adapted to the needs of a region where metal and the skill to shape it were equally scarce. The earliest description of the carts was recorded by Alexander Henry, a North West Company trader stationed at Pembina. In 1801 his men fashioned some small wooden carts with solid wheels sawed from tree trunks. In 1802 he noted that some of them had devised "a new sort of cart which facilitates transportation, hauling home meat, etc. They are about four feet high and perfectly straight; the spokes are perpendicular, without the least bending outward, and only four to each wheel." Later he commented that "This invention is worth four horses to us, as it would require five horses to carry as much on their backs as one will drag in each of those large carts."[17]

Over the years experience and ingenuity produced a number of changes in design, although not in the carts' basic construction of native wood. They were quickly adopted and adapted by a special segment of the Red River people — the métis or mixed-bloods. These restless offspring of more than a century of Indian-white contact in the fur trade of the Red River country formed a population separate from both European settlers and Native Americans. They lived mainly by making annual or semiannual expeditions in search of the herds of buffalo that supplied pemmican for the canoe brigades and the arctic wintering posts of the great fur companies. The entire métis community took part in these hunts. By the 1820s it was not uncommon to see large trains of more than 100 carts returning across the plains piled high with hides and dried meat.[18]

The largest permanent settlement of these people was at the mouth of the Pembina River, approximately on the 49th parallel. Their buffalo hunts customarily took them toward Devils Lake and the Missouri into what was then Dakota Indian territory. Both the Hudson's Bay and the North West companies maintained posts at the métis village of Pembina over the years, but in 1822 the consolidated firm determined to close the operation. This move was hastened by the arrival in 1823 of an American military and scientific expedition under the command of Major Stephen H. Long. Long's observations to determine the exact location of the border placed Pembina just within United States territory.[19]

The métis themselves were little disturbed by this discovery. Long circulated among them a petition which represented to Congress the condition and needs of the community and the status of its inhabitants as American citizens. Some of them signed it, saying they were satisfied with their new situation, but within a few months of Long's departure most of them were preparing to move north into British territory. The relocation had been planned by the Hudson's Bay Company, which offered the métis land at White Horse Plain on the Assiniboine River in what is now Manitoba.[20]

The Long expedition was the first official American venture into the Red River Valley. Its half-dozen "gentlemen" members, escorted by a handful of troops, had been chosen for their broad range of scientific and scholarly talents. They fulfilled the expedition's purpose by supplying the United States public with its first clear glimpse of this far northwestern country. Nevertheless their very presence raised before the Hudson's Bay Company the prospect of American competition along the border. Selkirk's vision of an expanding colony of farmers finding supplies and ultimately markets in the Mississippi Valley had faded with his death, leaving the 150-year-old firm to pursue its original purpose of making profits in fur. The removal of the métis from the temptations of free trade with the Americans was the company's first maneuver in a long, losing battle to raise a wall against the natural flow of commerce to the south.

Long's party traveled most of the way from Fort Snelling (then called Fort St. Anthony) to the Red River Settlement on horseback, closely following the Minnesota and Red rivers. The expedition visited the American Fur Company's post on the western shore of Big Stone Lake as well as the Columbia Fur Company's major establishment on the eastern shore of Lake Traverse. At the latter post Long met 13 families of discouraged Swiss and German settlers from the Selkirk Colony. They had determined to risk the journey in order to reach the gentler climate of the Mississippi Valley and the support of their fellow countrymen in Illinois and Indiana.[21]

They were not the first to make the trek southward. Two years earlier, in 1821, five desperate families had made their way from the colony to Fort Snelling in the company of Bailly or another party of drovers. They had received a humanitarian welcome from the fort's commander, who had allowed them to stay under the protection of the garrison and to build houses and plant gardens on the military reservation. The dangers of the journey were underlined, however, by the experience of David Tully, a stubborn Scottish blacksmith, who in about 1823 started south with his family and met swift death at the hands of a party of outlaw Dakota near present-day Grand Forks, North Dakota.[22]

The emigrants Long encountered were well armed. They had hired several métis guides with carts to haul their belongings on the first leg of the journey. At the height of land they stopped to build boats which they used to finish the trip down the Minnesota by water. They were the vanguard of a steady population movement from the Red River Settlement to the Mississippi Valley that peaked in 1826 but continued well into the 1830s and 1840s.

The initial waves of southward-bound migrants were drawn from the last band of colonists sent by Lord Selkirk in 1821. Recruited in Switzerland, these people were town-dwellers who had agreed to go to the Red River under a false impression of the country and the life that lay ahead of them. The miserable years they spent in the colony were climaxed by a winter of deep snow in 1825–26 and a sudden spring thaw that sent the Red River rampaging over its banks. For 22 days the flood rose, and as they looked out across the gray expanse of water where their hard-won fields and homes had been, the Swiss as a group decided to follow the venturesome handful of their countrymen who had already left.[23]

Nearly 200 started; others joined along the way. By the time the emigrant train reached the border it numbered close to 300 souls, including a few Scottish, Irish, and French-Canadian families. The Hudson's Bay Company, more relieved than sorry to see them go, wished them Godspeed and gave them provisions, an armed escort, a guide, and an interpreter to see them through the Dakota country. Most of them eventually settled near Galena, Illinois.[24]

A trickle of emigration continued in the years that followed. By 1835 the Indian agent at Fort Snelling had counted a total of 489 persons, and he wondered if the British colony would not soon be depopulated. An Irishman named John Corcoran kept a journal of his trip. He traveled with a party that left the forks of the Red and Assiniboine rivers on June 25, 1827. Passing Pembina on July 1, the members of the group spent the next two weeks traveling up the west side of the Red River. Their progress was punctuated by the crossing of such tributaries as the Salt (Forest), the Turtle, the Goose, the Maple, the Sheyenne, and the Wild Rice, as well as the Red River itself a little north of present-day Breckenridge. All river crossings were difficult and some were dangerous. At one of them Corcoran noted: "Made rafts of our carts. Crossed our baggage, women and children all safe with the exception of one box getting wet as some of them were immersed two feet below the surface of the water. Our women got wet also as they were immersed above the hips when crossing on a single cart." The men were not so lucky, for "As we shoved the carts into the water one after the other and mounted them to cross, they upset and whirled around several times, as if set in motion by some machine power." These people were unable to get boats at Lake Traverse and had to continue by cart as far as Lac qui Parle, where trader Joseph Renville had established a permanent post. There, after some debate and haggling, they exchanged the carts for three canoes in which they descended the Minnesota River, arriving at Fort Snelling on August 10.[25]

As the emigrants made their way south a sporadic flow of livestock continued to move north. In 1825 a final herd of cattle reached the Red River Colony. By then the market was nearing saturation, and the prices were disappointing. Three years later drovers from Missouri with a small flock of sheep were attacked and turned back by the Dakota near Big Stone Lake. In 1832 the Red River farmers united in a more serious effort to import sheep. A party of 10 men started south in November, traveling as far as Kentucky, the nearest place where they could buy the needed number of animals. Turning homeward the next spring with a flock of nearly 1,400, they drove the animals across Indiana, Illinois, and Iowa.[26]

Exhaustion and wild spear grass, which proved deadly to the sheep, reduced the flock to about 300. With these and some 30 horses the Canadians headed blindly through southern Minnesota, following a compass needle northward. At last they reached the Minnesota River and crossed at the first good fording place in order to pick up the well-marked trail that linked the fur posts at Traverse des Sioux, Lac qui Parle, and Lake Traverse. The final stage of the trip down the west side of the Red River was made under the protection of several Dakota chiefs who accompanied them to ensure their safety.[27]

By the mid-1830s the situation in the Red River Settlement had begun to change significantly. Despite the drain of migrants to the south, the population had grown. In the spring of 1834 it numbered about 2,600, plus more than 400 métis at White Horse Plain. Additions had come from traders, voyageurs, hunters, and guides thrown out of work following the merger of the Hudson's Bay and North West companies, from retired Hudson's Bay Company employees whose family ties with métis or Indian communities kept them in the country, and from the natural increase of large families among both the Selkirk settlers and the métis.[28]

Overcoming the repeated blows of grasshoppers and floods, agriculture had become well established. The needs of the community had long since been met, but markets for the surplus were lacking. One disgusted Irishman who moved south in 1835 reported that he had seen barley and other crops thrive in the fertile Red River Valley soil, but he could find little reason to plant them because there was no one to buy the harvested grain. Herds of livestock also had increased to the point where finding markets for the excess cattle and horses was a pressing problem. Nor was farming the only source of surplus goods. For most of the newcomers to the settlement, hunting and trapping had long been a way of life. Yet the only legal outlet for hides and furs was the Hudson's Bay Company, whose original royal charter, issued in 1670, had given it a monopoly throughout the lands tributary to Hudson Bay.[29]

The pressure soon created illegal outlets. During the 1820s the American Fur Company had built wintering posts along the border from Grand Portage to Pembina that offered an open invitation to Canadian traders and trappers. To counter this threat, the Hudson's Bay Company had encouraged certain independents to gather furs from the border area, which the firm bought at prices above those generally paid by the Americans. This practice ended in 1833 when the two companies reached a gentleman's agreement. American Fur pulled back from the border east of Pembina in return for a yearly subsidy of 300 pounds from the Hudson's Bay Company. Among those who suffered most from this sudden switch was Andrew McDermot, an Irish trader who had become the Red River Colony's leading independent merchant. He was ably supported by an associate, James Sinclair, the third son of a brilliant mixed-blood family. Sinclair had graduated from the University of Edinburgh and returned to the Red River country determined to succeed outside the ranks of the Hudson's Bay firm. While McDermot and Sinclair vigorously protested the change of policy through official channels, métis adventurers who were less conspicuous and therefore more daring, loaded carts, assembled herds, and headed south to pursue business with the Americans.[30]

In the summer of 1835 a party of traders and emigrants from the Red River arrived at the mouth of the Minnesota with 50 or 60 head of cattle and some two dozen horses. They found a ready buyer in Henry H. Sibley, the new manager of the American Fur Company's Dakota Indian trade, headquartered at Mendota across the river from Fort Snelling. Sibley had been hired following a reorganization of the company in 1834 which had given control of the entire upper Mississippi area to a semi-independent subsidiary known as the Western Outfit. At the head of this

James Sinclair, independent trader

organization was Joseph Rolette, the long-time Prairie du Chien trader. His junior partners were Sibley and Hercules L. Dousman, a son of Rolette's old rival, Michael Dousman. All three men had reason to be keenly aware of the potential of the Red River trade. They were restrained, however, by the agreement between their parent firm and the Hudson's Bay Company.[31]

The British monopoly's control of its fur trade empire was tightened in 1836 when the heirs of Lord Selkirk reconveyed to the company the land which had been granted for the colony. The government of the settlement was reorganized, and Hudson's Bay officials immediately asserted their increased authority by imposing a stiff tariff on all imported goods. Thus the so-called free traders whose carts and herds had begun to raise dust in the rutted tracks along the Minnesota River became outright smugglers.[32]

Smuggling was easy and profitable in the absence of British troops on the Red River, for the people's sympathies lay with the free traders, and the Hudson's Bay Company had no organized law-enforcement agency. Moreover the markets and the population on the American end of the route were rapidly increasing. Treaties signed in 1837 with the Dakota, Ojibway, and Winnebago tribes opened all land east of the Mississippi to white settlement. One of the first results was the enforced evacuation of "squatters" from the military reservation at Fort Snelling. The small community of *de facto* settlers — including a number of emigrant families from the Red River that had clustered under the protection of the fort's walls — moved down the Mississippi to take up land claims on the east bank at the first convenient steamboat landing below the fort. The settlement, soon known as "St. Paul's," immediately began to replace Mendota as the commercial center of the area, for the older trading station was still in Indian country where licensing was required and government regulation was ever-present.

The Red River free traders responded to the changes with increasing boldness. In June, 1839, James Sinclair himself arrived at Fort Snelling with a train of 40 or 50 carts. Probably in the early 1840s some of the Canadians began to avoid the long detour down the Minnesota River by striking out across country from the headwaters of the Red directly to the upper Mississippi. They followed a line of small lakes eastward to the valley of the Sauk River, crossing the Mississippi near present-day St. Cloud and turning south along the eastern bank to St. Paul. Although the distance was substantially shorter, this may not have been the only consideration in laying out the new route. The Yanktonai and Wahpeton Dakota living near Lake Traverse had always looked with suspicion on the traffic that passed with or without permission through their lands. Over the years several displays of open hostility had occurred in defiance of the leaders of these bands, who generally tried to prevent violence. In the spring of 1838, however, an altercation at the American Fur Company's Lake Traverse post resulted in the death of one employee and the serious wounding of another. Sibley retaliated by immediately closing the post and calling a halt to all trading activity beyond Lac qui Parle. Thus the assistance and implicit protection the Lake Traverse post had offered to travelers since the days of Robert Dickson no longer existed.[33]

The new trail held its own hazards. It skirted the very edge of the wooded country that for half a century had been the buffer zone between Dakota and Ojibway, and it ran just south of the boundary that had been accepted by the rival tribes at a treaty council held in 1825. For more than a decade relatively peaceful relations had prevailed along this line, but the late 1830s saw a gradual escalation of hostility that climaxed in 1839 in two pitched battles. European traders were theoretically uninvolved, but the Red River métis became unwilling parties to the struggle. Nearly all of them had family ties to the Ojibway or the closely related Cree. Moreover their yearly slaughter of buffalo had begun to alarm the plains Dakota, whose way of life depended on the herds.

An incident connected with one of the métis buffalo hunts in 1844 sparked serious trouble that led to the opening of yet another trail. In a case of mistaken identity, the métis attacked some young Dakota hunters whom they took for marauding Pawnee from the Missouri River. Several of the Dakota were killed before the error was discovered. Although the métis apologized and offered to make restitution, the wary and skeptical Dakota sought revenge. A brigade of Red River carts, which had traveled south on the Minnesota Valley Trail a few days earlier, was preparing to return when news of the affair reached St. Paul. At the same time fur traders and missionaries on the upper Minnesota warned that the Dakota were patrolling both trails and had already plundered a luckless party of Missouri drovers headed for Fort Snelling. After one false start and some hesitation the Red River traders decided to try a route that would take them back through Ojibway territory for the entire distance.[34]

One of these men was Peter Garrioch, a young Scottish-Cree mixed-blood. A sometime schoolteacher, fur trader, and theology student, Garrioch had made the trip between the Red River and the Mississippi at least four times and was well on his way to becoming one of the colony's most aggressive free traders. In 1844 he was in charge of goods and carts belonging to Sinclair, who was a relative by marriage. Also a member of the party was McDermot's nephew, John McLaughlin. Garrioch's diary offers a graphic picture of how the track that came to be known as the Woods Trail was hacked through the Minnesota forests in the bleak months of October and November.[35]

The party followed the east bank of the Mississippi north to an American Fur Company post on the Crow Wing River where they hoped to hire a guide. After waiting for several days, they concluded that no guide was to be had. Since the season was growing late, the men decided to push on "at all hazzards." Although the trader at Crow Wing was unable to provide either guide or provisions, he did lend them canoes to ferry their goods across the Mississippi. The empty carts were easily floated over, and after another delay while members of the party searched for strayed horses, they headed up the north bank of the Crow Wing River.[36]

On October 1 Garrioch recorded "A deal of cut-[t]ing and cleaving through brush and lying timber." The next day he noted that the work of trail breaking was "almost intolerable." Two of the party set out to find an easier path, but "every account they give of the face of the country before us, would be enough to dishearten any person not accustomed to crosses and difficulties." After 14 days of what Garrioch grimly described as "hard fighting," they had traveled only some 60 miles and found their provisions running dangerously low. Providentially, they encountered "a man of the Chipeways" who agreed to guide them as far as Otter Tail Lake. He further earned the $12 they paid him by hunting along the way to furnish them with game.[37]

When they arrived at Otter Tail Lake a week later, Garrioch's men were alarmed to find there a large camp of the Ojibway band known as Pillagers. Although the reputation of these people matched their name, they proved not only friendly but also eager to help and protect the travelers. Restocked with provisions and furnished with another guide, the party turned northward in better spirits. After 12 more days of struggle through brush and timber, Garrioch at last reported, "Unspeakably cheering to our almost wasted courage and patience, the vast and beautiful prairies we had longed fore [*sic*] burst suddenly upon our occulars this evening." By then, however, it was mid-November. The "vast and beautiful prairies" were soon swept by howling storms and deep snow, while the rivers ran with ice. Before reaching Pembina the men left several animals dead from hunger and exhaustion, burned the sides of their carts for fuel, and would probably have starved had they not encountered another group of Indians who shared their precious food supplies.[38]

Like Garrioch's party, other travelers on the Woods Trail over the years received timely aid from the Ojibway. Not all members of the tribe were overjoyed, however, at the free and easy crossing of their land by the traders. They pointed out that no permission had ever been asked for cutting a road. In 1846 a Hudson's Bay clerk on company business encountered two Ojibway hunters who sought to exchange a few furs for some ammunition and a drink. When he refused, explaining that he was not allowed to do business in American territory, they complained that the increasing traffic over the trail was frightening off the game and threatened to levy a toll on all traders.[39]

Norman W. Kittson in middle age

The 1840s saw further important changes in the organization of the upper Mississippi fur trade. When the American Fur Company failed in 1842, the Western Outfit was transferred to Pierre Chouteau, Jr., and Company of St. Louis. At the same time the aging Rolette was forced to turn over control of the outfit to his partners; he died shortly thereafter. Thus Dousman and Sibley, released from American Fur's pact with the Hudson's Bay Company, were free to expand the business.[40]

They moved quickly to do so. In July, 1843, Sibley signed a contract with Norman Wolfred Kittson, a Canadian-born scion of the fur trade who was to manage the business in the upper Minnesota Valley and on the plains to the west and north. The plan called for posts on the James and Sheyenne rivers as well as a new post at Big Stone Lake to replace the old one at Lake Traverse that had been abandoned five years earlier. It was hoped that these posts would produce a large supply of buffalo robes for which there was a booming market, but more ambitious goals were also unveiled. Probably in the fall of 1843 and perhaps again in the spring of 1844 Kittson traveled to the Red River Settlement, where he conferred with Sinclair and McDermot. He proposed to build an American post at Pembina, evidently hoping that Sinclair would manage it.[41]

The latter's relations with the Hudson's Bay Company had been under increasing strain for several years. Sinclair and McDermot had been among a few favored independent merchants who were allowed to import goods from Britain on the annual Hudson's Bay Company ships; they had also enjoyed the privilege of shipping tallow, which was one of the Red River community's only salable exports. The partners collected it from both métis and settlers and sent it north with the brigade of boats they dispatched annually to bring their imported goods from Hudson Bay. After repeated threats, both of these privileges were canceled in 1844 on the grounds that they produced inconvenience and loss to the company. A more important reason, no doubt, was the clandestine trade that Sinclair and his partner were carrying on over the trails to the south.[42]

The outbreak of hostilities between the Dakota and métis in the summer of 1844 seriously hampered Kittson. The Dakota objected to his carrying goods through their country to trade with the métis. He was unable to stock his new post as he wished; reports that he had been killed circulated in the Red River Settlement; and he was so late in arriving at Pembina that Sinclair had given up and made other plans for the next year. Nevertheless, the post was completed in time to welcome Garrioch's exhausted trail breakers as they came in on the heels of yet another snowstorm. Ever since news of their departure from

Crow Wing two months before had reached Pembina, their arrival had been anxiously awaited.[43]

Despite a lean first season, Kittson remained confident. He found that many Ojibway as well as métis frequented Pembina, that they were eager to hunt, and that the country abounded in muskrats — a staple of the upper Mississippi fur trade. To the west the wooded Turtle Mountain area yielded a variety of other pelts. To the east the Roseau River Valley and Lake of the Woods were prime country for mink, weasel, fisher, and marten. By the fall of 1845 Kittson was able to contract with Sinclair and McDermot "for all the furs which they may collect during the winter at a very fair price, delivered at this place." The "very fair price," which was to be paid in cash, was nearly 25 per cent over that of the Hudson's Bay Company, terms that Kittson estimated he would need between

Henry H. Sibley, seated, and Joseph Rolette, Jr., in about 1856

$2,000 and $2,500 to meet. He was also laying plans for a new post at Reed (Roseau) Lake to be managed by Joseph Rolette, Jr., the 25-year-old son of Sibley's former partner.[44]

Young Rolette, who had accompanied Kittson north in 1844, represented a continuation of the ties that had bound Prairie du Chien to the Red River Valley from the first years of the Selkirk Colony. Rolette's maternal grandfather, Henry M. Fisher, had been among the traders who migrated north from Prairie du Chien following the War of 1812. The elder Fisher died in 1827, but his son, also named Henry, continued as a trader for the Hudson's Bay Company. Another relative was young Rolette's cousin, Charles Brisbois, who had gone with the Fishers to the Red River Valley in 1815.[45]

Henry Fisher had visited Prairie du Chien in September, 1843, probably for a reunion with his recently widowed sister, Jane Rolette, who would soon become the wife of Hercules Dousman. At that time there had apparently been some talk of associating Fisher with the new Pembina venture proposed by Dousman, Sibley, and Kittson. In the end Fisher decided to stay with the Hudson's Bay Company. Nevertheless, Kittson probably felt a sense of betrayal as well as astonishment when early in the spring of 1846 he found Fisher not only building a post a short distance from his but also displaying an American fur-trading license. The betrayal was not on Fisher's part alone, for Ramsay Crooks, who continued as president of what remained of the American Fur Company, had long enjoyed a cordial relationship with Sir George Simpson, governor of the Hudson's Bay Company. Crooks still had potent political connections. He used them to co-operate with Simpson in securing the license for Fisher, who could claim American citizenship by virtue of his birth at Prairie du Chien.[46]

Determined and indignant, Kittson immediately sent a dispatch by dogsled to inform Sibley that the license was fraudulent and the post was being openly operated by the Hudson's Bay Company. He demanded help from the government officials at Fort Snelling or — lacking that — authority to drive Fisher out of the country himself. Neither was forthcoming. Nevertheless, the new post was short-lived. The boldest of many ploys adopted by the northern Goliath to crush Kittson's upstart competition, Fisher's post apparently failed to divert much trade from the American.[47]

His competition was unquestionably beginning to sting the British firm. "Eight thousand dollars will not make up the difference in their trade by means of our small opposition," Kittson told Sibley gleefully in 1846, "but this is not the worst. We have created quite a censation [sic] in our favor in their Colony, which is working strongly against them, and by a little exertion on our part, we must drive them into terms before long."[48] He was overly optimistic, but he had put his finger on the key issue. The Hudson's Bay Company could handle Kittson's competition — or learn to live with it. The real threat was from the people in its colony.

To restless Red River citizens, Kittson's very presence on the border opened vistas to the south. Supplying an enterprise as extensive as his called for a more organized system of transportation across the plains. Furs and hides collected through the winter and spring must reach the Mississippi in time for the steamboat season in order to be shipped to St. Louis and ultimately New York or New Orleans, for they were a perishable product, subject to damage from worms and rot. In return, a variety of manufactured goods, ammunition, food supplies, liquor, and tobacco must be ready and waiting for the overland haul back to Pembina. Hiring a crew of métis drivers and their carts, Kittson assembled a large brigade each spring. It would usually leave in late May or early June, and if the seasons were favorable, a month's steady travel would bring the carts to the rendezvous at Traverse des Sioux. There, if Sibley had done his part, a year's supply of trade goods would be waiting, along with the boats needed to carry the pelts the last 50 miles down the Minnesota River to Mendota. The water link spared the carts the most miserable stretch of the entire trail; it also kept Kittson's crew from dispersing for a spree in the whisky shops of St. Paul. The trader and his clerks might accompany the boats to Mendota, but his men occupied themselves at Traverse des Sioux preparing for the return trip.[49]

From Pembina the brigades followed the western plains trail most often traveled by both emigrants and traders up the North Dakota side of the Red River Valley. It generally kept to high ground about 20 miles from the river until it reached the upper end of the valley. There the path swung eastward to cross the upper Red or lower Bois de Sioux rivers at one of several commonly used fords. Having reached the eastern side, the brigades creaked southward across the prairie to Lac qui Parle and then followed the north bank of the Minnesota River until they reached the cutoff to Traverse des Sioux. Their route was dictated by various business considerations. For one thing, until 1847 Kittson continued — at least nomi-

nally — to supervise posts on the Sheyenne and James rivers, at Big Stone Lake, and at Lac qui Parle. In the earlier years carts loaded at these places sometimes joined the Pembina brigade on its way to Traverse des Sioux. For another, until 1854 Kittson was associated with Sibley and Chouteau, both of whom had extensive land holdings in prospective townsites at Mendota and Traverse des Sioux to which they were interested in maintaining traffic.

As the years went by, improvements in the trail generally consisted only of deeper ruts and a bewildering network of bypasses to avoid the worst sloughs and mudholes, although Kittson bridged a few of the river crossings from time to time. Offering security to smaller parties, his brigades were often accompanied by a variety of independent traders, drovers, and other travelers. But because some Canadians preferred shorter routes than that via Traverse des Sioux, travel also continued to grow over what came to be known in time as the Middle or Sauk River Trail and the Woods or Crow Wing Trail. Kittson also used the Middle Trail for some of his carts, especially during a cycle of wet weather and widespread flooding from 1849 to 1851. For winter trips, generally made on snowshoes or by dogsled, he used the Woods Trail or various Indian routes that went by way of Red, Cass, and Leech lakes.

Kittson was invariably accommodating about carrying mail. Even in winter he sent an occasional "express" by dogsled to the Mississippi settlements. Anyone in the Red River Colony whose need for communication with the outside world could not wait for the annual company ship through Hudson Bay used Kittson's services. This included the Hudson's Bay Company itself from time to time, for whatever form the competition might take in the frozen woods and plains along the border, the company's management maintained cordial relations with Sibley and made full use of his banking connections in St. Louis and New York.[50]

The closing years of the 1840s saw the final effort of the Hudson's Bay Company to block the economic tide flowing southward. Early in 1846 a meeting and widespread discussion among the free traders and métis produced a petition to the British queen complaining about the governing of the settlement but especially about the commercial monopoly that the company was trying to enforce. The petitioners pointed out that the firm's charter, which was nearly 180 years old, had been intended to protect it from competition by other British merchants. Noting that they were native-born citizens of the country, they

Dog train from Fort Garry with St. Paul's Summit Avenue in the background, about 1859

maintained that the company had no just power to prevent them from trading their own furs and other products to the Americans or anyone else. Sinclair carried the petition to London, where it soon became lost in the ponderous machinery of parliamentary politics.[51]

The company's management, led by the canny Simpson, had other ideas. He had been busy persuading the crown to send British troops to the Red River Colony on the grounds that the Oregon boundary dispute had increased tensions between the United States and Britain, and that the former had stationed a detachment of cavalry near Devils Lake in 1845. This small unit had been sent merely as a response to the hostilities between the métis and the Dakota, but Simpson hinted darkly at American plans to fortify the border at Pembina and take over the colony. His lobbying effort was so successful that some 350 British regulars arrived via Hudson Bay in August, 1846. Whether the company had the legal and moral right to forbid the wholesale smuggling of furs was no longer important. It now had the power to do so.[52]

Almost at once free trade ceased. Small-scale smuggling continued along the border, and no real effort was made to stop it. Sinclair and McDermot, however, bowed to necessity and withdrew from the fur business. McDermot, in retirement, was restored to the favor of the company's management. The urbane but adventurous Sinclair, who had done as much as any single man to establish commerce on the Red

River trails, remained independent. In 1854 he guided a train of emigrants which included his own family across the Canadian Rockies to Oregon. There he met death two years later from a Klikitat tribesman's bullet.[53]

Kittson prepared to tighten his belt, but he soon found that the decline in his profits from furs was partly balanced by the presence of the troops, which brought an unaccustomed flow of hard British cash into the tiny colony. Because they increased the demands for imported groceries and manufactured goods in general, Kittson soon found himself doing a brisk business in everything from champagne to sheet-iron stoves. Many of the free traders also continued to import general merchandise over the trails from the Mississippi.[54]

The Hudson's Bay Company, too, found the trails unexpectedly convenient. When word arrived that the troops were being sent, the company's supply ships had already sailed from Britain. It was necessary, therefore, to send buyers to St. Louis in the summer of 1846 to procure additional stores of sugar, tea, and other provisions. The mission was entrusted to Robert Clouston, a young clerk, and John P. Bourke, a veteran company employee. They chose to follow the Woods Trail to St. Paul, where Bourke became so seriously ill that he was forced to remain under the care of the surgeon at Fort Snelling while Clouston went on to St. Louis alone. On his return journey up the Mississippi, he found that low water was preventing steamboats from going above the mouth of the St. Croix. Moreover a deadly flu epidemic in the Red River Valley had slowed the departure of the promised train of carts which was to meet him in St. Paul. In this crisis Clouston appealed to Sibley, who offered to store the goods in his own warehouse at Mendota if necessary. Ultimately, however, the carts arrived and Clouston was able to complete his mission.[55]

The troops remained in the colony for two years while Kittson continued to prosper. Traffic over the Red River trails had never been heavier. St. Paul had grown from a steamboat landing, a log chapel, and a collection of whisky shops into a thriving river town and the capital of Minnesota Territory, established in 1849. The area now had a base of local government from which its political leaders could push effectively for greater control over the land and for stimulation of the Red River trade on which much of its commerce depended. On the border a growing community of métis was migrating back to Pembina from Canada. They found the American settlement convenient for both trade and buffalo hunting, but the main attraction was a mission church established there in 1848 by the Reverend Georges-Antoine Belcourt. The priest had been an articulate spokesman for the free traders and the métis in the Red River Colony until pressure from the Hudson's Bay Company had caused the Catholic church to withdraw him. His unexpected reappearance at Pembina signaled a new core of resistance to company authority as well as redoubled demands for free trade.[56]

Goaded to desperate action by the awakening forces he saw across the border as well as by the unrest in the colony, the chief factor of the Hudson's Bay Company in the Red River District had four métis smugglers arrested in May, 1849. His purpose was to set an example by convicting them in an open court trial. The attempt backfired. Angry métis surrounded the courthouse, making it clear to all that no conviction could be enforced. The first man charged, William Sayer, admitted his guilt. The jury agreed with him but recommended no penalty; the other cases were dismissed. An example had indeed been set, but it had demonstrated the company's impotence, not its authority. The métis crowd broke up with jubilant shouts of *"Le commerce est libre!"* And so it was.[57]

The decade of the 1850s saw transportation and commerce over the Red River trails come into their own. After the Sayer trial, the Hudson's Bay Company made no further attempt to stop free trade in the settlement. By 1856 St. Paul accounted for nearly half the value of all goods imported to the Red River. Year by year the brigades lengthened until trains of 200 or 300 carts, mostly driven for hire by their métis builders, were not uncommon. In 1857 a total of some 500 arrived in St. Paul. The estimated value of furs and skins shipped through the city that year was $183,000, of which about four-fifths came from the Red River region. Other items of freight often brought from the Red River country were pemmican, dried buffalo meat, moccasins, and skin garments fashioned by skilled Indian hands and worked with beads or porcupine quills. On their return north the brigades hauled a varied supply of general merchandise — staple groceries, tobacco, liquor, dry goods, clothing of all kinds, tools, hardware, guns, ammunition, farm implements, and even window glass.[58]

The cart trains were a distinctive sight that caught the eye and the pen of many a mid-century traveler. One writer recalled riding ahead of a train so that he could "look back at the line extending far over the plain, the spare cattle following, and horses galloping about with very Cossack-looking prickers after them, and the train winding its way, like a great snake, coming along very slowly, and then, when it got near enough, to hear the carts which, at a distance, sounded not unmusically, and then the lowing of the cattle, and the songs and voices of the men, until they at last got too near, and then it was bedlam again."[59]

On close inspection the convoy lost some of its picturesqueness and became colorful, comical, deafening, and at times brutal. The dress of the métis drivers was notable mainly for its variety, the only common elements being the brightly colored sashes and beaded moccasins. One might see a French capote, or hooded coat, constructed of blue homemade cloth studded with brass buttons and looking like "a frock coat with large skirts." Checked or plaid flannel shirts and woolen or buckskin trousers might be offset by fancy beaded shoulder belts from which were suspended a powder horn or a shot pouch. On their heads could be found a variety of gear, from a small blue "Scotch cap" to a broad-brimmed hat with a brightly colored band. "They seem such wild-looking fellows, but all blessed with splendid powers of conversation," a traveler observed. In the "polyglot jabber" of the camp he heard "fine broad Scotch," a scattering of Gaelic and Irish brogue, and a plentiful mixture of "rapidly uttered French *patois* that would drive a Parisian mad." A European ear probably had greater difficulty distinguishing the ever-present tones of Ojibway and Cree.[60]

Like the buffalo hunt, the trek to St. Paul was a

family affair among the métis. Women and children accompanied the train, many of the former driving their own carts. Jane Grey Swisshelm, St. Cloud's observant feminist newspaper editor, remarked that "The carts of the women are painted; and have a cover with other appearances of greater attention to comfort than is displayed in the carts appropriated to the men."[61]

The Red River cart looked like "a ramshackle, squeaky affair" to anyone unacquainted with its peculiar virtues. As one observer noted, "Each cart . . . waggles its own individual waggle, graceless and shaky, on the uneven ground." But to the experienced traveler it was "a marvel of mechanism." Designed for the wide variety of travel conditions it was sure to encounter, the cart was easy to draw through bogs, buoyant at river fords, strong on rock-strewn hills, and hard to upset in stumpy forests. The body was made of tough, well-seasoned oak. Although the particulars of construction varied with each cartmaker, most builders started with two squared twelve-foot poles. Six feet of their lengths served as the shafts for harnessing the ox, while the other six feet supported the frame of the cart. Crosspieces were firmly mortised into the shafts to underlay the floor, and upright rails were fitted into holes. Front, side, and tailboards to hold the load completed the cart's body.[62]

The five-foot-high wheels were the most unusual feature. To lend stability to the vehicle, they were dished outward so radically that it looked as if the outer rims were "about to part company with the spokes and hub." The three-to-five-inch-wide wooden tire was made from several pieces of bent oak fitted loosely together, so that the spaces between them served as expansion joints to take up the shock when the wheel struck a rock or stump. Though many an observer must have wondered whether "the fellow who made these joints had been quite himself when he completed this wooden monstrosity," the looseness of construction saved many a wheel from shattering. After the wheels, the oak or poplar axle was the most important part of the cart, for it bore the weight of the heavy load. Carefully trimmed and adjusted to prevent friction, the axle was lashed to the cart with dampened strips of buffalo hide which shrank as they dried, holding the axle firmly. As many as five or six axles might be replaced in a single cart during the course of a trip to St. Paul. When one broke, another was simply cut from a nearby tree.

The Red River cart was not only sturdy, it was also versatile. At night the buffalo-hide or canvas cover could be thrown over the cart, making a compact tent for the driver, who had no need to carry tent poles or pins. When the convoy reached a river too deep to ford, the carts could be easily converted into makeshift boats. One method was to place in a row several detached wheels, concave side up, lashing them together at the points where they touched. Four pieces of wood were then tied to the outer rims, forming a rectangular framework. Waterproof buffalo hides, sewed together with thread made from buffalo sinews, were lashed to the frame. This skin boat "floated like a duck" with a load of up to 800 pounds.

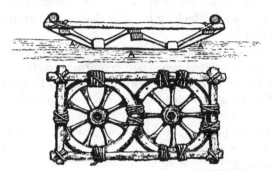

Front and top views of a Red River cart-wheel scow

In other cases, the cart itself was used as a raft, with the wheels stowed under the box and the canvas or skin cart cover tied around it to protect the goods. Even when a stream could be forded, there was always the danger of upsetting the cart on the steep banks. In such cases a line was tied to the middle of the axle and wrapped around a convenient tree so ox and cart could be let down the slope gradually. On the opposite side the same system led them up the bank. If the cart did turn over, it was easily righted again. Broken pieces of cart or harness were mended with *shaganappi*, a rope made from buffalo hide cut into strips a half-inch to an inch wide, or *babiche*, a twine cut from deerskin.[63]

Either an ox or a horse could be harnessed to the cart, depending on the requirements of the journey. In addition to having more strength, an ox was better than a horse in a marsh, for its cloven hoof would spread, giving it a firmer foothold in the mud. A horse, besides moving along faster with a moderate load, was better on a rocky trail or steep bank, where its unshod hooves and natural agility came into play. The oxen used were a small, dark-colored breed of uncertain origin. The horses were Indian ponies with "short barrels, sturdy legs, long manes, and tails which touched their fetlocks." They "disdained oats," never having eaten anything but prairie grass. After

American stagecoach and freighting companies began to ship goods over the trails in the late 1850s, mules were also used.[64]

Large convoys were divided into brigades of from four to ten carts, and each animal was tied by a strap to the cart ahead of it. This made it possible for one driver to handle several carts by goading or whipping the lead animal. With oxen the straps often rubbed the flesh at the base of the horns until their heads were covered with blood, but this never stopped the drivers from keeping a steady pace of 18 to 20 miles a day. "Many and mighty were the whacks they dealt the poor brutes whenever they were tempted off the track by a juicy-looking bit of herbage," reported one traveler.[65]

Packing the 800 to 1,000 pounds of freight the Red River cart carried was a job requiring practice. The load had to be evenly distributed and easy to unpack, while the accessories needed on the trip had to be stowed where they would be readily accessible. The ax, used for cutting firewood and new axles, was hung by leather straps on the sideboards of the cart. The driver's gun was strapped to the side rails, pointing into the air at a 45-degree angle to avoid accidents, since it was kept loaded and ready to be snatched up in an instant. Kettles, nested inside one another, were hung from the bottom of the axle. Other indispensable equipment included a long-handled frying pan, an auger, a square, needles, knives, extra *shaganappi*, buffalo robes, and clothes in waterproof bags. Special problems in packing were no doubt entailed by some of the more unusual items freighted over the trails. For example, in 1849 a piano that had come by ship from Britain was sent south to the Mississippi, following its owner to Oregon, and in 1858 the machinery for a textile mill was hauled by cart to the Red River Colony. By the late 1850s reapers, mowers, and other new-fangled, horse-powered farm machinery were also being dismantled for shipment.[66]

Riding in a Red River cart presented its own set of hazards. There was only one way for a person to do so without "being pitched onto the pony, having his right or left ribs cracked against the side rail, or turning a somersault over the tailboard of the cart." It was necessary for the passenger to be "seated in front on its floor, with your legs hanging down near the horse's tail. If you are luxurious, tie a broad piece of shaganappi from rail to rail to support your back, put an extra folded blanket under you, sway your body slightly with [the horse's] jog-trot, and you need not envy the occupants of a coach and four."[67]

The squeak of the Red River cart became prover-

bial. The "hellish" sound of the ungreased wooden wheel rubbing against the wooden axle could allegedly be heard three miles away; when it drew near, one sensitive soul maintained, the noise "makes your blood run cold." Some travelers whose nerves were not as steady as those of their fellows reduced the racket by scraping the grease from their frying pans — or, in one case, fat from a luckless skunk they killed — onto the axle. But such efforts seem to have been the exception. When a brigade of carts moved together on the road to St. Paul, "the noise was deafening — a continual creak, squeak, groan, and moan, from a hundred and twenty pairs of wooden wheels innocent of grease." A St. Anthony woman remembered the passing of the oxcart trains vividly: "One morning I was at church. . . . The minister had just given out the text when the squeaking of the Red River carts was faintly heard. He hastily said, 'To be discoursed on next Sunday,' for nothing but this noise could be heard when they were passing."[68]

The great cart trains of the 1850s established no new trails; the routes they followed were those laid out in earlier years, although several interconnecting links came into more common use. In 1854, when Sibley retired from the fur trade, Kittson dropped the Minnesota Valley route, and thereafter nearly all Red River traffic shifted to the Middle and Woods trails. The Middle Trail, being by far the easier of the two, was the most traveled. It became the one generally meant when "the Red River Trail" was referred to. Because in later years it was no longer the middle of three trails, it was also called the Plains Trail in contrast to the Woods Trail. In 1856 promoters of towns in the lower Minnesota Valley tried to divert some of the traffic away from St. Paul by opening a trail from Henderson to the Bois de Sioux River by way of Glencoe, Hutchinson, and Cedar Island Lake. Apparently it was used by one or two small trains the following summer but seldom again.[69]

The Middle Trail proper extended from the Mississippi at St. Cloud or Sauk Rapids to the Otter Tail River. From there several alternatives were possible for the traveler headed northward. He could keep to the south of the Otter Tail and cross the Bois de Sioux above the junction of these two streams, or he could ford the Otter Tail and cross the Red a few miles downstream at Graham's Point. Two routes then led north: one followed closely along the riverbank on the west side; the other path swung inland, keeping to the firm, gravelly ridges formed by the beach lines of ancient Lake Agassiz, which filled the Red River Valley in early postglacial times.

THE HISTORY OF THE TRAILS 17

From the western end of the Middle Trail it was also possible to stay on the east side of the Red River by taking a connecting route to the northeast after crossing the Otter Tail and picking up the northern extension of the Woods Trail some distance beyond present-day Detroit Lakes. Like its counterpart on the west side, this route followed the beach ridges, which, according to one traveler, were "almost as good as a turnpike road" and "as smooth and as dry as the sidewalks of Broadway."[70] A stage and wagon road, developed in later years, followed the east bank of the Red River as far north as the settlement of Georgetown at the mouth of the Buffalo River. Beyond that, however, travel by cart close to the Red was difficult.

Confusion about the locations of river crossings and trails has sometimes been caused by the varying names applied to the Red River and its tributaries. Early Canadian traders, following the customs of their Cree and Ojibway guides, considered Red Lake to be the source of the Red River. Hence when they spoke of the upper Red River they usually meant the Red Lake River. The present-day Red above Grand Forks was often called the Sioux River. Travelers approaching from the south, however, saw the source of the northward-flowing Red as either Lake Traverse or Otter Tail Lake. Therefore many early Minnesota writers referred to the Otter Tail River as the Red, reserving the name Sioux (or Bois de Sioux) for the comparatively small stream that drains Lake Traverse. Today, of course, the Red River proper begins at the junction of these two streams.[71]

A characteristic of all the Red River trails was their tendency to hug geographic landmarks. Because snow, fog, or rain could render the road suddenly invisible, travelers could not risk grand strides across the featureless plains. Wood and water, as one traveler put it, were the "fundamental data of life. By them we lived, and moved, and had our being."[72] A camp without these two elements was a camp without supper or breakfast, so travel consisted of leaps between places where they could be found. These considerations account for the fact that the trails clung to river valleys wherever possible, despite the difficulties created by marshes and woodlands. It was no accident that the three great routes through Minnesota were known for the rivers they followed — the Minnesota, the Sauk, and the Crow Wing. Nor was it an accident that all of them followed paths long used by Indian people.

Minnesota's politicians, of whom Sibley was the acknowledged leader throughout most of the 1850s, did

their utmost to promote the Red River trade and to assert the presence of American government and civil authority on the Canadian border. The first result of their efforts was a military expedition in the summer of 1849 to survey the Red River Valley and recommend a site for a fort there. Led by Major Samuel Woods, commandant of Fort Snelling, and accompanied by Captain John Pope of the Corps of Topographical Engineers, the detachment traveled via the Middle Trail to the upper Red River, then crossed to the west bank and followed Kittson's trail to Pembina. After talking with Kittson and with Father Belcourt and noting the vast distances and emptiness of the country, the officers suggested that not one, but two forts were necessary. They recommended locations at Pembina and on the upper Red River at Graham's Point. Woods and Pope disagreed, however, as to which should be built first. As a result, seven years passed before another expedition under Colonel Charles F. Smith was sent to select a site for the fort later erected near Graham's Point. Not until 1857 did construction begin on what became Fort Abercrombie. Also fruitless for the time being was an 1849 recommendation by Alexander Ramsey, governor of Minnesota Territory, that the trails should be improved. More successful was an effort to get a post office at Pembina in 1850, a move which further strengthened the dependence of the Red River settlers upon the United States. In 1851 an American customs officer was also stationed at the border.[73]

The same year saw an unsuccessful effort to buy the Red River Valley from its Indian owners. In September, immediately after concluding treaties with the Dakota for the purchase of southern Minnesota, Ramsey and a large official party traveled to Pembina to parley with the Red Lake and Pembina bands of Ojibway. An agreement was extracted from the reluctant tribesmen, after which Ramsey visited the Red River Colony and the Hudson's Bay Company headquarters at Lower Fort Garry. Minnesotans were disappointed, however, in their hope of opening the Pembina area to white settlement, for Congress refused to ratify the treaty. Probably the keenest regret was felt by Norman Kittson, who had exerted all his influence over his customers to bring about the successful negotiations and who stood to collect about $30,000 for alleged debts owed him by the Ojibway.[74]

Kittson's disappointment was no doubt cushioned by his continuing prosperity in the border trade. In 1852 he moved his main post from Pembina to St. Joseph, some 30 miles to the west, to avoid the recurring Red River floods which had inundated his buildings each spring for several years. At Pembina he left the junior Rolette, who invested some money in the business and graduated from the rank of clerk to the status of semi-independent trader. The same year saw both men elected to the Minnesota territorial legislature, Kittson taking a seat in the council (senate) and Rolette in the house. It was the first of several terms for both. They made the long winter journey by dog-sled to attend the sessions in St. Paul. Together their influence was greater than might have been expected, and they played significant roles in Sibley's political fortunes. Kittson was devoted to his chief, while Rolette, like Sibley, was "a Douglas Democrat to the spinal column." No one knew the exact size of their constituency, but one fact about it was clear: it contained few opposition votes.[75]

A quiet, shrewd man, affable and somewhat dapper, Kittson was not the stuff of which legends are made. His only notable weakness was a passion for fast horses. He carefully hedged his risks in the fur trade with real estate investments in St. Paul. When Sibley withdrew from the trade in 1854, Kittson formed a partnership with William H. Forbes, another of Sibley's former clerks, and took over the St. Paul end of the business — the purchase and forwarding of goods and the collecting and selling of furs. In 1855 he moved to the city, leaving to Rolette the management of his trading posts and the title "King of the Border."[76]

"Jolly Joe" continued to wear this crown with characteristic flamboyance throughout his life — and the life of the Red River trails. Rolette was a boon to eastern journalists in search of colorful western characters. He never neglected to cultivate the legend of himself. On occasion he wore Indian finery, was known to give impromptu demonstrations of Ojibway songs and dances, and identified himself firmly with the métis community. In fact, however, his heritage was almost entirely French and British, his only traceable Indian ancestor being an Ottawa great-great-great-grandmother. He had been educated in eastern private academies under the watchful eye of American Fur Company president Ramsay Crooks, and his appreciation of territorial and national issues far exceeded that of the ordinary backwoodsman. Among his genuine contributions to Minnesota politics was his firm opposition, along with that of other traders and métis legislators, to a law that would have required the bonding of all the territory's free Black residents. In this he violated party lines and won the grudging respect of Republicans.[77]

Far better known was a caper in which he absconded with a bill that would have moved the capital from St. Paul to the new Minnesota Valley town of St. Peter. This prank sprang not only from personal loyalties (probably to Kittson among others) but also from Rolette's inveterate love of outrageous practical jokes and the attention they drew. Equally well known were his generosity, his improvidence, and his backwoods habit of trusting a neighbor with anything he owned. He drank lustily but also abstained for long periods. Probably the best description of him was penned by Manton Marble, a correspondent for the *New York Evening Post*, who traveled over the Red River trails to Pembina in 1859.

"Short, muscular, a bullety head, the neck and chest of a young buffalo bull, small hands and feet . . . full bearded, cap, shirt, natty neckerchief, belt, trowsers, and dandy little moccasins — so he looks to the eye," wrote Marble. "Inside of all this there is a man of character . . . who asserts himself always, whatever the right or wrong of the assertion. Of unfailing good spirits, brimful of humor, . . . sticking to his belief in a breezy, healthy way, and believing first and always in Joe Rolette."[78]

With his superb horses and his crack team of sled dogs, heralded by jingling harness bells and hearty shouts, Rolette was touted as the master of the Red River trails.[79] Those who knew the country, however, turned elsewhere for a protector and guide. The man they chose most often was Pierre Bottineau. If the trails had a master, it was this dark, six-foot métis with piercing eyes and hawklike face.

Born in the Red River Settlement, Bottineau was the son of an Ojibway mother and a French voyageur father. For more than 30 years he traveled the rivers and marshes, the beach ridges and coteaux bordering his native valley as well as the plains stretching westward. He guided emigrants in the 1830s, traders in the 1840s, and land speculators in the 1850s. Garrioch's party tried unsuccessfully to engage him for its trail-breaking trip in 1844; he accompanied Ramsey to Pembina in 1851; he led railroad survey teams across the northern plains in 1853 and 1869; he guided gold seekers bound for the Fraser River in what is now British Columbia in 1859; he shepherded a wagon train of emigrants from Minnesota to Montana in 1862; and he accompanied Sibley's military expedition against the warring Dakota in 1863.[80]

Bottineau himself left no memoirs of his many brushes with death from charging buffalo, Dakota bullets, and blizzards roaring out of Saskatchewan. Others who remembered, however, included the young trader Martin McLeod.[81] In March, 1837, the 20-

Pierre Bottineau in the 1850s

year-old Bottineau was hired by McLeod and two other inexperienced Canadians who were impatient to leave the Red River Settlement and make their way back to civilization. Using a dog team, they started south over the still-frozen plains. In the vicinity of North Dakota's Wild Rice River a sudden spring blizzard overtook them. Bottineau became separated from his companions in the fury of the storm, but he succeeded in finding shelter and lighting a fire.

McLeod recalled how "I found myself at the bottom of a ravine more than 20 ft deep from which I had to use the greatest exertion to save myself from being suffocated by the snow which was drifting down upon me. Upon gaining the edge of the ravine (which I effected with the greatest difficulty having my snow shoes still on, as my hands were too cold to untie the strings of them which were frozen) I found the poor faithful dogs with their traineau buried in a snow bank." Too cold to light a fire, McLeod burrowed into the snow, where he spent the night with the dogs, rubbing his feet to keep them from freezing. His buffalo robes and the dogs' warmth saved him to be rescued the next morning by Bottineau.

The third member of the party was never found, and the fourth was so badly frozen that he could not travel. Leaving him in a hastily thrown up shelter with provisions, firewood, and blankets, Bottineau

and McLeod set out for the American Fur Company station at Lake Traverse. Two days later they reached the post, Bottineau using blows from his rifle butt to keep the exhausted and freezing McLeod on his feet. Supplied with horses, a cart, and another man, the guide immediately returned for the injured companion left behind but found only a corpse.

McLeod, who recorded the grim tale in his diary, changed his mind about returning to Montreal, took employment in the fur business, and eventually became one of Sibley's most trusted traders. Bottineau soon moved with his family to Fort Snelling. Within a few years he took up a valuable claim along the Mississippi in the village of St. Anthony. In the late 1870s, after travel over the trails had ceased and the city of Minneapolis had engulfed his land, he went back to the Red River Valley, where he promoted a successful colony of French-Canadian settlers near the Red Lake River.

Rivaling Bottineau as a frontiersman and guide was James McKay, who was known to the English and French in the Red River Settlement as "Jeemie," and to the Dakota of the plains as "Jimichi." Born in Saskatchewan of Indian, French, and Scottish descent, McKay became a legend among the Red River people, who admired his strength and skill. In later years his command of Indian languages, his even-

James McKay about 1870

handed diplomacy, and his ties to all the elements in the divided community of early Manitoba led to a distinguished political career. He served at various times as speaker of the legislative council, president of the executive council, and minister of agriculture for the new province.[82]

Educated in the Red River Settlement, McKay entered the service of the Hudson's Bay Company at an early age. In the 1850s, when Sir George Simpson began to make almost annual treks over the trails to the Mississippi, McKay was entrusted with the task of accommodating the governor's notorious taste for speedy travel. With relays of horses pulling a light carriage, the plainsman whisked Simpson across Minnesota at a pace that set records: "Jeemie McKay was proud of the fact that, always on the tenth day of their start from Crow Wing at the stroke of noon from the Fort Garry bell, he landed Sir George at the steps of the Chief Factor's House."[83]

A man of enormous bulk and catlike grace, McKay was equally at home lifting a Red River cart out of the mire, ferrying Sir George across a stream on his shoulders, or treading a measure in a ballroom. "Immensely broadchested and muscular, though not tall, he weighed eighteen stone; yet in spite of his stoutness he was exceedingly hardy and active and a wonderful horseman," observed a fellow traveler. His face, "somewhat Assyrian in type," was handsome, with "aquiline nose; piercing dark grey eyes; long dark-brown hair, beard, and moustaches." The same writer, who had never before met a wearer of moccasins, was amused to watch this "grand and massive man" pace the corridors of his St. Paul hotel noiselessly, "while excitable little Yankees in shiny boots creaked and stamped about like so many busy steam-engines."[84]

McKay's polish and gallantry captivated the daughters of James Sinclair, who made the trip over the Woods Trail in 1850 on their way home from a boarding school in Illinois. The Sinclair party encountered him at the crossing of the Red Lake River, where the cart in which 18-year-old Harriet and 15-year-old Maria were riding became stuck in midstream. McKay dashed into the water, ignoring his fine broadcloth trousers and beaded moccasins. Unhitching the pony, he got between the shafts himself, heaved with his powerful shoulders, and personally pulled them across.[85]

The Sinclairs were probably the only young women to make the long trek by cart in search of education. The journey was not an unusual one, however, for sons of the Red River Colony. One such traveler was the 13-year-old son of a métis miller named Louis Riel. Riel's young namesake set out in June, 1858, accompanied by two other youths and the mother superior of the Grey Nuns, who served as teachers in the little community of St. Boniface. The three promising boys had been chosen by the bishop of the settlement to attend college in distant Quebec. A month's travel by cart took them to St. Paul and their first glimpse of city streets and steamboats. Ten years later young Louis returned over much the same route, successful in his education, but deeply embittered by the racial and religious prejudices he had encountered in eastern Canada.[86]

Although by the mid-1850s there had been no fundamental change in the mode of transportation over the Red River trails, their economic advantages over the cumbersome northern route through Lake Winnipeg and the Nelson or Hayes rivers to the arctic waters of Hudson Bay increased year by year. The reason lay in the next step of the journey, for the 19th-century revolution in transportation was fast engulfing the Mississippi Valley. In 1847 Hercules Dousman told his brother-in-law, Henry Fisher, "There are now four steamboats running constantly to St. Peters [Mendota] and the trip from Red River is done in so short a time to that place that you can give us a visit in very little time and without as much trouble as formerly." Six years later the Prairie du Chien merchant and financier, still urging Fisher to visit, observed that "we now see People from Red River almost every week."[87] In 1852 scheduled packet service on the Mississippi had begun, and by 1857 the shipping season saw over 1,000 arrivals at the St. Paul levee. Travelers could also continue by steamboat above the Falls of St. Anthony as far as Sauk Rapids on the upper Mississippi, where weekly service began in 1851. The first railroad reached the Mississippi at Rock Island in 1854, closely followed by other lines extending to Galena, Prairie du Chien, and La Crosse. Thus it was possible to ship goods between Europe and St. Paul at a fraction of the former time and expense.

No one was more keenly aware of these developments than Sir George Simpson of the Hudson's Bay Company. Although for practical purposes the monopoly conferred by its charter no longer existed, the company had succeeded for a few years in outdistancing the pack of free traders that snapped at its heels. Nevertheless, the number of competitors was steadily increasing, and they were penetrating ever more deeply into the rich northern fur regions far from the border. As the cost of imported American goods decreased relative to those shipped by the company from England, it became clear that a change would have to be made.[88]

Simpson once again turned to his old friend Ramsay Crooks, who agreed to become the New York agent for the Hudson's Bay Company. In the closing months of 1857 Crooks negotiated with the United States Treasury Department an arrangement by which the company's goods sealed and bonded, could be transported through the country duty-free. A trial shipment, sent to St. Paul in the summer of 1858, was carried north by a brigade of carts under the efficient direction of James McKay. The results were so satisfactory that Simpson at once began to make more permanent arrangements that would allow the company virtually to abandon its Hudson Bay route.[89]

This purely commercial decision coincided with several other events that compounded its impact on Minnesota. In August, 1857, a committee of the British House of Commons released a lengthy report recommending that the territories hitherto governed by the Hudson's Bay Company be annexed to Canada and opened to settlement. The announcement created more excitement in St. Paul than it did in Canada, for Minnesotans concluded with frontier optimism that the transfer was virtually an accomplished fact and that emigration to the Red River country would soon be pouring northward over the trails. Their wishful thinking was no doubt helped along by dire need, for in that year Minnesota, as well as the rest of the country, was prostrated by the financial panic and depression of 1857.[90]

Still more sensational news reached St. Paul the following summer. Gold had been discovered on the Fraser River. Immediately St. Paul outfitters and businessmen envisioned a rush of prospectors to the Pacific slope of western Canada. Promoters pointed to the course of the Red River connecting through Lake Winnipeg with the Saskatchewan, which provided — at least on the map — an all-water route to the foothills of the Rockies. Several meetings, dubbed the "Fraser River Convention," were held in St. Paul during 1858, and the enthusiasm they generated snowballed into two locally sponsored schemes for giving destiny a shove.[91]

One of these was an expedition to demonstrate the feasibility of a St. Paul-Saskatchewan route to the Fraser River gold fields. Hastily put together with limited planning and unlimited confidence, it left St. Paul in June, 1859, and got as far as Pembina before breaking up. A handful of its members, striking out on

their own, eventually reached the Columbia River and were lucky enough to arrive safely at Fort Walla Walla in Washington Territory. The others, among whom were several publicists and newspapermen, returned to St. Paul.[92]

The second and more substantial undertaking was the beginning of steamboat service on the Red River. This effort was initially funded by the St. Paul Chamber of Commerce, which offered $2,000 to anyone who would launch the first boat. The bonus was collected by Anson Northup, who owned a tiny steamer he had bought for use on the Mississippi between Little Falls and present-day Grand Rapids. Early in 1859, while the streams and bogs along the

The "Anson Northup," first steamboat on the Red River

trails were still frozen, he dismantled the craft, cut timber for a new hull, and, assembling 34 teams and a crew of some 60 men, hauled everything from Crow Wing to the upper Red River. There, working at top speed, they put together a steamboat that was best described as "a lumbering old pine-basket." Northup named it for himself and set out for Fort Garry. After a gala welcome in the Red River Settlement and an excursion on Lake Winnipeg, the "Anson Northup" returned upriver, where its captain moored it under the protection of United States troops who were engaged in building long-delayed Fort Abercrombie near Graham's Point.[93]

While Northup was at work on his vessel, Governor Simpson made a hurried stop in St. Paul. There he found that in the course of the winter several small firms had merged to form the Minnesota Stage Company. Under the leadership of two brothers, James C. and Henry C. Burbank, it was preparing to commence stagecoach and freight service to the upper Red River. The line would presumably connect with the new steamboat. Simpson studied the situation, but he decided to cling to using his company's own cart trains. Under the system he set up, Hudson's Bay northbound goods would go by steamboat on the Mississippi as far as St. Cloud, by cart across to the firm's new depot on the upper Red River opposite the mouth of the Sheyenne, and thence by bateau to Fort Garry.[94]

Early in June, 1859, a party of road builders employed by the Burbanks' company left St. Cloud. Their purpose was to improve for stage travel a rudimentary road that had been put through the year before as far as Fort Abercrombie. Within three weeks some 160 miles of it had been made passable for stages. The first coach loaded with passengers followed on the heels of the road crew. At Alexandria it met Captain Northup on his way back to St. Paul to collect payment from the Chamber of Commerce. At Fort Abercrombie the stage party found Northup's steamboat tied to the bank and deserted. While the disappointed but resourceful managers of the stage line were building a bateau to float their passengers the rest of the way to the Red River Settlement, they were visited by none other than Governor Simpson, on his way east again via St. Paul. Sir George admired the steamboat, shook his head over Northup's abrupt departure, and suggested glibly that the stage company should buy and operate the boat. Then he departed at his usual whirlwind pace.[95]

Once in St. Paul, Simpson lost no time in proposing to the Burbanks an undercover arrangement by which the Hudson's Bay and Minnesota Stage companies would unite in buying and operating the "Anson Northup." The participation of the British firm was to remain secret, and other customers would also be served by the steamboat — but at higher rates. The Burbanks, who desperately needed the steamboat connection to make their new stage line pay, agreed at once. Thus the Minnesota Stage Company acquired the craft, rechristened it the "Pioneer," and ran it between the Red River Settlement and the Hudson's Bay Company's new establishment opposite the mouth of the Sheyenne. This place, at first called Sheyenne, was soon rechristened, appropriately enough, Georgetown in honor of the governor.[96]

Once again in 1859 the comparative speed and economy of the St. Paul route proved its value to the Hudson's Bay Company. During the following winter Simpson took the further step of contracting with the Burbanks to handle the firm's overland freight. The fur company advanced money for additional improvements in the stage road. The next year saw its shipments carried from the Mississippi to the Red River in heavy, canvas-covered freight wagons instead of creaking Red River carts. The carts and the trails continued to be used, however, by many of the company's competitors.[97]

In 1860 a rival steamboatman tried to take one of his craft up the Minnesota River and over the height of land to Lake Traverse. After the boat stuck fast about eight miles below Big Stone Lake, he gave up the effort. The Burbanks promptly bought the abandoned steamboat, dismantled it, and hauled the machinery overland to Georgetown during the winter. There a new hull was built, and the "International" was launched in the fall of 1861. The timing was fortunate, for during the next winter the "Pioneer" sank and could not be raised.[98]

As the decade of the 1860s opened, Minnesota seemed poised on the threshold of unprecedented commercial expansion. Statehood had been achieved in 1858. The Hudson's Bay Company was under contract to ship 250 tons of merchandise annually through St. Paul. Minnesota had become the acknowledged gateway to the Canadian northwest, and expectations remained high for the early opening of that area to immigration and settlement. Although business was still suffering from the effects of depression, claim shanties continued to spring up like mushrooms in the valleys of the Minnesota and Sauk rivers. Townsites along the stage road to the Red River were sorting themselves into those that would become vanished dreams and those that would survive as rural centers, while along the upper Red River itself new townsites continued to appear.[99]

The line of military protection had been pushed northward and westward with the establishment of Fort Gaines (later Ripley) in 1848–49, Fort Ridgely in 1854, and Fort Abercrombie in 1857–58. Along the east bank of the Mississippi the Red River Trail between St. Paul and Crow Wing had been replaced by a military road constructed between 1851 and 1858, and an extension designed to supplant the Woods Trail as far as its connecting link with the Middle Trail had been completed almost to Wadena before federal appropriations ran out in 1858.[100]

Nevertheless, there were hints by 1861 that the course of empire might have pitfalls. It was slowly becoming apparent to the Burbanks and their partners that their interests differed widely from those of the Hudson's Bay Company: "We wanted immigration and trade; they did not want immigration nor mails nor any one to trade in the Hudson Bay Company's territory but themselves."[101] Having once reaped for itself the economic benefits of the Minnesota route, the British giant blocked any further expansion of the steamboating and transfer business. It was also content to see the matter of annexation of the western territories to Canada delayed by one political hurdle after another.

A further barrier to the expansion of commercial ties between the Red River Settlement and St. Paul had been consistently ignored or bypassed. This was the continuing ownership of the intervening land by Indian people. No agreement had ever been sought or given for the passage of cart trains through the lands of the Dakota or the Ojibway. The stage road had been built over territory already ceded to the United States, but steamboat traffic on the river passed through areas to which the tribes still held title. In 1861 the Ojibway called this awkward fact to the attention of the Burbank company in a letter demanding money "to quiet the spirits of their fathers." With a pointed touch of metaphor, they claimed that these spirits had been disturbed by the unearthly screeching of the steamboat whistles. The boats, they said, were also driving away the game and killing the fish. The owners of the line passed the problem of property rights to the United States Office of Indian Affairs, and the Hudson's Bay Company recruited its erstwhile rival, Norman Kittson, to operate the steamboats and use his experience and diplomacy with the Ojibway.[102]

By 1862, however, Minnesota was called upon without warning to pay the bill for years of bullying and double-dealing on the question of Indian rights. During August and September the Dakota War flamed like a wind-driven prairie fire across southern Minnesota and into the Red River Valley. Settlers in the vicinity of Breckenridge and along the western end of the stage road were attacked; a stage was captured and its driver slain; some 80 persons from Georgetown and the surrounding area took refuge at Fort Abercrombie; and the fort itself lay under siege for 26 days.[103]

Kittson, caught at Georgetown with an entire shipment of Hudson's Bay Company goods worth about $25,000, prepared to stand his ground against the Dakota. After waiting for some days, he put the goods aboard the "International" and started down the river. The overloaded boat ran aground. Kittson

was forced to abandon it, taking the freight on by wagon and cart. Near present-day Grand Forks he encountered an assemblage of Ojibway who had for weeks suspended hunting and other activities while awaiting the arrival of United States treaty commissioners to negotiate for their land. The commissioners had long since retreated before the Dakota threat, but no one had notified the Ojibway. Many of them were hungry and all were angry. Over Kittson's protests, they confiscated part of the freight and helped themselves to supplies.[104]

The rations proved expensive in the long run. The following summer the commissioners arrived, led by Alexander Ramsey and accompanied by a detachment of mounted troops. At a treaty council held in late September, 1863, at the spot where the Woods Trail crossed the Red Lake River, the commissioners used the Kittson incident as an excuse to threaten the Ojibway with dire punishment if they hesitated to sign a treaty. Ramsey first proposed an agreement that would have allowed free navigation of the Red River and given to the United States a corridor through the valley. For this he offered only $20,000, and he could hardly have been surprised at the stinging answer of Little Rock, the Ojibway spokesman: "If you had wanted a right of way over the roads and rivers you would have consulted us before you took it."[105]

As finally drawn, the treaty ceded all of the valley on both sides of the river from the Canadian border south to the Wild Rice on the east and to the Sheyenne on the west. It amounted to 9,470,000 acres, including some of the most fertile soil on earth. The payment was to be $510,000, of which $100,000 would go to Kittson, the Hudson's Bay Company, and other traders in compensation for Ojibway "depredations." Ramsey later boasted that "No territorial acquisitions of equal intrinsic value have been made from the Indians at so low a rate per acre." Despite threats, several leaders of the Red Lake band refused to sign. Ultimately, supported by Episcopal Bishop Henry B. Whipple, they forced the Indian Office to partially rewrite the agreement and scale down the plum given to the traders.

By the end of 1863 the remaining hostile Dakota had been hunted beyond the Missouri and the Ojibway had given up all claim to the Red River Valley, but commerce was slow to revive. The memory of death, sudden and without warning, hung over the borderland traversed by the trails. The Burbanks found it nearly impossible to hire teamsters for the route without a military escort, and none was available. Steamboat navigation, too, was held up, though less by fear of the Dakota than by low water. The "International," freed from its sandbar, had been taken up to Fort Abercrombie, where it remained until the spring of 1864. In this emergency the métis oxcarts once again came into their own. The Burbanks agreed to haul the Hudson's Bay Company goods from St. Paul as far as Crow Wing, from which point they were sent by cart over the difficult but relatively secure Woods Trail.[106]

The Burbank contract ran out in 1863 and was not renewed. Kittson bought out the partners' half interest in the "International" to become the American associate of the Hudson's Bay Company in the steamboat business. On the overland end of the route, the managers of the British firm contracted briefly with a St. Cloud freighter who proved no more satisfactory than the Burbanks. Thereafter they resigned themselves once more to assembling and conducting cart brigades. Continued drought throughout 1864 and 1865 hampered navigation so severely that most of the commerce between St. Paul and Fort Garry went the entire way by cart. This included not only the Hudson's Bay Company shipments, but an ever-increasing amount of other freight, bringing the volume of traffic over the trails to an all-time peak in the late 1860s. According to a St. Cloud newspaper, more than 1,400 carts arrived there in 1865. The following year St. Paul businessmen estimated that "The Red River trade, as carried on by the half breed traders of the upper Red River as far as Fort Garry, amounts to about $150,000 and is annually increasing. About one thousand of their carts, each drawn by a single ox in harness, come down once a year." In 1869 the *Alexandria Post* reported that as many as 2,500 carts had passed through to St. Cloud carrying 600 tons of freight for the Hudson's Bay Company alone.[107]

Swelling the traffic even further were wagon and cart trains carrying supplies to the new forts being built to control the Dakota on the distant plains — Fort Wadsworth in 1864 and Forts Ransom and Totten in 1867. Where practical, the military trains followed established cart trails. In time, these became known as "government roads" — as did the route up the Minnesota Valley from Fort Ridgely to Fort Abercrombie and beyond. Elsewhere wholly new paths were broken — the Fort Wadsworth Trail, for example, which left the stage road near Sauk Centre and struck directly west through present-day Glenwood and Browns Valley.[108]

During the mid-1860s the Hudson's Bay Company toyed briefly with the idea of bypassing St. Paul in favor of Superior, Wisconsin, from which a new road would be built to Crow Wing. The idea was quickly dropped, however, after the St. Paul and Pacific Railway opened a line to St. Cloud late in 1866. By then it was apparent that railroads would soon eliminate cart traffic over the trails, for with the end of the Civil War, money and men were being released for a great westward push.[109]

After completion of its branch to meet the Red River traffic at St. Cloud, the St. Paul and Pacific began extending its main line from Minneapolis directly westward toward Breckenridge. As the distance between the end of the tracks and the Red River began to shrink, many cart trains chose to meet the railroad at its terminus rather than travel all the way to St. Cloud. The line reached Willmar in 1869, Benson in 1870, and Morris early the next year. Each village was inundated for a season by carts and wagons, lowing oxen, shouting drivers, and clouds of dust. By the end of 1871 the tracks had at last reached the Red River at Breckenridge, and in 1872 the Northern Pacific passed through Moorhead on its way to the Pacific Coast.[110]

As the railroads pushed west, so did farmers. In the Sauk Valley, where only occasional homesteads had broken the sweep of prairie in 1859, fields and fences were almost continuous by the mid-1860s. In 1866 Norwegian and Swedish immigrants were reported to be taking up land as far west as the Pomme de Terre River. They proved to be only the vanguard of a flood of Scandinavian settlers that poured into the upper Red River Valley in the years that followed. The state's busiest land offices between 1865 and 1871 were at St. Cloud and Alexandria.[111]

Change also caught up at last with the Red River Settlement. The Confederation of Canada was created by the British North America Act in 1867, and in 1869 the former Hudson's Bay Company territories were transferred to it. In the meantime anxiety and discontent had been growing among the Red River people, especially among the métis. A severe grasshopper plague in 1867 and 1868 had ruined the settlement's crops and caused widespread hunger and hardship. Aggravating the situation was the disappearance of buffalo from the eastern plains, for the shrinking herds had been driven westward by military operations, advancing settlement, and indiscriminate slaughter. When the Canadian government, anticipating the opening of the territory to eager land seekers, sent surveyors to the Red River Settlement during the summer of 1869, the métis at once became suspicious. Their own land claims, though well estab-

Red River carts at a railroad station

lished, were often unmarked and informal. Since neither they nor any other settlers had been consulted in the transfer of the territory to Canadian rule, they feared that their land rights would be ignored.[112]

Led by the young Louis Riel, who had returned to the settlement the year before, the métis at first protested to the local authorities. When no action was forthcoming, they blocked the movements of the crews, bringing the survey to a halt early in October In the meantime William McDougall, the new governor appointed to take over administration of the territory when its transfer from the Hudson's Bay Company became official on December 1, 1869, was already traveling from Ottawa by way of Minnesota. News of the métis action reached him at Fort Abercrombie, but he took little notice until he reached the border at Pembina. There he was met by a messenger who handed him a letter ordering him not to enter the country. It was signed by the "National Committee of the Métis of Red River," whose secretary was Louis Riel. McDougall blustered his way as far as the Hudson's Bay Company store two miles north of the border. From there he was firmly escorted back by an armed body of métis.[113]

The insurgent National Committee, which was supported at least tacitly by most of the Red River community, remained in control for more than six months. All that Riel and his followers really demanded were open negotiations with the Canadian government and some guarantee of the rights of the métis. No recognition was granted them. However,

the Canadian Parliament conceded the right of the Red River Settlement to enter the Confederation with full political rights by creating the Province of Manitoba early in 1870. The métis provisional government was dispersed the following summer by an armed expedition dispatched through the wilderness from Lake Superior, and Riel, a hunted man, fled to St. Joseph.[114]

Minnesotans watched the dramatic events of 1869–70 with close attention and a few fumbling, *sub rosa* attempts at intervention. Many of them hoped that the end result would be annexation of the Red River country to the United States. Also hoping to use the métis for their own purposes were members of the Irish nationalist group known as Fenians, who had previously organized several armed raids into eastern Canada. Their Minnesota leader, William B. O'Donoghue, became one of Riel's supporters and advisers, and a year after the collapse of the métis rebellion, O'Donoghue led some 35 men in a futile "invasion" across the border at Pembina.[115]

Early in the previous year a quieter and far more important invasion of the Red River country had taken place. It was conducted alone by a young St. Paul forwarding agent and commission merchant named James J. Hill. After Kittson had returned to the Red River Valley in the mid-1860s to enter the steamboat business with the Hudson's Bay Company, Hill had become his St. Paul agent in the shipping of goods and furs. Along with Kittson's business, the Canadian-born Hill also acquired the accounts of numerous other independent traders in the Red River Settlement, and by 1870 he was handling furs worth upward of $100,000 annually.[116]

The trip Hill made to the Red River Valley in March, 1870, was undertaken partly as a service to the Canadian government and partly to satisfy his own curiosity about the country, its business prospects, and the effects of the métis insurrection. He traveled by stage as far as Georgetown and the rest of the way by dogsled, following the Red River and crossing it several times. In spite of the hardships he suffered from wintry weather and a faithless guide, he became convinced that the valley had a great future. Along the trail, moreover, he encountered Donald A. Smith, who held the position formerly filled by Simpson as head of the Hudson's Bay Company operations in North America. The two men talked at length, strengthening a casual acquaintance they had already made in St. Paul.

That summer Hill built flatboats to take goods down the Red River and organized a company to carry on "a merchandising and transportation business." During the winter of 1870–71 the new firm of Hill and Griggs constructed a steamboat for service on the Red River, and Hill succeeded in persuading the United States Treasury Department that his was the only bona fide American company legally qualified to carry goods in bond across the border. The new steamer, christened the "Selkirk," made its first trip in April, 1871. By June the Hudson's Bay Company had hastily withdrawn from the steamboat business, turning the "International" over to Kittson. After a single season of competition, Kittson and Hill joined forces in organizing the Red River Transportation Company to monopolize steamboat service on the river and charge what the traffic would bear.

Their timing was precise, for in that year steel rails crossed the Red River and freight rolled along them to the steamboat landings. With no more fanfare than the whistle of the first locomotive, a way of life for the métis and a chapter in history ended. When the cart trains vanished, so, in large measure, did the Red River trails. In a few places they continued to carry local traffic, but for the most part they became choked with weeds or were swallowed by plowed fields.

The panic and depression of 1873 brought railroad expansion to a sudden halt and forced both the Northern Pacific and the St. Paul and Pacific into bankruptcy. Hill and Kittson, teamed with Donald Smith and backed financially by the Bank of Montreal, succeeded in seizing control of the St. Paul and Pacific. They reorganized it as the St. Paul, Minneapolis and Manitoba, aimed, as the name implied, northward rather than westward. Hill, with unprecedented determination and speed, pushed the line to the border in 1878. There it connected with a branch of the Canadian Pacific extending south from the burgeoning city of Winnipeg. Until the main line of the Canadian Pacific reached Winnipeg from the east four years later, the St. Paul, Minneapolis and Manitoba carried (for a price) nearly all the traffic of the Canadian northwest.

Thus Lord Selkirk's prophecy of 1817 was fulfilled in full measure. As he had perceived, the natural flow of commerce, like the rivers, ran north and south in the heart of the North American continent. But the cross-grain of politics and ethnicity continued to predominate. In Selkirk's own generation the enterprise of eastern Canada, embodied in the North West Company, had climbed over the barrier of the Laurentian Shield on the thin shells of birch-bark canoes and the backs of sweating voyageurs to establish a continent-wide business. Sixty years later Canada again reached west with equal tenacity to build a railroad over and through the solid rock that divided its eastern and western regions and to reinforce the slender lines of political control with stronger ties of economic dependence. In the 20th century, however, trade and the rivers continue to flow north and south. The prairie provinces of Canada continue to look southward for markets and manufactured goods, and the populous Mississippi Valley still looks north — if no longer for beaver and buffalo, then for timber products and thick black oil.

2 ~ THE MANITOBA TRAILS

THE POLYGLOT COMMUNITY fathered by Selkirk and the Canadian fur trade near the confluence of the Red and Assiniboine rivers determined the character of the Red River trails. If the Red River Settlement had not grown up where it did or if it had evolved in another era, the trails might never have played a role in the history of the Northwest. The first crucial factor was the site of the settlement only 60 miles from the United States border. To the north lay the watery empire of the Hudson's Bay Company stretching over 600 rugged miles to York Factory on Hudson Bay. To the south only 400 miles of rolling prairie separated the settlement from St. Paul and free trade. Accentuating the southward orientation was the course of the Red River, which provided a natural link to the waters of the Mississippi. St. Paul was both the nearest available market and the most accessible supply point.

It was not only geography that turned the enterprising Red River settler's mind to the south. The trails were a spontaneous outgrowth of conflicts and ties within the settlement — conflicts with the monopolistic supervision of the Hudson's Bay Company and ties with the old network of free traders on the Mississippi. The community's diffuse ethnic, religious, and geographical character mirrored the complex origin of the Red River trails. Just as no one person or company originated the trade to St. Paul, no one link bound together the elements of the Red River population. Although the looming presence of the Hudson's Bay Company dominated its economic life, the settlement was as deeply divided between loyalty and opposition to the firm as it was divided along cultural lines. These stresses, as well as individual enterprise and the simple need for goods, found their outlet along the dusty paths to St. Paul.

Two main trails ran from the Red River Settlement to the border. They traversed a region devoid of landmarks, "a boundless, treeless ocean of grass, seemingly a perfect level," varied only by the wooded banks of rivers meandering through the rich soil. On the east side of the Red River a trail swung away from the settlement to follow the dry gravel ridges of glacial Lake Agassiz's beaches. Farther south it connected with a detour to Pembina and with the Woods Trail. On the west side of the Red lay a more frequented route from the settlement to Pembina. From it a branch cut over the prairie to St. Joseph in what is now North Dakota, and south of the border it connected with the North Dakota and Woods trails. Not only was the western trail the one usually used by the oxcart brigades, it was also the main road linking together the dispersed community that was the Red River Settlement.[1]

A muddy Red River cart in Winnipeg about 1870

27

The various components of the settlement straggled along the banks of the Red River from Lake Winnipeg to the border and up the Assiniboine to Portage la Prairie. About 20 miles down the Red from its junction with the Assiniboine stood Lower Fort Garry, the stone citadel built by Sir George Simpson in 1831 as his monument in the West. A little above this fort were St. Andrew's Rapids, and below it to the north the Red flowed into Lake Winnipeg.

The point where the two rivers met (within modern Winnipeg) was called "the forks." Here stood Upper Fort Garry, the Hudson's Bay Company's administrative headquarters in Assiniboia. Two miles to the north on the banks of the Red was Point Douglas, the site of Lord Selkirk's fort and the governmental center of his colony. A "sort of scattered town" grew up around the forks, but the familiar symbols of town life — streets, sidewalks, hotels, and businesses — were missing.[2]

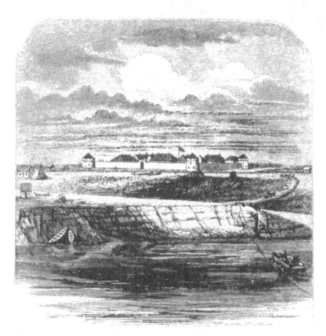

Fort Garry, about 1859

The Red River Settlement was wholly unlike an American frontier town in that it had no central core, no commercial center. Farms lined the banks of the Red and the Assiniboine, giving the area "the appearance of a long suburban village — such as you might see near our [American] eastern sea-board, or such as you find exhibited in pictures of English country villages," wrote the visiting territorial governor of Minnesota in 1851. One party of travelers, arriving at Upper Fort Garry as late as 1860, searched in vain for "the nearest part of the settlement" until they were told that they were standing at the center of the community, which stretched away from them on either side, looking "about the same for twenty or thirty miles." There was no "downtown" because none was needed. The internal economy of the settlement was based on barter under the total supervision of the Hudson's Bay Company. Fur trading and farming were the community's only viable economic activities and they were (at least on the surface) controlled by one firm.[3]

The settlement was actually an amalgamation of several different communities divided by language and religion. On the west side of the Red south of the Assiniboine and along the east side south of the Seine River was the French village. It was composed of two groups: the métis descendants of early voyageurs and their Indian wives, and French-Canadian immigrants from Quebec who for a time formed a farming community distinct from the seminomadic métis. The latter, though more numerous, were only part-time residents. Although they did some farming, their principal resource was the buffalo. These French groups composed the Roman Catholic parishes that later evolved into the cities of St. Boniface and St. Norbert. Also living along the Seine in the years before 1826 were the Swiss and German immigrants sent to the New World by Selkirk.[4]

On the west side of the Red River, clustered around Lower and Upper Fort Garry and spreading up the Assiniboine lived a community of retired Hudson's Bay Company employees who had chosen to remain in the Red River country with their Indian wives and English-speaking métis families. These people formed the aristocracy of the settlement. They were comparatively well off, having held responsible company positions over many years, and most of them belonged to the Church of England.

The Highland Scots of the Selkirk Colony were also concentrated on the west side of the Red. Primarily farmers, they cultivated their lots in the community of Kildonan north of Point Douglas in what one historian referred to as "careful poverty." In religious affiliation, they were Presbyterians. Other Protestant denominations took root in the settlement with the advent of English-speaking immigrants from Ontario in the 1860s and 1870s, adding to the cultural variety.

Despite the ethnic disparity of the settlement, its land-use patterns were surprisingly similar throughout, reflecting those found in Quebec and the Scottish Highlands. As in Quebec, the river was the life line, and each farmer owned frontage for water and trans-

TRAILS IN WINNIPEG

portation. The farms stretched back from the river for two miles or more. Near the water might be five acres of intensively cultivated land with a foot and bridle path winding along the shore. Next might come a few acres of auxiliary farm land, common grazing land, and then prairie hay land. The river lots were divided and redivided among a farmer's sons, each of whom must have a bit of frontage. Thus the lots became narrower and narrower with passing generations, prompting visitors from Ontario and the United States to remark that the Red River settlers "farmed on lanes." In 1851 an American observed that "each of these narrow farms [had] their dwellings and the farm out-buildings spread only along the river front, with lawns sloping to the water's edge, and shrubbery and vines liberally trained around them, and trees inter-mingled." Away from the river stretched "the fertile prairies, carpeted over with wild-flowers, lying a beautiful and unprofitable waste, save for grazing purposes."[5]

The Red River Trail on the west side of the river skirted the area of intensive cultivation just at the point where the common grazing land began. A traveler passing along it was presented with a scene of pastoral industry on one side and open prairie on the other. An Old World quality pervaded the collage of buildings visible from the trail. A visitor in 1851 spoke of "churches peeping above the foliage of the trees in the distance, white-washed schoolhouses glistening here and there amidst sunlight and green; gentle-men's houses of pretentious dimensions and grassy lawns and elaborate fencing, the seats of retired officers of the Hudson's Bay Company occasionally interspersed; here an English bishop's parsonage, with a boarding or high school near by; and over there a Catholic bishop's massive cathedral." Modest log houses with thatched or moss roofs stood beside more elaborate whitewashed or limestone structures in French or Ontario Georgian styles. Adding a pic-turesque touch to the medley were the "numerous

The Red River near Point Douglas about 1822, painted by Peter Rindisbacher

wind-mills, nearly twenty in all, which on every point of land made by the turns and bends in the river, stretched out their huge sails athwart the horizon." Steepled stone churches dotted the banks of the Red from the forks to Lake Winnipeg. Dominating the east bank at the forks was the twin-towered Catholic cathedral of St. Boniface, and facing it on the west was Upper Fort Garry, the imposing stone edifice erected by the Hudson's Bay Company in the 1830s.[6]

Over the years two structures known as Upper Fort Garry were built upon the "elevated bank" where the "confluence of the Assiniboin[e] and Red rivers washed the base of the bluff." The first one seems to have been an uninspiring sight in 1825 when fur trader Alexander Ross described it. "Instead of a place walled and fortified, as I had expected, I saw nothing but a few wooden houses huddled together without palisades, or any regard to taste or even comfort," he wrote. "To this cluster of huts were, however, appended two long bastions in the same style as the other buildings. These buildings, according to the custom of the country, were used as dwellings and warehouses for carrying on the trade of the place." By 1831 floods and time had reduced this fort to a "very dilapidated state," and Sir George Simpson decided "to set about erecting a good, solid, comfortable establishment at once" farther down the Red River. The result was Lower Fort Garry, begun in 1831, and still standing. Restored by the Canadian government, it is now a popular historic site open to visitors.[7]

The old site at the mouth of the Assiniboine was not abandoned, however, for in 1835 work also began on another stone fort to replace the rotting buildings there. The second Upper Fort Garry enclosed a rectangular space measuring 240 by 280 feet, with "rounded, bastion-like towers . . . pierced for small artillery" at the four corners. The buildings inside its walls — offices, residences, warehouses, and a retail store — were "built of stone or axe-hewn logs, and two and a half stories high." A 465-acre common around the fort was set aside by the Hudson's Bay Company as a camping place for visiting Indians and plains traders. Today only one gateway of Upper Fort Garry remains standing in downtown Winnipeg.[8]

Oxcart brigades seldom gathered to start from any one particular point; they simply accumulated while meandering south through the settlement. A network of trails converging at the forks from the north, east, and west fed in traffic from the outlying areas of St. Andrew's, Ste. Anne, and Portage la Prairie. Some carts might carry sugar, powder, or dry goods to trade along the way at Pembina and St. Joseph, but most were piled high with the staples of the St. Paul trade — furs, buffalo robes and meat, pemmican, and moccasins. Setting out from Upper Fort Garry in 1860, one caravan was comprised of "half-a-dozen Red-river carts, with a most promiscuous assortment of baggage, peltry, and squeak, . . . a stray ox and pony or two, a number of armed horsemen, and a troop of friends from the settlement, come, as is their wont, to see their friends off." By the time this group reached the southern end of the settlement it had grown to two dozen carts, a dozen mounted warriors, and "numerous cattle and ponies dangling along for half a mile" behind.[9]

Some carts began their journey from the settlement at the ferry across the Assiniboine. This dubious convenience was the object of much comment and not a little complaint over the years. In 1861 its equipment consisted of "two scows worked on ropes," plus "a canoe and passenger skiff" in such a drastic state of disrepair that "every step of the horses, or motion of the carts, deranged the boarding." If stepped on by an unwary ox, the end of a floor board might go down, while the other end flew up against the face of some neighboring beast. In the ensuing chaos, the passengers would be "shouting for mercy and assistance, the boatmen contemplating a leap into the water, and the scow floating in midchannel of the river."[10]

Once across the Assiniboine, the carts plunged into a belt of bushland that extended for several miles south of the river. From this stretch of the trail a traveler could still look back to catch a glimpse of St. Boniface Cathedral to the north and the woods along the Assiniboine "stretching away, until lost in the western horizon." On a hot day the brush provided welcome shade until the carts emerged onto "the sweeping level prairie." At this point the trail cut off some wide bends of the Red River, and travelers had to take care not to be marooned at nightfall far from water and wood. Marshes, abounding on either side of the road, were covered in summer with water lilies, ducks, and brown mud hens.[11]

By the 1850s the farms of the French métis were scattered along the Red River more than half the way to Pembina. A traveler on the trail who brought the latest news and spoke a little French was "always sure of the best they had in the way of bed and board. . . . One's horses too were always included in the generous hospitality." The farms of the settlers followed every bend of the tortuous Red, and many of the points formed by the river had names. Pointe Coupée, Rat Point, Great Salt Point, Grand Point, and the Two Points were prominent landmarks on the way south. The distance to St. Norbert at the mouth of the Rivière Sale (or Stinking River) was nine miles by road and sixteen by river. In 1857, and probably earlier, a ferry was maintained at the mouth of the Sale. It was here in 1869 that the Red River métis under Louis Riel erected a barricade closing off the Pembina Trail. The barrier was set up to prevent William McDougall from entering the settlement to as-

sume the post of lieutenant governor of the Northwest Territory. South of St. Norbert farms became less and less frequent until the last French settlement at Ste. Agathe was passed. After that travel sometimes became more difficult. An American who made the journey in 1851 complained that the road was "a mass of tenacious mud and water" interspersed with patches of "tall wet grass."[12]

But when the weather was good, travelers sometimes succumbed to the luxury of boredom. "As in canoeing, with few exceptions, one day is much like another, only here the weather is not allowed in the least to interfere with movement," wrote an American scientist who rode south with the carts. "We are always up by daybreak, and travel an hour or two before we breakfast; another spell of travel, and then a longer rest, as the cattle must be allowed to graze to their content. . . . And so day after day passes by, its monotony rarely relieved by any stirring events, excepting when it becomes necessary to cross a river. Then there is always some fun."[13]

The Morris River (also called Scratching and Gratias River) was the scene of a good deal of such "fun" over the years. This bad, muddy crossing had been the site of North West and XY Company fur posts as early as 1801. It was still giving trouble in 1850 when Edward S. Wortley, Earl of Wharncliffe, passed this way. Fancifully the earl noted in his diary that the river was "called in the Indian tongue, stick in the mud river." He had ample reason to know that the name was appropriate, for he found Father Belcourt, the missionary priest from Pembina, stuck there. "His cart was in the middle of the stream; his two horses on the other side, and himself in the middle of the water working away at pulling the cart out of the mud," wrote Wharncliffe. "However he could not move it an inch, and he was an absurd sight, as the

Cathedral of St. Boniface, about 1859

MANITOBA TRAILS

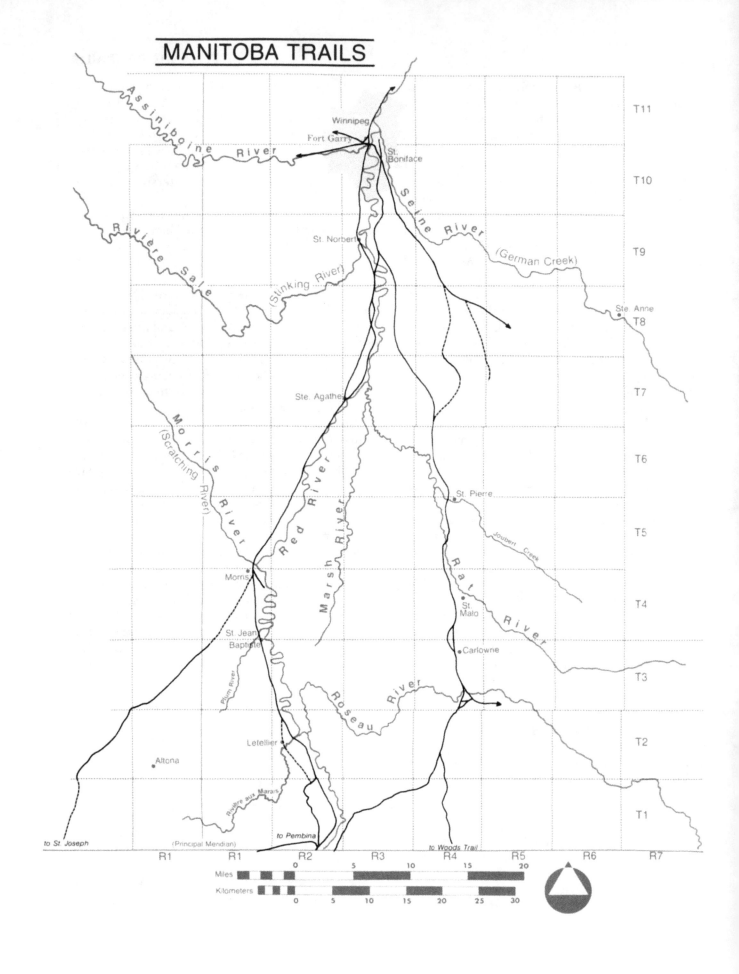

Assiniboine   River

Riviere Sale

(Stinking River)

Winnipeg

Fort Garry

St. Boniface

Seine River

(German Creek)

St. Norbert

Ste. Anne

Morris River

(Scratching River)

Ste. Agathe

Red River

Marsh River

St. Pierre

Joubert Creek

Morris

Rat River

St. Malo

St. Jean Baptiste

Plum River

Carlowne

Roseau River

Letellier

Altona

Riviere aux Marais

to St. Joseph

(Principal Meridian)

to Pembina

to Woods Trail

R1   R1   R2   R3   R4   R5   R6   R7

T11

T10

T9

T8

T7

T6

T5

T4

T3

T2

T1

Miles   0   5   10   15   20

Kilometers   0   5   10   15   20   25   30

drops streamed down his face from exertion; his black gown being tucked up round his waist, he altogether presented such a curious spectacle that I stood on the bank, & laughed at him." Then following the code of backwoods chivalry, Wharncliffe's party extracted the priest's cart from the river and sped him on his way. By 1857 a floating bridge and scow had been installed, but some passengers were not sure the additions were an improvement. "In crossing Scratching River . . . we find a house, and an apology for a ferry in the shape of a rickety scow, three-fourths full of water, [and] shaky stakes to which to fasten the ferry-ropes," one writer complained. Today travelers can cross the Morris River on a modern highway bridge located slightly upstream from the notorious ford.[14]

Beyond the Morris River in later years a branch of the trail wandered off southwest to St. Joseph, while the older route to Pembina continued south across the Plum and Marais (Marsh) rivers. According to one writer, the latter crossing was a "treacherous morass" that merited its name. Half a mile north of the 49th parallel the trail passed Fort Pembina, a Hudson's Bay Company post established about 1845 and maintained into the 1870s. Major Samuel Woods, who saw it in 1849, wrote that "The English Fur Company's trading post is about *two hundred* yards from the line on their territory, consisting of a small 'shanty,' but they now have under erection very extensive buildings." By 1859 the post had grown to "a substantial enclosure, with stout walls and bastions." Here in its heyday travelers could count on a hearty welcome on the second night of their trip south, but by 1876, when stagecoaches were plying the old west bank trail, the fort had dwindled to "a few wooden houses surrounded by fences."[15]

The trail on the east side of the Red was neither so old nor so heavily traveled as the one on the west side, but it had several advantages. Used after 1844 in conjunction with the Woods Trail, it was safer from Dakota war parties, less open to prairie fires, better supplied with wood, and less muddy because it ran along the gravelly beach ridges. Its disadvantages were its isolation from settlement and the large streams which had to be forded. The main east side route ran from the forks along the Red to a point south of St. Norbert. Then it moved gradually away from the river and the farms along it, through "a swampy country interspersed with clumps of willows," until it struck the higher ground of a beach ridge.

An alternative trail followed the Seine River from St. Boniface toward Ste. Anne, then headed south to join the main trail on the ridge. From there the east side route continued south along the boundary between the prairie on the west and the forest that stretched east to Lake of the Woods, crossing Joubert Creek at present St. Pierre. Five miles farther on lay the Rat River — "a very difficult stream to traverse in high water; the banks being steep and the bed of the river soft."[16]

Following the left bank of Rat River, the trail passed a few miles west of St. Malo. It branched briefly when it reached the Rivière du Milieu, a "narrow stream thinly skirted with clumps of willows and small poplar" near present Carlowrie. Then after crossing five miles of prairie, the trail reached the stony bed of the Roseau River.

On the south side of the Roseau it branched. If a Red River traveler wished to stop at Pembina, as many did, he here turned west along the south side of the Roseau River. If he wished to bypass Pembina and reach the Woods Trail by the most direct route, he continued southeast "along the summit of some high ridges varying in breadth from 100 to 300 yards." In either case, the scenery changed scarcely at all. "To the eastward hills [,] knolls and swamps bounded the view, while to the West, spread out an extensive plain or rather swamp, bounded on the verge of the horizon by the woods of the Red River."

The process of modernization began to overtake the Red River trails of Manitoba in 1874, when the Pembina Branch of the Canadian Pacific Railroad was authorized. Before long the old west bank route was "duplicated in the iron track of the railway." In 1913 this trail's triple ruts were obliterated when portions of it were paved with asphalt. Now Manitoba Highway 75 follows the west bank trail, especially from Winnipeg to St. Norbert and from Ste. Agathe to the junction with Highway 14 south of St. Jean Baptiste. From St. Norbert to Ste. Agathe there seem to have been two trails at different times, one of which the highway follows more closely than the other. South of the junction of Highways 75 and 14, the modern road heads away from the river, while the old trail hugged the bank more closely. On the east side, portions of the alternative Seine River Trail are followed by present Highway 59. A marker east of Niverville, where Provincial Road 311 now meets Highway 59, commemorates a settlement that grew up on this Red River Trail. On both the east and west sides the journey to the 49th parallel, which took two days or more by oxcart, can now be driven by auto in an hour and a half.[17]

3 ~ THE NORTH DAKOTA TRAILS

AFTER CROSSING into the United States travelers from the Red River Settlement faced the second, and much longer, lap of their trip to St. Paul. Two major routes and an intricate web of connections formed the system of Red River trails in what is now North Dakota. One — the River Trail — was a continuation of the west bank route from Manitoba which hugged the Red all the way from Winnipeg to the Bois de Sioux. The second route was the Ridge Trail. From the Canadian border it climbed the coteau bounding the western watershed of the Red and emerged onto the endless sea of grass that marked the eastern edge of the Great Plains. The grandeur of the open prairie dominated the journey for as much as 175 miles before the trail descended to the river valley and whatever ford of the Red was chosen. At the completion of his journey over the North Dakota plains, one traveler felt that he had been "dead a hundred years or so, and had woke . . . into another existence, in a strange, new world, in emerging from the sleepy days and sleepless nights of a journey down the Red River valley."[1]

In the north, the North Dakota trails diverged from two focal points: Pembina and St. Joseph. Pembina, the little border town founded on smuggling, boundary disputes, and trade wars, had been the site of trading posts from the time Peter Grant of the North West Company established himself opposite the

mouth of the Pembina River in the 1790s. He was succeeded by Charles J. B. Chaboillez, who built a post on the south side of the Pembina River in North Dakota, and by Alexander Henry, who arrived in 1801 and stayed for seven years, managing the North West Company's interests in the entire Red River region from his post on the north bank of the Pembina. During Henry's tenure a sizable mixed-blood community began to grow up around the post. The population was further increased by the advent in 1811 of the Selkirk settlers, who spent their first few winters at Pembina to take advantage of the protection offered by the métis community. In 1818, when Father Sévère Dumoulin arrived to establish a mission school and church, he counted 300 parishioners in the village.[2]

The métis of Pembina called themselves *gens libres*, or freemen, in somewhat defiant contrast to the *engagés* of the Hudson's Bay Company across the border. Farming was not in much favor among them; trapping and the annual bison hunt were their main occupations. The hunts organized at Pembina were huge civil and military enterprises which rivaled or surpassed the treks to St. Paul in size and importance to the community. Before setting out with their families, parties of several hundred men elected cap-

One man could drive four carts on the prairie

34

tains to control the hunt and agreed upon rules and regulations to direct it. Then virtually the entire métis population departed in their carts for weeks or months of hunting on the open prairie, returning only when the carts were filled with a year's supply of buffalo meat. Life in Pembina revolved around the departure and arrival of the oxcart trains from and to St. Paul or the hunts on the plains.[3]

The town's first era of prosperity ended in the spring of 1823 when the Hudson's Bay Company closed the only remaining trading post at Pembina and withdrew north of the border. Major Stephen H. Long's party, which visited the village during the summer, reported that 350 souls still lived there in 60 log cabins, but that the Catholic mission church was "fast going to decay." The inhabitants struck the American visitors as having a "very low rank in the scale of civilization." In succeeding years Pembina was nearly deserted. Then a slow trickle of métis began to return, partly to "free themselves from disadvantageous restrictions" on trade imposed by the Hudson's Bay Company, and partly because of their "lingering fondness for the place of their birth." With the establishment in 1844 of Norman Kittson's trading post-cum-smuggling depot on or near the site of Alexander Henry's old post, the village began to prosper again. By the late 1840s it boasted 511 men, 515 women, 300 oxen, and 600 carts.[4]

To observers unaccustomed to frontier life, Pembina seemed to be in a perpetual state of imminent decay. Major Samuel Woods, arriving there in 1849, was surprised to find not even a "collection of huts, with the appearance of a village." Kittson's post, the school, the chapel, and some miscellaneous sheds were the only wooden buildings in sight. The inhabitants lived Indian-style in skin or bark lodges set up

Pembina about 1822, painted by Peter Rindisbacher

outside Kittson's fence. Their way of life was actually more practical than most visitors gave it credit for, because the lodges could be easily moved when the recurring spring floods washed over the site. The métis lodges were ranged along the banks of the Pembina River and the Ojibway lived along the Red.[5]

In 1850 Kittson's house, "a large long log hut," stood at one end of a quadrangular courtyard of cabins, "stables, stores for peltry, & for goods to be given in exchange for peltry." A blacksmith shop and icehouse completed the ensemble. The cabins were built of logs chinked with mud and straw and thatched with grass; the sides of the trading post were shingled with bark, making the building look like a huge Ojibway lodge. One visitor, after weeks of travel on the prairie, thought the establishment possessed "a general appearance of thrift, comfort, and industry."

The leading white citizen in the little community was the missionary, Father Georges-Antoine Belcourt, who lived in "a large, two-story frame-house, situated alongside of a rude log-church . . . upon the high ground about half a mile back from the river" between Kittson's post and the border. From there he kept a suspicious eye on the small Hudson's Bay Company post 200 yards north of the 49th parallel. Violently partisan against the British monopoly, Belcourt joined Kittson in besieging the American government with pleas for military protection and a customs commissioner at Pembina. The latter request was granted in 1850; the former, despite the long series of military expeditions that filed through Pembina, was not granted until the Dakota War in the 1860s.[6]

A mass migration from Pembina to escape the spreading waters during the disastrous flood years of the early 1850s induced both Kittson and Belcourt to move their main bases up the Pembina River to St. Joseph. The Pembina trading post was left in charge of Joseph Rolette, Jr., who ruled the village like a feudal lord surrounded by hounds and horses. Although Pembina survived to play an important role in the politics of Minnesota Territory, its days as a trading metropolis were numbered. A visitor in 1856 noted laconically that the village had again "gone to decay."[7]

Just as visitors over the decades concurred on Pembina's impending demise, they also agreed that St. Joseph had barely been born. Actually St. Joseph was nearly as old as its downstream neighbor. It was the location of the North West Company's Hair Hills post, founded by Michel Langlois in 1801. After that date a small mixed-blood community seems to have

Manitoba
North Dakota

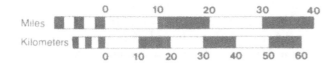

NORTH DAKOTA
TRAILS

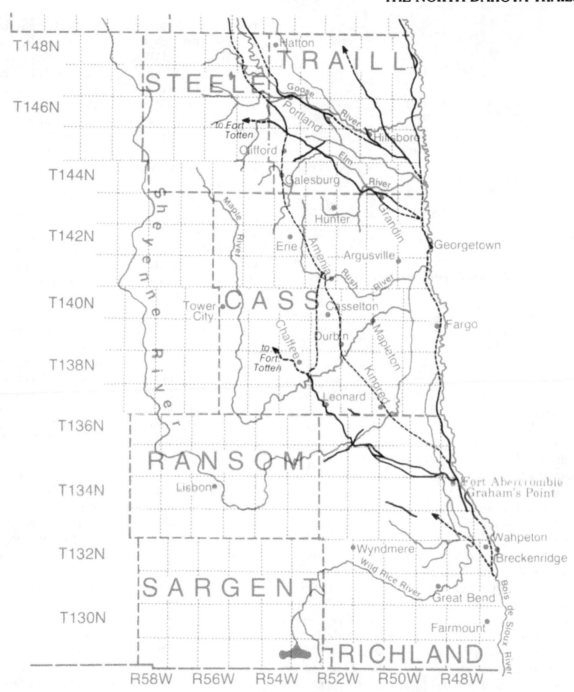

NORTH DAKOTA
TRAILS

View of St. Joseph from Pembina Mountain about 1859

formed on the site, a picturesque spot beside wooded Pembina Mountain, about 30 miles up the Pembina River. When Father Belcourt built a mill there in 1856, St. Joseph was flourishing, with a population of 1,500 French-Canadian, Cree, Ojibway, and Assiniboin métis. Some 80 to 100 substantial log houses clustered about the mountain, while barley and oat fields dotted the lowlands to the east. With Kittson's removal to St. Paul and Belcourt's recall from service in the Northwest in 1859, the community lost its two most notable white citizens, but it remained a thriving métis town. Just as Pembina played its part in politics to the south, St. Joseph assumed a role in politics to the north. When Manitoba went through the agonies of enfranchisement in 1869–70, the town several times served as Louis Riel's haven across the border in those trouble-filled years.[8]

As early as 1851 a visitor to St. Joseph, out of aversion to "exhausting the whole calender of saints, and making every one of them stand as godfather to every town . . . in the territory," tried to persuade Kittson to change the village's name. The suggestion did not bear fruit until many years later when Scandinavian settlers arrived at the old townsite. St. Joseph survives today as Walhalla, North Dakota. Two historic trading-post buildings, including one of Kittson's, still stand there, and Father Belcourt's bell hangs in the steeple of Walhalla's Roman Catholic church.[9]

The cart trail along the north side of the Pembina River leading from Pembina to St. Joseph became a well-worn path while these villages flourished. From St. Joseph, trails branched out to the buffalo-hunting grounds near Devils Lake and to the Ridge Trail leading south toward St. Paul. Often cart trains from

Pembina would proceed first to St. Joseph, then angle southeast through the "shocking marshes" between the Tongue and Pembina rivers. From the steep, muddy banks of the Tongue they could look back for a last view of Pembina Mountain, conspicuous over the plain because of its wooded slopes. Then they turned south along the bluffs to join the Ridge Trail near Mountain, North Dakota. The ford of the Tongue, now flooded by the Renwick Dam, is situated in Icelandic State Park, just west of Akra, North Dakota.[10]

Another well-used trail crossed the Pembina River at Pembina and followed the southern bank of the Tongue through a flat, marshy area dotted with "poplar islands" — thick groves of young trees which looked like islands rising out of the ocean of grass. Passing through present Cavalier, it climbed into the highlands and turned south along the Ridge Trail proper.[11]

The Ridge Trail, or "back country route," was the more important of the two trails in North Dakota. Despite the fact that it required a detour to the west, it had several advantages over the River Trail. For one thing it was drier, because it followed the highlands out of reach of the flooding Red. Even in wet years when standing water covered the benches between the bluffs, travel was easier because the ridges were sandier and less liable to form deep quagmires than the soil in the valley. In addition the tributaries of the Red were easier to ford near their sources, and the relative scarcity of mosquitoes on the higher ridges was a major consideration. Even the lack of woods could be advantageous, for the open country allowed an uninterrupted view over long distances. Prairie travelers had mixed feelings toward gullies, woods, and hills that could provide shelter but might also conceal enemies. On the treeless plains the impersonal forces of nature were known dangers; in the forest other human beings offered hidden threats.[12]

Wayfarers on the North Dakota plains found it impossible to resist images of the sea in describing their surroundings. Even the terminology suggested water travel. "Coteau," derived from the French word for "coast," was used to describe the long line of the hills, "sweeping in a gentle arc like curve from north to south as far as the vision can extend," and looking like nothing so much as land rising from a sea of grass. "Traverse," the French-Canadian voyageurs' word for a trip across a wind-swept lake, was applied to a trail's short leaps across open prairie. The comparison was apt; journeying over the plains on foot or on horseback was reminiscent of the dangers inherent in venturing out on open water in frail canoes. The traveler was at the mercy of the weather; he had no landmarks to navigate by; his judgment was often confused by mirages; and he had to make the leap in a single day, for spending a night exposed to the piercing plains wind without either water or wood was scarcely more desirable than sleeping on an open lake. In bad weather, a group might have to endure long days of delay in the shelter of a valley before chancing a traverse.[13]

But in good weather, a sense of exhilaration often rewarded the traveler who ventured over the rolling land under a cloudless sky of vivid blue. "The security one feels in knowing that there are no concealed dangers, so vast is the extent which the eyes takes in; no difficulties of road; . . . the tempest that can be seen from its beginning to its end; the beautiful modifications of the changing clouds; the curious looming of objects between earth and sky" — all these contributed to the sense of spacious freedom. The night was scarcely less impressive. "As far as the eye can reach on every side sweep the level lines, slowly darkening as they approach the horizon. Nothing obstructs or limits the view of the sky. A whole hemisphere of stars look down upon you," wrote a journalist who followed the Ridge Trail in 1859. Among the experienced fraternity, Red River plains travel must have acquired a mystique resembling that among seafarers.[14]

Fire was a constant hazard on the plains, not only because of the obvious dangers from smoke and flame, but also because it deprived horses and oxen of grass to eat. In late summer and autumn, when fires "frequently darkened the heavens for days together," a constant lookout had to be kept, for the velocity of a fire driven by wind through the withered grass "defies the fleetest horse." Under some circumstances escape from the flames was possible only by setting fire to the grass down-wind and following the flames as they progressed. Lightning was another common danger. Members of Major Woods's military expedition found that their iron tent poles served as lightning rods; many a Red River caravan caught in a storm must have blessed the fact that their carts had not a trace of iron about them.[15]

On the plains, weather seemed larger than life. Robert Clouston, traveling in August, 1846, described how a "dark, portentous cloud" overtook his party with uncanny swiftness: "We were travelling along the ridge . . . without any wood near us and we had barely time to fasten our horses to some low bushes and to cover our baggage and guns, when the storm burst upon us . . . the thunder — crash following crash in quick succession — seemed to rend the very heavens and the vivid glare of the lightning affected our sight with a painful feeling of heat & while the rain and hail fell in torrents — I believe that each feared that the next flash might send him to eternity: people may laugh and joke (as we did) about such things in retrospect, but I never heard one say, that while such a storm was raging around him, he could jest on the subject."

On the first leg of the journey south, from the Tongue to the Forest River, there were so many streams to cross that gathering wood for campfires was not a problem. Fords were the best known and most consistent places along the trail; between them the routes might vary. The tributaries of the Park River, given descriptive names such as Cart, Steephill, and Clear Water, were the first streams the traveler encountered. Far away to the east, the distant line of timber marking the course of the Red could be seen. "We plunge from a shore of wood in the morning to bury ourselves for a few hours in a sea of grass, and to emerge at evening on apparently the same dark shore again," wrote one traveler. The succession of prairie

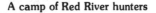

A camp of Red River hunters

and stream imparted a sense of monotony to this leg of the trail in the hot summer of 1859, when the Nobles expedition crossed it. Every day they forded a tributary of the Red, "first a line of blue on the northern horizon, resolving itself into trees which we gradually neared [and crossed], emerging on the other side to another stretch of open prairie, terminated at the distance of twenty or thirty miles by another timbered stream."[16]

Crossing into Walsh County, the trail ran parallel to and west of present State Highway 32 to its intersection with Highway 17, after which it followed the east side of the north branch of the Forest River (then called Big Salt or Saline) to the crossing at present Fordville. This was the most rugged stretch of the Ridge Trail. On the rolling prairie were scattered granite boulders dropped by the glaciers, many of them painted by the Indians with stripes or "a blood-red hand." On the southern bank of the Forest another trail from Pembina joined the Ridge Trail. In 1849 Captain John Pope labeled it "Kittson's New Road."[17]

At the Forest River parties often stopped to gather wood for the traverse to the Turtle. Between these two streams lay another rugged stretch of "high, broken prairie." Two miles southwest of present McCanna, the Ridge Trail's route intersected that of a later east-west stage road from Grand Forks to Fort Totten at Devils Lake. The spot where the stage road crossed U.S. Highway 2 is marked about five miles east of Niagara; nearly four miles farther southeast the Ridge Trail crossed the highway almost exactly at the ford of the Turtle River's south branch. On the banks of the Turtle travelers encountered Indian mounds which they thought resembled "a rude attempt at a field-work." Tradition held that the area was an old battleground between the Dakota and the Ojibway, and that the earthworks were built by the latter for defense.[18]

South of the Turtle the trail encountered some of the many tributaries of the Goose River, each marked by abrupt banks cut deep into the prairie. Between streams the land remained as flat "as if it had been adjusted in its horizontal by a spirit-level." When Goose River was reached, its high, wooded banks presented a handsome contrast to the otherwise featureless country.

Here several branches developed in the trail in later years. One route, probably used after 1860 by cart trains traveling via Georgetown, followed the north bank of the Little Goose River to the site of the present State Highway 18 bridge, at which point the trail forded the stream. Crossing the Goose River's south branch at Portland, it continued along the south bank to join the River Trail near the mouth of the Elm. Another branch from Georgetown followed the southern bank of the Elm River, crossing the Ridge Trail north of present Clifford, and continuing to Devils Lake. After 1867 this became the route used by the military between Georgetown and Fort Totten. It is possible that this military road followed an even older path linking the Ridge Trail with the ford of the Red at the mouth of the Sheyenne River. The Elm River route seems to have been the one described by the Nobles expedition in July, 1859, as rising from the "low marshy surface, intersected with numerous *coulees* and bad sloughs" along the Red onto "immense plateaux," where it met the Ridge Trail amid a profusion of wild flowers.[19]

But the oldest and most important branch of the Ridge Trail kept to the west side of the Little Goose River, passing several miles west of Portland. South of the Goose, its route becomes uncertain, since the two trails from Georgetown largely superseded it in later years, and the old route had disappeared into the prairie grass by the time the state was surveyed. We know that it cut across high, flat prairie in a "grande traverse" to the Rush (Rivière La Prelle to the French) nearly 30 miles away. Halfway between the Goose and Rush, it reached the edge of a gentle slope where travelers sometimes paused to admire the view. "We came upon a cluster of hills of considerable elevation," Major Woods wrote on his trip north, "and after ascending them, we could see off to the west and south west their continuation; but in our direction, west of north — they extended but a few miles, and a flat country was still before us."[20]

South of the Rush the land dropped in elevation, for here the trail no longer followed the highest part of the coteau. The traverse to the Maple was made over a "large flat Prairie" in dry years and an interminable marsh in wet ones. After "a hard days work under a burning sun, and through clouds of mosquitoes" travelers arrived at the Maple River, which they seem to have crossed at several places. The best known is the historic Watson Crossing now marked opposite St. Peter's Lutheran Church three miles south and one mile east of Chaffee. An earlier crossing apparently existed farther down the Maple, where Major Woods in 1849 found that one of the bridges built by Kittson had washed out. In 1851, when Governor Alexander Ramsey's party used the Watson Crossing, they were following a "new road, and a good one, made during a season of high water." The Watson ford was much frequented in later years as part of a military route between Forts Abercrombie and Totten.[21]

The largest river to be crossed in North Dakota was the "rapid turbid" Sheyenne, which boasted at least three fords. The highest of these was the most used. It was known in the early days as the "Butte de Sable" crossing, so named for the sand hills nearby; it was called Nolan's crossing for Anthony Nolan, a homesteader who settled near it in the 1860s. Located in Barrie Township, Richland County, where the Sheyenne "emerges from the highlands," it was bridged each year by the cart brigades with rough logs which washed away in the first spring freshet. The crossing was a picturesque spot, with high bluffs on the south side from which the traveler could see the Sheyenne "rolling rapidly about two hundred feet below, and a vast expanse of rolling prairie away off to the north." Later the ford was heavily used by traffic on the Fort Totten-Fort Abercrombie road. It was located where State Highway 18 now bridges the Sheyenne.[22]

From the Nolan ford, three trails led to the Red. One angled southeast to meet the Bois de Sioux four to six miles above its mouth, where an easy ford took travelers into Minnesota. The other two were parallel routes leading to the old ford of the Red at Graham's Point — named for Duncan Graham, who had operated a fur post there early in the 19th century.

Near this well-used crossing, Major Woods in 1849 recommended the construction of a military post, to be placed at "the prettiest location in the country," a protected spot a mile or two north of Graham's Point where "the prairie comes up to the water's edge, and extends as far as the eye can reach north, west, and south." Eight years elapsed before the post that became Fort Abercrombie was authorized by the War Department. Then Lieutenant Colonel John J. Abercrombie was dispatched with a company of the 20th United States Infantry to build it on a narrow neck of land surrounded by the Red River on three sides. Later, because of repeated flooding, the post was moved to higher ground a few hundred yards away. A heavy belt of oak, elm, ash, and basswood extended along the river, and the soldiers used this timber to hew the unimposing log buildings. "Rough place, this Abercrombie!" a visiting St. Paul journalist remarked sarcastically in 1859. "Ten thousand dollars expended to make one moderately-sized cottage on the prairie, for the quarters of [the] commanding officer . . . and the residue gone into a number of low mud-chinked log huts for the subordinate and private fry, arranged in the form of a square under the big trees of Graham's Point, to frighten the Indians." Though the fort was besieged briefly during the Dakota War of 1862, it proved more useful as a steamboat terminal, stagecoach stop, and hotel for travelers to the Red River than as the stronghold its name suggested. The fort is now partially restored in a park at Abercrombie, North Dakota.[23]

The west bank River Trail from Pembina to the Bois de Sioux River was active both earlier and later than the Ridge Trail, but it was not as often used during the height of Red River traffic. The reason for this was largely topographical. The trail ran through alluvial bottom land along the west bank of the Red, more or less near the timber belt lining the river. Its route was thus on a flat plain "subject to inundations that at periods of years turn nearly the whole valley for hundreds of miles . . . into an inland sea." Even in dry years the river bottom was riddled with sinkholes of stagnant surface water and intersected by ravines. The little tributaries of the Red, easily forded on the Ridge Trail, were here "as bad as the most inextricable Red River mud can make them." Even in the best of times, the trail was only practical in autumn and winter when the marshes were either dry or frozen.[24]

Fort Abercrombie
in 1862,
by Robert O. Sweeney

In 1832 when Robert Campbell traveled south from the Red River Settlement, he stated that no River Trail existed south of Pembina, but that his party "followed the course of the river from point to point." By 1836 a trail had come into being, for in that year a trader going north struck a well-defined path along the river. During the next year the Red River schoolteacher Peter Garrioch recorded a trip south over the route with a brigade of carts. The journey was punctuated by laborious crossings of the tributaries of the Red, each accomplished by constructing a temporary bridge. The landmarks on this trail were the loops or "points" of the winding Red, many of which had names. Grand Point near Drayton, Walnut Point north of Manvel, and Turtle Point east of Hillsboro were among the most prominent.[25]

After leaving Pembina experienced travelers hurried past the first two tributaries of the Red — the Park and Forest rivers — because their waters were so heavily impregnated with salt they could not be used for cooking or drinking. Many a miserable night was spent by unwary wayfarers who camped on these streams. Drawing south past the Turtle River, the cart trains reached English Coulee, a landmark near present Grand Forks. This dry ravine was then known as Tully's Creek for David Tully, the Red River blacksmith who met his death there about 1823. Soon after crossing Tully's Creek, the cart trains passed the Grand Forks, where the Red and Red Lake rivers meet. Early travelers invested this spot with an importance it no longer possesses, for Canadians, who believed the source of Red River to be Red Lake, considered this the point where they left the Red and began to follow what they called the Sioux River south.[26]

Beyond the Grand Forks, travelers entered "the heart of the wilderness, and consequently [were] in the very centre of danger." One party adopted the following precautions to avoid an unpleasant encounter with the Dakota: "(1) Start about 3 A.M. (2)

Breakfast about 9, if wood and water were convenient. (3) Camp near sundown. (4) Two to keep watch over camp and horses every night. Generally after our evening meal, we moved off some distance before lying down for the night in case the smoke from our fire would be seen by the Indians." Another group took care to sleep at a little distance from their carts "because Indians generally fire under a cart thinking that people invariably use such shelter." The danger was particularly acute as travelers neared the junction of the Otter Tail and Bois de Sioux, an area considered "debatable land" between the Ojibway and Dakota during the 1830s.[27]

The River Trail re-emerged as a major route with the beginning of steamboat navigation on the Red in 1859. In response to steamboat service, tiny settlements began to spring up along the shores of the river, and the old trail was the only land link between them. After regular postal service was inaugurated between Fort Abercrombie and St. Paul in 1859, mail was carried over the River Trail all the way to the Canadian settlements. Throughout the 1860s the mail went in an intermittent, "go-as-you-please" way by foot, cart, and dog team. All this changed in 1871 when Russell Blakeley's Minnesota Stage Company received a contract to carry the mail to Winnipeg. Improvements were forthwith made in the road, bridges were built, and the new stage route was opened in September, 1871. Stage stops were made at all the settlements then in existence on both sides of the river: Pembina, Twelve-Mile Point near Joliette, Bowesmont-Long Point four miles north of Drayton, Kelly Point or Girard's Station at Acton, Turtle River station north of Manvel, Grand Forks, Buffalo Coulee, Frog Point, Goose Prairie, Elm River, Georgetown, Oak Point, Twenty-Four-Mile Point, McCauleyville, and Breckenridge. In a few years daily postal service was established, and the old cart trail became a well-traveled stagecoach road.[28]

4 ~ THE MINNESOTA VALLEY TRAIL

IN THE MINNESOTA VALLEY, the original avenue of travel was the Minnesota River itself. Unlike the Red, the Minnesota was easily navigable for canoes and keelboats — in wet years from Mendota to Lac qui Parle and in dry years to Patterson's Rapids in Renville County or to Traverse des Sioux in Nicollet County. Though in later years the cart trails extended progressively farther and farther down the valley toward St. Paul, the river always remained a formidable rival for their traffic. The first immigrants to trek south from the Selkirk Settlement abandoned their carts at the Minnesota's headwaters and completed their journey in dugout canoes. By 1835 the American Fur Company's boats met the southbound carts at Patterson's Rapids, and throughout the 1840s and 1850s Traverse des Sioux was the rendezvous point between cart and keelboat. Only in the last years of the Red River trails did any considerable number of carts make the trip all the way to Mendota.[1]

The Minnesota Valley route was the earliest of the Red River trails across Minnesota, and it remained the principal one throughout the 1840s and early 1850s until it was supplanted by the two shorter northerly routes. Though the Minnesota Valley Trail was by far the longest of the three, entailing a wide detour to the south, it had many advantages. It was safer in bad weather, for the river was a constant landmark, and wood and water were always available.

The country was less lonely, for as early as the 1830s the valley was dotted with fur posts, missions, and Dakota villages — and in the later years, with two government agencies and a fort. As the carts moved south, furs from the many American Fur Company posts along the way could be added to the caravan. Not least important, the route traversed a region wholly claimed by the Dakota, which lay well south of the disputed no man's land between that tribe and the Ojibway. In the years before clashes over buffalo hunting created enmity between the Dakota and métis in the 1840s, the plains tribe offered friendship, trade, and protection to the passing cart trains.[2]

The Minnesota Valley trails along both the north and south banks of the river followed Indian paths that had been used from the earliest times, and it is impossible to define at what point they developed into cart trails. As the commencement of cart traffic is obscure, so its termination is clouded by the fact that most of the trails became government roads during the 1850s. For example, the establishment of Fort Ridgely in 1853 was the occasion for the improvement of the trail from Traverse des Sioux to the fort; the founding of Fort Abercrombie on the Red River in 1858 probably inspired an upgrading of the cart road along the north side of the Minnesota from Fort

Métis drivers using horse-pulled carts

43

Ridgely to the Bois de Sioux; and the old trail along the south side of the river in Redwood and Yellow Medicine counties seems to have received similar attention with the establishment of the Upper and Lower Sioux agencies in 1854. In many places the trails depicted on the maps in this chapter show the routes after their conversion to government and military uses. Undoubtedly these developments produced some minor variations in the older routes, but, in general, the outlines were the same.[3]

There was a definite seasonal pattern to the usage of the main trails on the north side of the Minnesota Valley. Holding close to the rivers and lakes was a winter trail for local and bad-weather travel. This river-bottom route was impractical in spring and summer when the water was high, so an alternative developed on the prairie along the edge of the bluffs lining the valley. Still another trail ran along the south side of the Minnesota River as far east as the mouth of the Cottonwood at present New Ulm. There both trails left the Minnesota to take a short cut across the prairie instead of following the stream's southernmost bend. Since most cart brigades made their journeys in the summer months, it can be assumed that the dry bluff trails were those most often used. The one on the north bank was undoubtedly preferred, for it was shorter and more convenient, but parties who had reason to visit the valley's fur posts or missions probably used the south side. Certainly many explorers and others did so. Only at two places did the trails break away from the river altogether: at Traverse des Sioux and near Lakes Traverse and Big Stone.[4]

Cart trains that had completed the long journey south over the North Dakota trails crossed the Bois de

The Bois de Sioux River, about 1853

Sioux River into present Minnesota and traveled along the east bank to a spot north of present-day Wheaton. The Bois de Sioux could be forded almost anywhere along its length. In some years it was little more than a trench in the prairie, with a muddy bottom and steep banks, while in others it could reach "swimming depth for horses." When Lieutenant Colonel John Abercrombie traveled this way in 1858, he noticed but did not use a ford halfway between the mouths of the Rabbit and Otter Tail rivers. Instead his troops built a bridge just above the mouth of the Rabbit to avoid crossing the bad slough there. The Bois de Sioux Valley had no trees, except for the occasional "isles des bois" or "islands of wood" that gave the river its name, and this part of the trail was considered a traverse. "Nothing but a boundless prospect presented itself to our view," wrote a Red River mixed-blood who passed this way with an 1837 cart train. "Nothing but one continuous stretch of wild and barren plains! Not a tree of the most solitary or diminutive kind could be discerned throughout the vast extent of this beautiful prairie; and nothing but a little brush or scrub, occasionally scattered over its surface . . . gave variety to the almost universal sameness of scenery."[5]

North of the Mustinka River (called the Rabbit River in early days, this being the meaning of its Dakota name) the trail branched. The eastern route set out on a long traverse across the prairie through the present sites of Wheaton, Graceville, and Clinton, returning to the safety of a river valley only at Lac qui Parle. This was the route taken by the cart trains when they wished to bypass Lake Traverse and go down the north side of the Minnesota. It struck one traveler as being a "barren, groveless and howling prairie" the whole way, but in reality it wound by a number of prairie lakes and crossed the continental divide near Clinton in the vicinity of "the first hills we had the pleasure of seeing since we left R[ed] R[iver] S[ettlement]."[6]

The western route followed the Bois de Sioux to the shores of Mud Lake (then called Buffalo Lake), crossed the sluggish Mustinka, and continued along a high ridge paralleling Lake Traverse, which lay in a broad valley more than 100 feet below the prairie. From here the western horizon was bounded by the distant outline of the Coteau des Prairies, the height of land dividing the waters of the Minnesota from those of the Missouri.[7]

Fur posts had existed at this southernmost source of the Red River since at least 1800, when Robert Dickson set up shop at Lake Traverse. Later the Co-

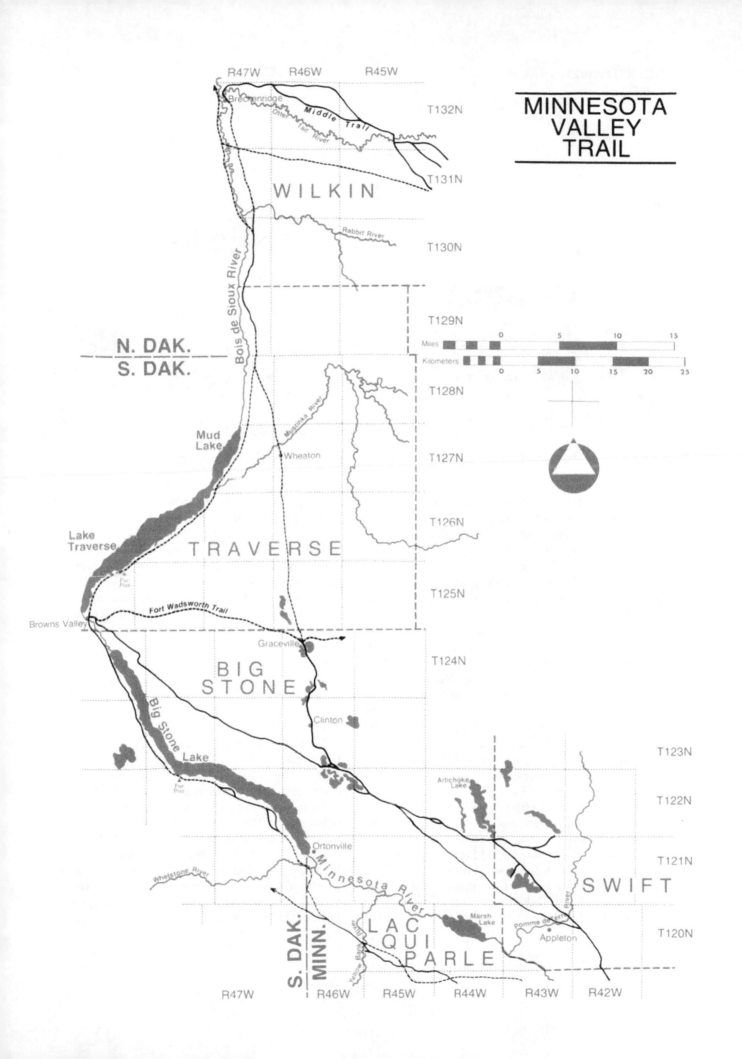

MINNESOTA VALLEY TRAIL

A Dakota village and platform for the dead near the stockaded Columbia Fur Company post at Lake Traverse in 1823

lumbia Fur Company took over, apparently building its post on the same site, "beautifully situated on the edge of the lake and at the base of the hills" opposite a small island. Despite its scenic location, the Lake Traverse post was apparently an unprepossessing structure. "The houses, which are built of logs & covered with bark & earth, are enclosed by a sorry stockade," wrote a member of Major Long's party in 1823. The huts, only "sufficient to accommodate thos[e] necessary to carry on the affairs of the establishment," had parchment windows through which "a mild light" was admitted. Nor was life comfortable there. When the fastidious English geologist George W. Featherstonhaugh visited the post in 1835, he said that the resident trader treated him to a "disgusting" meal "of the coarsest kind . . . a few broken plates, placed on a filthy board, with what he called coffee, and maize bread to correspond."[8]

Cart trains sometimes paused at the Lake Traverse post to pick up furs bound for Mendota or to take advantage of the protection of the Dakota band living there. From Lake Traverse two routes could be used: one on the northeast side of Big Stone Lake and one on the southwest. A third also converged on Lake Traverse in later years — the military trail to Fort Wadsworth in South Dakota. Whether it followed the route of an older Red River trail in this area is not

known, but it would have been a connecting link rather than a major trail. Both paths to the south crossed the low continental divide separating the waters of Hudson Bay from those of the Gulf of Mexico just after leaving Lake Traverse. Here from time immemorial the Indians had placed two weather-beaten buffalo skulls where travelers paused to smoke a pipe at the divide. "Should I gain nothing else by traveling," a Red River colonist reflected after crossing the divide, "I have gained at least this much, viz, that I have had the pleasure of seeing water running to[ward] both poles. . . . Thus, said I, should Newton never have been born, I could at least have known that this our world was not as flat as a pancake."[9]

Continuing on the west side of Big Stone Lake, one trail ran along the bluffs about a quarter-mile from the water. When Featherstonhaugh went this way he was impressed by the charm of the scene: "I suddenly came to an abrupt and lofty bank, and looking down, beheld one of the most beautiful lakes I had ever seen in North America, describing for a great distance very graceful curves, with fine bluffs about 200 feet in height, and well-grown woods covering the slope beneath me down to the water's edge. . . . Gaining the upland, [I] had a very beautiful ride along the west bank of this charming lake."[10]

Hazen Mooers, who was to become one of the grand old men of the Minnesota fur trade, was working for the American Fur Company at a post near present Hartford Beach in Roberts County, South Dakota, as early as 1823. Situated on the shores of Big Stone, the post catered to a Dakota band who lived nearby and planted their gardens on a rocky island in the lake. In the 1840s Martin McLeod had a post on this lake which may have stood on the same spot. Today the sites of the fur posts and the Indian village on the shore can be seen in wayside parks on Roberts County Road 109.[11]

The trail on the northeast side of Big Stone Lake could be more hazardous, for it crossed open prairie. A winter trail that kept closer to the lake may have existed but no record remains. The halfway point on the prairie trail was a place called both Les Grosses Isles and Lake of Big Islands, about 20 miles by road from the Pomme de Terre River. The names probably referred to a stand of trees surrounding a group of prairie lakes south of present Clinton. The traverse from Wheaton also passed this spot. A party of travelers caught on the unprotected plain in an October sleet storm was almost reduced to burning its cart before reaching the shelter of Les Grosses Isles. "My situation became exceedingly painful," one of their number remarked; "my whole exterior, as well as the head and neck of the mare, was covered with a glazing of ice; night was advancing, and we were without a guide, upon a dreary and shelterless moor of very great extent." Finally the party's horses, wise from long experience, found the stand of trees.[12]

The next landmark along the trail was Lac qui Parle, where a fur post, mission, and Indian village were situated at the lower end of the lake. If they were on the north bank, the carts had to ford only the Pomme de Terre River, "a most beautiful crystal stream of water" with a firm gravel bed, before reaching the site of present Milan, where a branch of the trail led to the buildings at the foot of the lake. If the carts were on the south side, the Whetstone and the Yellow Bank (then called Hra Wahkan or "Spirit Mountain") rivers had to be forded. Along this stretch many of the glacial boulders that gave Big Stone Lake its name could be seen, some painted and decorated by the Dakota. Drawing east down the gradual slope to Lac qui Parle, travelers slowly lost sight of the Coteau des Prairies as it dropped from view beyond the western horizon.[13]

Many a Red River cart train gladly paused at the Lac qui Parle trading post of Joseph Renville on the north side of the Minnesota River. This veteran French-Dakota fur trader's establishment was, according to the French explorer Joseph N. Nicollet, "the only place open with hospitality to the travelers who cross these vast deserted regions of the northwestern United States. He gives, with all the excellence of his spirit, not only hospitality but official protection that is always necessary in these quarters." The protection of Joseph Renville was not to be taken lightly! A member by marriage of the Wahpeton band, he not only had friends and relatives throughout the tribe, but he also maintained his own bodyguard of warriors to protect himself and his property from invasions by the unfriendly Ojibway. Having established himself opposite the Wahpeton village at Lac qui Parle in 1826, he lived for the two decades until his death in a stockaded post complete with bastion and watchtower that came to be known as Fort Renville. The log post had a storehouse for trade goods, two dwellings, and a resident population of fleas "so plenty that they could almost walk away with our blankets." The room where Renville received guests had "a large open fireplace, in which his Frenchmen, or 'French-boys,' as they were called by the Indians, piled up an enormous quantity of wood of a cold day. . . . A bench ran almost around the entire room, on which they sat or reclined. Mr. Renville usually sat on a chair in the middle of the room." In this setting, the trader lived "in a barbaric splendor quite like an African king."[14]

Under Renville's protection was a Protestant mission established in 1835 by Dr. Thomas S. Williamson. In small log buildings beneath the bluffs about a mile from Fort Renville, the missionaries held services, taught classes, translated the Bible into the Dakota language, farmed, and tried their best to "civilize" the independent Dakota. Many a tired Red River trader praised the "kindness and sociability" of the missionaries who invited him to partake of food and worship. In turn, the missionaries depended upon the cart caravans to carry their mail to Mendota. During the summer months, one missionary recalled, the carts passed so frequently that "we received our mail as often as once in five or six weeks" instead of the usual three to five months.[15]

After Renville's death in 1846, the irreligious Martin McLeod took over the fur business at Lac qui Parle, building his post on the southwest side of the river. Hostility to the mission increased among the Dakota once Renville's devout influence was removed. In 1854, having been largely unsuccessful, the missionaries abandoned Lac qui Parle and moved to the Upper Sioux Agency. The sites of Fort Renville

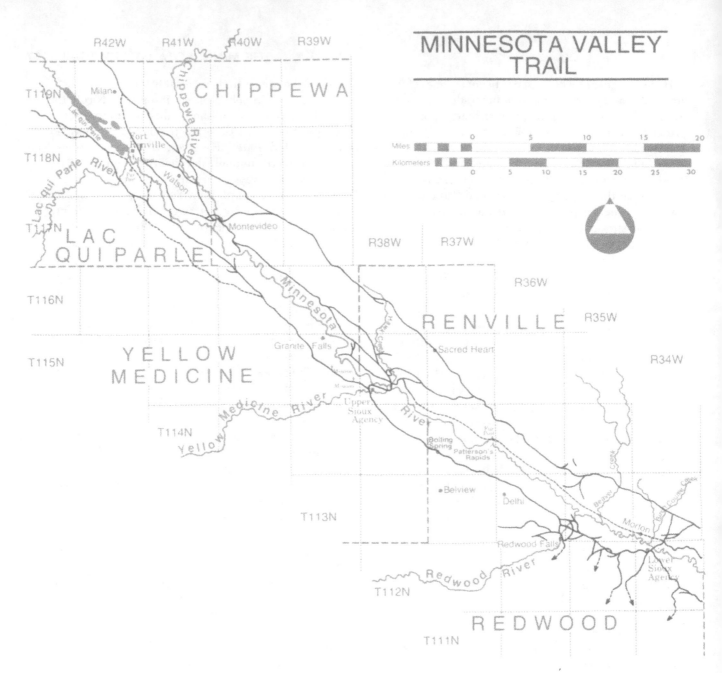

and the mission are marked on Chippewa County Road 13 northwest of Montevideo, and the mission church has been reconstructed in a state wayside.

Since the mission and fort were below the bluffs, they were invisible from the main trail along the north bank. But a short detour to the edge of the bluff provided a fine view of what one traveler from Red River thought was "the loveliest spot we saw on our journey." The Minnesota Valley, "as usual about two miles wide, lay before me to the south. To the west was the lake, about eight miles long, all the lowlands adjacent to it being very well wooded, with the upland prairie in the distance. In front of the height where I stood was the alluvial land with the fort and the village, this last consisting of forty-eight Nacotah

[*Dakota*] skin lodges, and twelve large bark-covered teebees, with Indians strolling about in every direction."[16]

From the opposite side of the river, Fort Renville could be reached by the first good ford of the Minnesota at the east end of Lac qui Parle. The south shore trail then veered away from the Minnesota, crossing over the high, white sandbanks of the Lac qui Parle River (Beaver River to the traders, and Watapan Intapa to the Dakota) and continuing south across the prairie.

The long stretch from Lac qui Parle to Traverse des Sioux was a well-beaten path, "usually good enough for any vehicle from a Red river Buggy ie. a wooden cart . . . to a four horse coach." The journey could be made in less than a week on horseback, but it took seven days with oxen and up to twelve days in bad weather. The Minnesota and its tributaries were lined with river-bottom forest — elm, ash, and cottonwood — with occasional oak openings extending up onto the prairie. On the north side, timber was scanty and scattered, but the south side was heavily wooded throughout Yellow Medicine, Redwood, and Brown counties. The river bottoms sheltered a multitude of small lakes, "not generally beautiful," commented Nicollet, "but they are rich in game, in wild rice, and other useful plants."[17]

The curse of the Minnesota Valley was the mosquitoes, which travelers swore were worse here than any other place on the trail. The swarms of insects could be so thick that "they choked down every expression that would consign them to the shades. It was impossible to talk without inhaling them." The animals suffered most acutely. "I rode a cream-colored horse," one man wrote, "and was unable to distinguish the color of the animal so thickly was he covered." At night sleep was totally impossible without the protection of a mosquito net or a smudge fire made from rotten wood covered with dry and green grass. Even then the travelers lay awake listening to the sound of mosquitoes pattering against their tents like falling rain. The insects were not merely a nuisance, they were a real menace. If the horses or oxen were so tortured by mosquitoes that they could not eat, they soon grew too weak to draw the carts.[18]

Although in later years at least three crossings existed on the Minnesota between Lac qui Parle and the mouth of the Chippewa River at present Montevideo, no dependable ford seems to have been used in the early part of the 19th century. On the other hand, two good crossings of the Chippewa could be found within five miles of the Lac qui Parle Mission. These two solid, sandy fords were used by the missionaries and traders to reach the main trail along the bluff. Between the Chippewa River and thickly wooded Hawk Creek (called Rivière l'Eau de Vie by the traders) lay 25 miles of prairie. Hawk Creek could be forded northwest of Sacred Heart where traces of the old route could still be seen in the 1930s. On the south bank trail another easy ford led across the Yellow Medicine River where it ran into the Minnesota over a solid, pebbly bed.[19]

On the high banks near the mouth of the Yellow Medicine in the 1850s was a cluster of government and mission buildings connected with the Upper Sioux Agency. In 1852 the Pajutazee (meaning "yel-

Drivers pose with hide-covered, cargo-laden carts

low medicine") Mission was founded by Thomas Williamson at the Dakota village there, and a few years later construction began on the agency, which served as one of the two administrative centers on the Dakota reservations created by the treaties of 1851. In 1854 missionary Stephen R. Riggs also moved from Lac qui Parle to Yellow Medicine where he opened the Hazelwood Mission about three miles from Williamson's. The trail along the south bank passed all of these landmarks, and it was heavily used for government and mission business until the Dakota War in 1862 destroyed all three establishments. The site of the partially restored Upper Sioux Agency can now be reached from State Highway 67.[20]

In the Minnesota River between the mouths of the Yellow Medicine and the Redwood lay Patterson's Rapids, where Joseph R. Brown operated a trading post in the 1840s. Here the south bank trail ran over a "level prairie." A notable feature along this stretch was the Boiling Spring (now marked just off Redwood County Road 7, four miles north of Belview), near which travelers often camped. A bit farther on, east of present Delhi, Redwood County has marked a segment of the trail which can still be seen where it crosses County Road 17.[21]

The "wide and romantic valley" at the mouth of the Redwood River was a sight many travelers must have paused to admire. "The beautiful and diversified vegetation, springing luxuriantly on the banks of both streams, the rapid current of the waters rushing to one common point, formed a landscape, which . . . appeared to us as smiling and as beautiful as any we had ever beheld," wrote a member of Major Long's party in 1823. The location of a Dakota village in the early days, the mouth of the Redwood was considered for the site of a second Indian center, but when the Lower Sioux Agency was established in 1854, it was placed several miles farther down the Minnesota River. There near the large Dakota village of Little Crow lived the agent and his staff as well as a number of traders.[22]

Today the role of the Lower Agency in the history of the Minnesota Valley and the Dakota War is carefully explained in a modern interpretive center on Redwood County Road 2, eight miles southeast of Redwood Falls. Also to be found on County Road 2 six miles north of Morgan is a marker for a portion of the Minnesota Valley Trail. A few miles farther on in present Brown County, the south bank route passed a lone cottonwood tree, a well-known landmark now recalled only in the name of Lone Tree Lake.

On the north side the trail crossed an "immense and almost interminable plain" between Hawk and Little Rock creeks. Stephen R. Riggs, one of the missionaries who often passed this way, commented that "With all its green and blue and gold, the prairie gets to be an old story. The little elevations and depressions are just such as you have seen a hundred times before, and you begin to wish for something different from simple beauty. Then, too, the sun shines out with unwonted force. It blazes and scratches and blisters, and you begin to long for 'the shadow of a great rock in a weary land.'" In this section of the trail two major streams had to be forded — Beaver and Birch Coulee creeks. Then, entering present Nicollet County, the route ran over a "level and elevated prairie." On an oak-covered bluff here, during the last two years of cart traffic, Fort Ridgely was built to defend the frontier and watch over the Dakota reservations on the Minnesota River. Now the fort's site is preserved and open to visitors in Fort Ridgely State Park.[23]

South of Fort Ridgely a branch of the trail neared the river at the mouth of Little Rock Creek. In 1835 Hazen Mooers, by then an independent trader, was busy building a post here on the south side of the Minnesota River — a post where hospitality was extended to the passing cart trains. At Little Rock the Red River schoolteacher Peter Garrioch and four friends on their way to Mendota in 1837 paused to build a canoe to carry them the rest of the way. Sleeping in Mooers' post after weeks on the trail, Garrioch proclaimed that they were "as dignified as lords, as cheerful as monkeys, and as snug as so many bedbugs." Mooers was not, however, allowed to remain in unchallenged possession of the site for long. By

1838 an American Fur Company post under Joseph Laframboise was open at the mouth of the creek, on the north side of the river. It, too, became a noted stopping point. Going east it was the last post before the long jump to Traverse des Sioux, and for many years it was the last post before Lac qui Parle for those traveling in the opposite direction. Laframboise's stockaded cluster of buildings was situated about 200 yards from the river near "a bold point . . . covered with huge granite rocks, some the size of medium dwelling houses." Besides being a haven in the wilderness, the post was said to be "one of the most beautiful and imposing upon the river."[24]

Past Little Rock the north bank trail lay "along the side of the bluff at the only height where a nearly level straight course could be obtained," closely following the route of present Nicollet County Road 5. The south bank trail also ran along the bluff until reaching the site of present New Ulm, where it descended into the valley. Pausing at the edge of the bluff, the admiring explorer Joseph Nicollet wrote: "The view to the south seems limitless, the verdure losing itself far away in the azure of the sky. The spectacle is full of grandeur because of its simplicity. . . . To the east of the plateau is a skirt of woods lining the Cottonwood; it is only a mile from us and soon disappears to reappear from time to time in the distance. In the west, the tops of the trees that run along the rise, bordering the left bank of the Minnesota, form a long black band along the horizon."[25]

The trail descended from the bluff to reach an old and important ford of the Minnesota River just below the mouth of the Cottonwood. On the way it passed the village of the Dakota Chief Sleepy Eyes, then crossed a ravine in the south-central part of present New Ulm. In later years a ferry existed above the mouth of the Cottonwood (which has changed position in recent times), but the important early crossing was a quarter-mile below. Though the bed of the Minnesota here was solid and rocky, the water was sometimes so deep that carts had to be unloaded for the ford. On the other side, the south bank and the north bank trails united for the final traverse famous as Traverse des Sioux.

There were two possible ways to make the traverse. One went north of Swan Lake along what is now Nicollet County Road 5; the other swept in a gentle arc south of the lake along the approximate route of present State Highway 99. Both trails existed at least as early as 1838. The traveler's choice probably depended upon the wetness of the season, the weather, and whether he was coming from the north or the south bank trail.

The land over which the traverse ran was "not grand, unless mere space can be called grand," but it had its charms. "Rolling prairies stretched on every hand of the horizon, sprinkled with flowers, and with groves frequently in sight. There was always a gem of a lake at the grove, sometimes not more than a hundred acres or so, sometimes several miles in extent." Trees were almost invariably to be found clustered on the east side of the lakes, because the prevailing winds blew from the west in the autumn when prairie fires swept through. The trails moved in short jumps from lake to lake, Swan, Middle, Goose, and Timber being the most important. In late summer or in a dry year these expanses of water were often so choked with grass that they seemed like little more than a group of ponds. But the seasons never seemed to affect the marshes, which were the bane of the traverse. The trails wound crazily to and fro in an attempt to avoid the worst of them, but they never seem to quite succeed in doing so. A missionary crossing the Wewe Shecha or "bad swamp" said that the earth "so bent and shook under the tramp of our teams, that we could almost believe it would break through and let us into the earth's centre." Even by 1853, when an improved road was being built over this stretch, great care had to be taken to avoid this "big slough."[26]

As the trails neared the settlement of Traverse des Sioux they plunged into a stand of woods, emerging to descend the gentle terraced bluff to the Minnesota River. For many years the cart brigades ended their journey here, amid Indian lodges and fields of corn, beans, and potatoes. The small Sisseton village at Traverse des Sioux was situated "upon a wide slope of prairie, which rose gradually from the banks of the river and extended far, far back, covered with luxuriant grass." The location had been known from the earliest days as the site of a good ford of the Minnesota — a ford with a hard sandy bottom, easy grades on both banks, and water only as deep as a man's chest. Here Louis Provençalle, also called Le Blanc, established a fur post in the 1820s, remaining a fixture of the locale until his death about 1850. And here in 1840 Martin McLeod opened a rival post, and Stephen Riggs in 1843 established a mission.[27]

Traverse des Sioux gained lasting notoriety in 1851 as the site of treaty negotiations with the Dakota, but its importance for the Red River trails was as a transfer point. Here during the trails' early years goods hauled slowly south by oxcart were loaded onto keelboats for the final leg of the trip down the Minnesota to Mendota. As late as 1853 Traverse des Sioux's main function was symbolized by the "165 carts [which] can be seen at a time, loaded with the imports from the North." The site, which was platted as a town in 1855, can now be seen in Traverse des Sioux State Park, two miles north of St. Peter on U.S. Highway 169.[28]

There was a good reason why the carts did not often travel beyond Traverse des Sioux. North of this point the Minnesota River flowed through the heart of Les Bois Francs, or "the Big Woods," a broad belt of hardwoods that once covered south-central Minnesota. The route through these woods was swampy, humid, and hilly, making cart traffic difficult. In 1835,

Sketch of cart outside trader's cabin at Traverse des Sioux by Frank B. Mayer, 1851

despite the fact that the path through the Big Woods was "almost impassible [sic]," a group of immigrants from Red River made it through with 50 or 60 head of cattle. Two years later not even a horse could get through, but in 1838 John C. Frémont managed to transport several carts from Mendota to Traverse des Sioux. This must have been an unusual feat, for in 1840 it was "regarded as absolutely impossible to take any wheeled vehicle through by land to Fort Snelling" from the Traverse.[29]

During the following decade, traffic became more frequent. The trail along the Minnesota as it eventually evolved, according to Martin McLeod, avoided "the continual meanderings of this winding stream," but kept "nearly paralell [sic] to it on its south[east] side." By 1854 a road had been surveyed along the route of the trail, and mail was being carried over it whenever steamboats could not get up the river. A modern traveler can follow the general route of the trail from Le Sueur to Shakopee on U.S. Highway 169.[30]

The trail did not plunge directly into the Big Woods at Traverse des Sioux. After fording the river to the east side, travelers proceeded through the wooded bottom lands for a few miles, then emerged onto a distinctive prairie known in early days as Prairie de Pierre au Flèche, later shortened to Prairie la Flèche or "Arrow Prairie." This grassy expanse stretched roughly between the present towns of Ottawa and Le Sueur. It was once the gathering place of the Sisseton when they left for buffalo hunts or wild-rice expeditions, or when they waited for the traders who came up the Minnesota. Glacial deposits of granite boulders could be found in this area; one was described as "painted on the top with red & crowned with a grass fillet." At the southern end of the prairie stood an

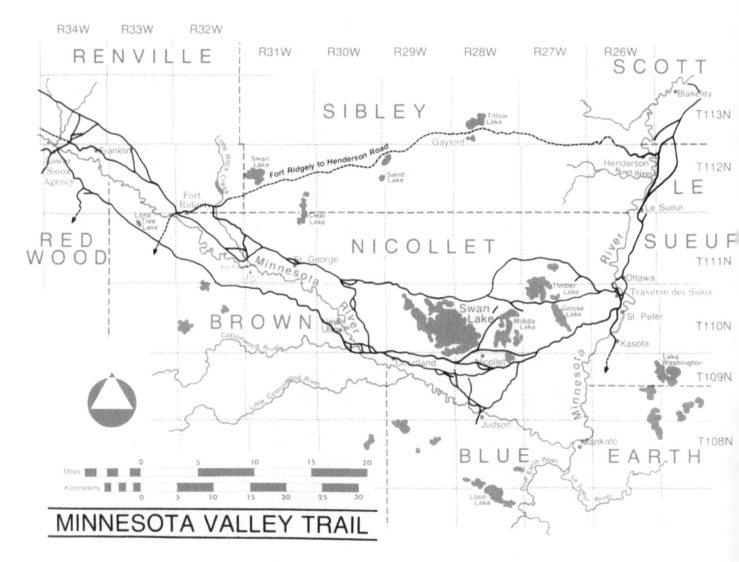

MINNESOTA VALLEY TRAIL

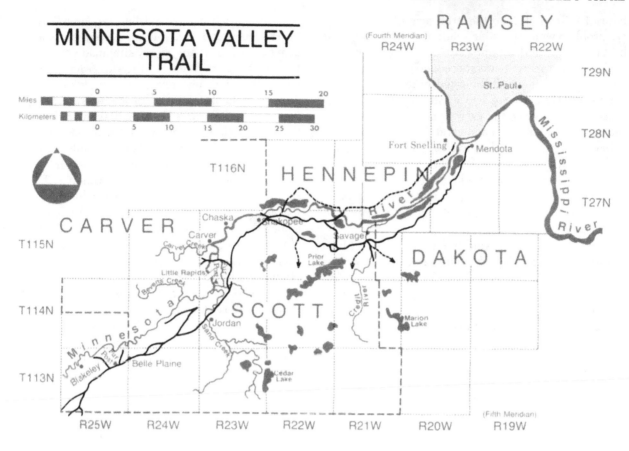

unusual bluff known as the White Rock, rising 60 to 80 feet above the silent river.[31]

North of Le Sueur there were two alternatives: one trail headed across the prairie toward the bluff, where it plunged into the Big Woods. The other continued along the river bottom for a way, then ascended a steep, 200-foot hill known as the "Grande Côte." Though the grade was very difficult for a cart, the traveler was rewarded at the top of the hill by "one of the grandest scenes in all Minnesota or the North West. Over an immense forest of many miles in extent the eye ranges and embraces with distinctness the distant outline of the beautiful Prair[i]e La fleche 30 miles in circumference surrounded with timber. On the opposite the terraced prair[i]e of Traverse des Sioux is distinc[t]ly visable [sic] and in the far distance the groves and prair[i]es near the mouth of the Blue earth, 35 miles distant."[32]

Turning away from this scene, the trail entered the woods, leaving the river to seek higher ground. It did not, however, manage to avoid the swamps covered in summer with luxuriant grass, which were hidden in the forest. One poetic journalist was charmed by this section of the trail, with its small "Lakes without names, like polished mirrors flashing through the countless pillars of a fairy palace." The scene was less enchanting to an oxcart driver who spent the night in the woods, noting that "The wolves were very thick."

The trail emerged from the Big Woods near Blakeley, where it crossed "a little gurgling stream" then called the Rivière du Bois Franc, now Robert Creek. Beyond lay a "broad and beautiful prairie" known as Belle Plaine, the site of the Dakota village of Bras Cassé ("Broken Arm") in the 1830s and later the home of trader Louis Robert. At Robert's comfortable log house, which seemed to "'guard the portals' of the big woods," many travelers of the 1850s stopped to dine on pork and beans before continuing on their way.[33]

After the beauties of Belle Plaine, the trail abruptly entered a swamp, through which "by a perversity peculiar to the topographical engineers of the fur trade, the road has passed from the most remote period in spite of the allowing range [of] level uplands with[in] gun shot," wrote a journalist. Sunny weather might dry up the marsh, but it took only an hour of rain to fill it to the brim again. "Every step is a problem whose possible solution is sadly intimated by the relic[s] of dead horses strewn around you."

This grisly spectacle was succeeded by a more pleasant one when the trail emerged onto Sand Prairie, where a Dakota village had existed on a ridge near present Jordan since the early 1800s. The sandy hills that gave the prairie its name stretched along the river valley. A few miles farther was the Wahpeton village at Little Rapids, one of the oldest continually occupied habitation and trading sites on the Minnesota. From at least 1826 to 1838 Jean Baptiste Faribault traded there as did others, including Louis Robert in the 1850s.[34]

Leaving the river to avoid the dense growth of butternut, linden, maple, ash, and elm near the bottom lands, the trail proceeded through alternating prairie and oak groves on the final lap of the journey. Shakopee, a Dakota village named for the line of Indian leaders who presided over it, was near the east end of the present city of the same name. Nearby stood a trading post run by Oliver Faribault in the 1840s and a mission established by Samuel W. Pond in 1847. A good ford of the Minnesota somewhat above Shakopee (later a ferry site) made it possible for the cart trains to follow two routes from there to the end of their journey, one on either side of the river. The north bank trail was probably used by groups whose destination was Fort Snelling or St. Paul rather than Mendota, for it connected with the ferry across the Mississippi at the base of the bluff where Fort Snelling stood. A majority of carts, however, probably continued on the south bank to Mendota. This trail ran along a dry prairie ridge than which "no better road could be." It passed several Dakota villages, among them Good Road's and Black Dog's, with fields of vegetables growing in the rich soil of the river bottom. On the approximate route of present State Highway 13, the cart caravans passed through the "rich luxuriance" of the Minnesota Valley and the "small clustering groves" on its bluffs, winding their way at last to their destination — the American Fur Company's stone warehouse near Henry Sibley's house nestling below the bluff at Mendota.[35]

5 ~ THE WOODS TRAIL

THE EASTERNMOST RED RIVER TRAIL, unlike the others in the network, was pioneered by men going north to the Red River Settlement from St. Paul. In the cold autumn of 1844 the Red River free trader Peter Garrioch and his companions were marooned in Minnesota by hostile Dakota who were patrolling the existing trails. Determined to reach home before winter set in, the Garrioch party decided to seek a safe road that would keep within Ojibway territory for the entire distance. As Norman Kittson recalled the incident 11 years later, the "route was cut out by a very small party on their way to Red river, and they were guided entirely by the openings, or where they would have less labor or cutting to do, frequently going some distance out of their way merely to take advantage of a small prairie patch or opening. The season was a remarkably dry one, and [the trip was made] late in the fall; consequently, it was unnecessary to avoid the swamps." The prospect of avoiding the Dakota country at this time quickly made the route popular; the very next year a group of some 80 carts going south from Canada followed Garrioch's tracks. But the failure of the original trail blazers to avoid marshy spots became a major disadvantage in later years, and the route acquired a reputation for wetness rivaling that of the boggy Middle Trail.[1]

Garrioch's path became known as the Woods Trail because it was the only Red River route which passed through many miles of forest. The name was, however, an exaggeration; only the section from Detroit Lake to Crow Wing was wooded. The rest of the trail threaded its way through a varied landscape. From Pembina it crossed the Red to the east bank, where it traversed a "low savannah country dotted with willow bluffs" and then a "Level high treeless prairie." Proceeding along beach ridges of glacial Lake Agassiz, it wound south past tributaries of the Red on the very eastern border of the valley. At Detroit Lake it entered the forest, following first the Otter Tail and then the Leaf and Crow Wing rivers to the east. At the point where the Crow Wing River joined the Mississippi, the trail reached the trading village of Crow Wing. Because this settlement was for many years the most important one on the route, the Woods Trail was often referred to as the Crow Wing Trail. South of this settlement the path pushed over the sandy prairie on the east bank of the Mississippi to Sauk Rapids, where it merged with the Middle Trail for the rest of the journey to St. Paul.[2]

Garrioch and his companions established a trail, strictly speaking, only between Crow Wing and Detroit Lake. From that point north they traveled, according to the trader, "in a circumlocutionary manner," amid dying horses and dwindling supplies, until

Red River carts passing along the bank of a river

they crossed the Red north of Grand Forks near the mouth of the Forest River. The section of the trail that ran along the beach ridges from Detroit Lake to Pembina was probably developed by experienced carters who knew how to pick their way through the prairies. One tradition attaches the name of William Hallett, a Red River trader and sometime road builder, to the opening of the Woods Trail, and he may have had a hand in charting this northern section. Whatever its origin, the portion along the beach ridges was apparently well established by 1846, when Robert Clouston traveled south over it.[3]

During the 1850s an attempt was made to improve sections of the Woods Trail as part of the network of United States military roads in Minnesota. In 1855 Congress appropriated $10,000 to cut out timber on the trail from Fort Ripley as far as the Wild Rice River. E. A. Holmes, the engineer sent to survey the route, returned with a low opinion of the 125 miles he covered. "The present road is extremely crooked," he wrote, "and in few cases runs where it would in case of a location being made at any future time." He advised that "Cutting timber alone on the existing route would do little to improve the means of transit."[4]

With Holmes' report in hand, Captain James H. Simpson of the United States Army Corps of Topographical Engineers was moved to substitute a proposal for a shorter and better route. After Congress approved the change in 1857, a second survey was conducted, and in 1858 construction was begun on the first segment — the 37 miles between Fort Ripley and the crossing of the Crow Wing River. After 29 miles had been completed, the money ran out. As a result the new road ended at the Grand Marais, some eight miles east of the old Wadena trading post. The Red River Addition, as the road was optimistically called, cut seven miles off the distance and was described by its builder as "a great improvement on the old trail."

The stretch of the Woods Trail between Fort Ripley and Sauk Rapids also received attention as part of a longer military road linking the fort with Point Douglas in Washington County by way of St. Paul. Begun in 1852, this road was not completed until 1858, although it was heavily used in the intervening period. It closely followed the original path of the Woods Trail.[5]

There were several ways to approach the northern beach-ridge portion of the route. When coming from Fort Garry on the eastern Manitoba Trail, one could avoid Pembina entirely by crossing the boundary in T164N, R49W and following the Gladstone beach south to join the main Woods Trail at Two Rivers (or Deux Rivières), passing west of Lancaster and east of Hallock on a diagonal across Kittson County. Coming from Pembina, travelers could also go due east, until they struck the trail from Manitoba. Another winter and dry-season branch may have run along the then-wooded east bank of the Red River in Kittson County. Supposedly used as early as 1850, this route followed the river from the Canadian boundary south through present St. Vincent to the mouth of Two Rivers, then turned east along the Two Rivers' south bank to join the main Woods Trail near Hallock.[6]

The most-used branch angled southeast from Pembina to Two Rivers. From an early date a ferry was maintained at Pembina to aid carts crossing the Red. The trail then rolled on parallel to and south of present U.S. Highway 75, "through a beautiful level prairie studded with willow bushes" to the north branch of Two Rivers at present Northcote, where the ford was marked by a nearby aspen bluff. Another crossing (the middle branch of Two Rivers) had to be made at the northern edge of present Hallock. Both of these streams, with their steep bluffs and "muddy, miry banks and bottoms," had to be negotiated before wayfarers from Pembina could call it a day, for it was a rule of prairie travel to camp on the far side of a river so that "the morning's start may be made with dry clothes and fresh horses." Local sources indicate that several miles of old ruts can still be seen between the branches of Two Rivers north of Hallock.[7]

Past Two Rivers, the trail continued south through "rich but bare and level prairie" which was aptly described by an Englishman in 1859. "It is strange to find oneself on an apparently flat disc of grass, nothing but grass meeting the plain horizon-line all around," he wrote. "One feels as if crawling about in view of high Heaven on a circular table punched out from the world and stuck on a spike." As travelers approached the Tamarac (or Pine) River, the prairie soil became sandier and "a distinct rise by ridges" became apparent, "at the base of which the river flowed." One party noticed grasshopper eggs "in vast numbers on the surface of the ground" before they reached their camping spot on the Tamarac. In a wet season like the spring of 1859 the area near that river could be "a miserable country, swamp following swamp," full of the incessant "chirping and croaking uproar" of frogs and the "doleful, throat-gargling cry" of numberless cranes. To these sounds were added "the shrieks of the ungreased cart-wheels, which moaned and screamed like a discontented panther." Nor was it

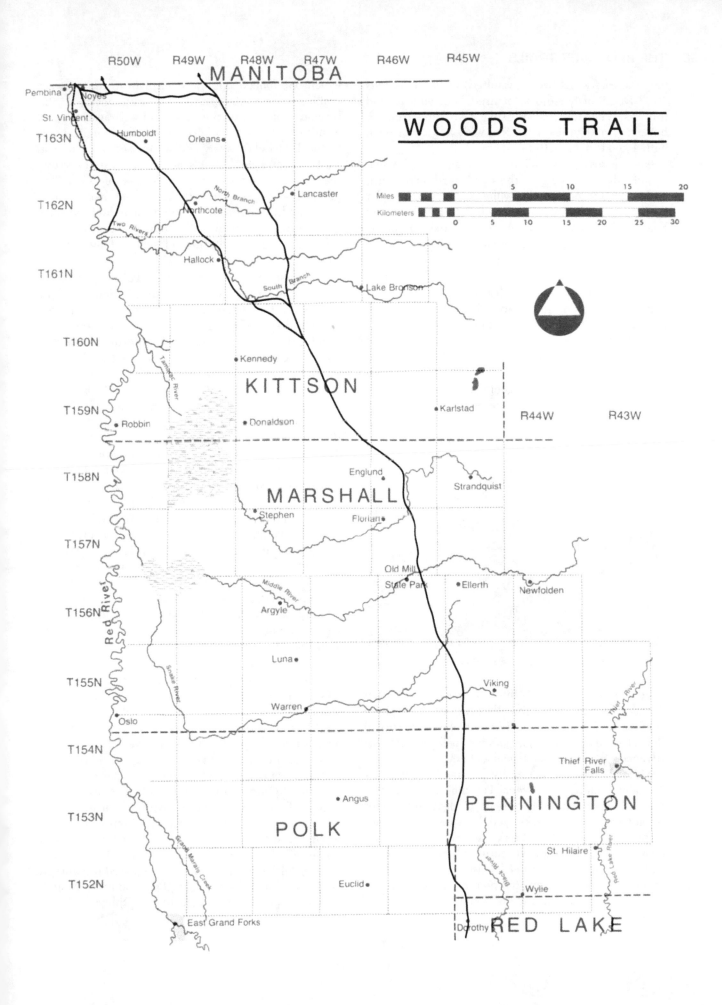

only the ears which were assaulted, for the tenacious "Bull-Dogs" of horseflies tortured both animals and humans. The Tamarac crossing gave little trouble, however; in 1859 it was 15 feet wide and a foot deep with a good rocky bottom.[8]

Once across, the trail began to follow "the fine gravel ridges, running in the main north and south, with a growth of aspen[,] willow and balsam poplar flanking them." These swamp-lined, tree-bordered beach ridges offered the three essentials of prairie travel — wood, water, and grass. "Ducks and prairie chicken constantly flying up, good encampments anywhere to right or left of track, safety from prairie fires, which cannot run in such a country, and the best of pasturage" added to the appeal of this section. The trail meandered along the McCauleyville beach, crossing the Middle and Snake rivers. At the Snake it picked up the parallel Campbell beach for a few miles before returning to the McCauleyville ridge through Pennington County. The geological features of the route did not escape some perceptive cart drivers.

A family preparing a meal in camp

"The eye no sooner rests upon [a beach ridge], than the idea forms in the mind, that it must at one time have been the bank of an immense lake," observed Robert Clouston in 1846, 30 years before geologists advanced the theory of glacial Lake Agassiz.[9]

Middle River, so named by fur traders because it was about halfway between Pembina and the Red Lake River, was a "small stream of clear, cold water — flowing over a rocky bed between high, well wooded banks." The Snake River, often called La Rivière Serpent, flowed "between steep sand-banks and hills." In a dry summer it was reduced to a series of stagnant pools, making it a poor camping place. On the south bank was an Indian mound, from the top of

which one looked upon a level plain to the south, a "rolling prairie interspersed with hummocks of poplar and willows" to the east, and a faraway line of woods on the western horizon. It was a long traverse to the Red Lake River, and in dry seasons water as well as wood could be scarce. One thirsty group searched in vain for even a trickle of water while "the grass rustled beneath our horses' feet like autumn leaves and the hot southerly wind scorched our faces like the air from a furnace." The Red Lake River was a refreshing sight at the end of such a long summer day.[10]

In Marshall, Pennington, and Polk counties are some of the longest and least changed stretches of the Red River trails that can still be driven today. Although the Woods Trail along the McCauleyville beach ridge cannot be followed in northern Marshall County, County Road 114 on the parallel Campbell beach only a mile to the east provides a good sense of the terrain. The trail crossed the Middle River approximately three-fourths of a mile east of Old Mill State Park. Just south of the Middle River it is now a dirt road which becomes Marshall County Road 114. The trail can be followed on 114 and adjoining less-improved roads nearly all the way to the Snake River. Beyond the Snake, Marshall County Road 38 again picks up the general course of the trail as far as the south branch of the Snake, where it veered off to the west. In Pennington County the trail is now a dirt road running south from County Road 8 past the Goose Lake Wildlife Area, cutting off a small corner of Polk County and returning to Pennington to meet Pennington County Road 10 near the Red Lake County border. The trail then paralleled Red Lake County Road 3 to Dorothy before turning east to the Red Lake River.

The Old Crossing of the Red Lake River was a place of some importance in Minnesota history. Claimed by both the Dakota and the Ojibway, the valley of the Red Lake River was a perilous region where an attack was always expected and often delivered. At least one group of travelers was requested by its métis guides not to fire any guns within 10 or 12 miles of the river so as not to "attract the attention of any stray parties of Sioux who might possibly be within hearing." In the 1850s Joe Rolette built a trading house at the Old Crossing and proposed to found a "magnificent city" to be called Douglas. A compliant state legislature, of which Rolette was a member, designated the townsite as the seat of Polk County in 1858, coolly ignoring the fact that the land belonged to the Ojibway. But the

Negotiating the tricky Old Crossing of the Red Lake River, 1859

willows that sheltered our tents, and as I watched its swift and turbid current, I could not but wish that everything were safe across."[13]

Getting over the Red Lake River could be a difficult undertaking at any time of year. A well-equipped party in 1857 had no problems; they sent their baggage across in two small canoes, swam their horses, and hauled their carts across with ropes. But those who made the attempt in higher water and without canoes had to make careful preparations. "We emptied the cart," wrote a journalist in 1859, "laid bars on the top, piled our goods and chattels upon them, weighting the upper side so that the current might not tip the cart over, and, one of us standing upon the same side, with [our horse] harnessed between the shafts, we entered the water."

But once in the water, the difficulties had only begun. To those who did not know "the secret of the ford," the crossing might well prove disastrous. A Canadian traveler described his puzzlement at seeing "the deep tracks of loaded carts [going] straight over the gravel shore and into the water" with similar tracks leading out directly opposite on the far side — yet in between the river was far too deep to ford. After several hours of effort, he at last discovered the key: "The carts had indeed entered straight into the water at the foot of the sloping bank we had descended, but, once in, they had turned up-stream to make the crossing in a horse shoe fashion which brought them out directly on the opposite side, where again a sloping bank formed the best path for ascent and descent." Even this method of crossing was impossible when the water was high. "In spring the river is at least twenty feet deep here," one passer-by noted; "at this season cattle are made to swim over and vehicles are rafted across." Rolette's ferry would have been a welcome convenience.[14]

tribe balked, refusing to let Rolette operate a ferry there, and his plan was stillborn.[11]

White settlement in the area did not become legal until 1864 after Senator Alexander Ramsey and his retinue came to the crossing to negotiate a treaty with the Red Lake and Pembina bands of Ojibway. Although the Old Crossing was on the Woods Trail, the Ramsey party did not follow that path. Instead they took a roundabout route via the Middle Trail to Fort Abercrombie, down the Red River to Georgetown, and then northeast to the crossing. Part of the treaty grounds and the old ford now lie within Old Crossing Treaty State Wayside, and the village of Huot occupies the spot once destined to be Douglas.[12]

The Old Crossing was a habitual camping spot despite its location in a war zone. From the river bluff on the north side, where Red Lake County Road 104 now climbs the hill, the trail commanded a beautiful view of the stream and "La grande Prairie — a treeless waste stretching out before us until lost in the distance." The "thick groves of Oak, Poplar, Elm, Whitewood and Iron-wood" through which the trail wound down to the ford provided all the firewood a party could want. Despite the beauty of the surroundings, one wayfarer probably did not sleep well, for "All night long the wolves made doleful music in the wood on the other side of the . . . River" while the "stream rolled on in heavy flood a few yards below the

From the Red Lake River the trail continued south over a prairie, "rising in steps at long intervals apart" and completely "lifeless, with the exception of two enormous grey cranes, who were stalking majestically through a swamp," wrote Clouston in 1846. Between Turtle Creek and the Sand Hill River in 1857 it was even more desolate, having burned black as far as the eye could see. East of Melvin the trail can now be followed along a sandy road which meets State Highway 102 at Maple Creek. From there it paralleled the highway to the ford of the Sand Hill River at Fertile, where in 1859 "eminences of pure Sand . . . thrown up to the height of several hundred feet" gave the river its name.[15]

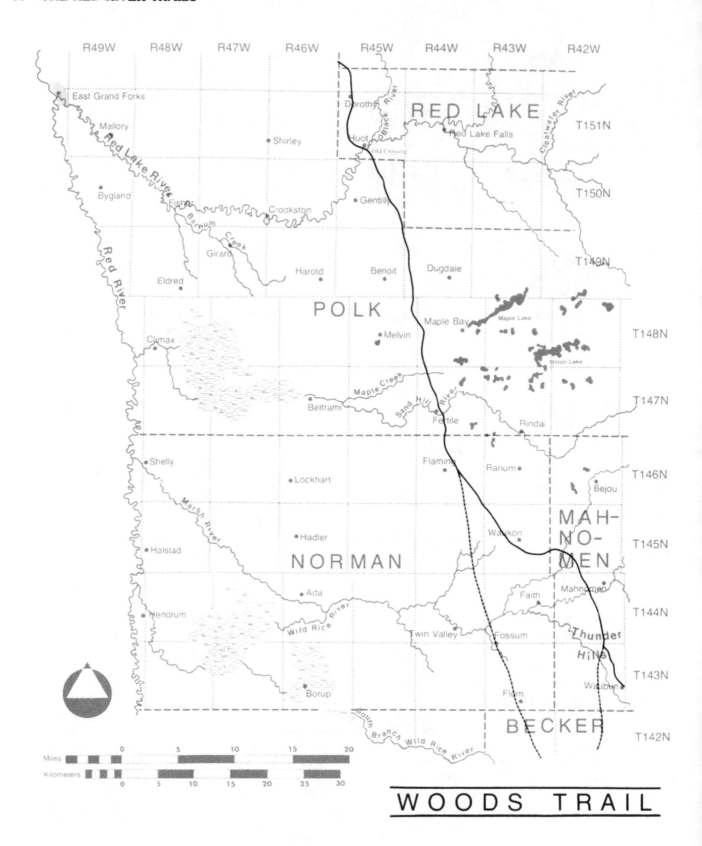

WOODS TRAIL

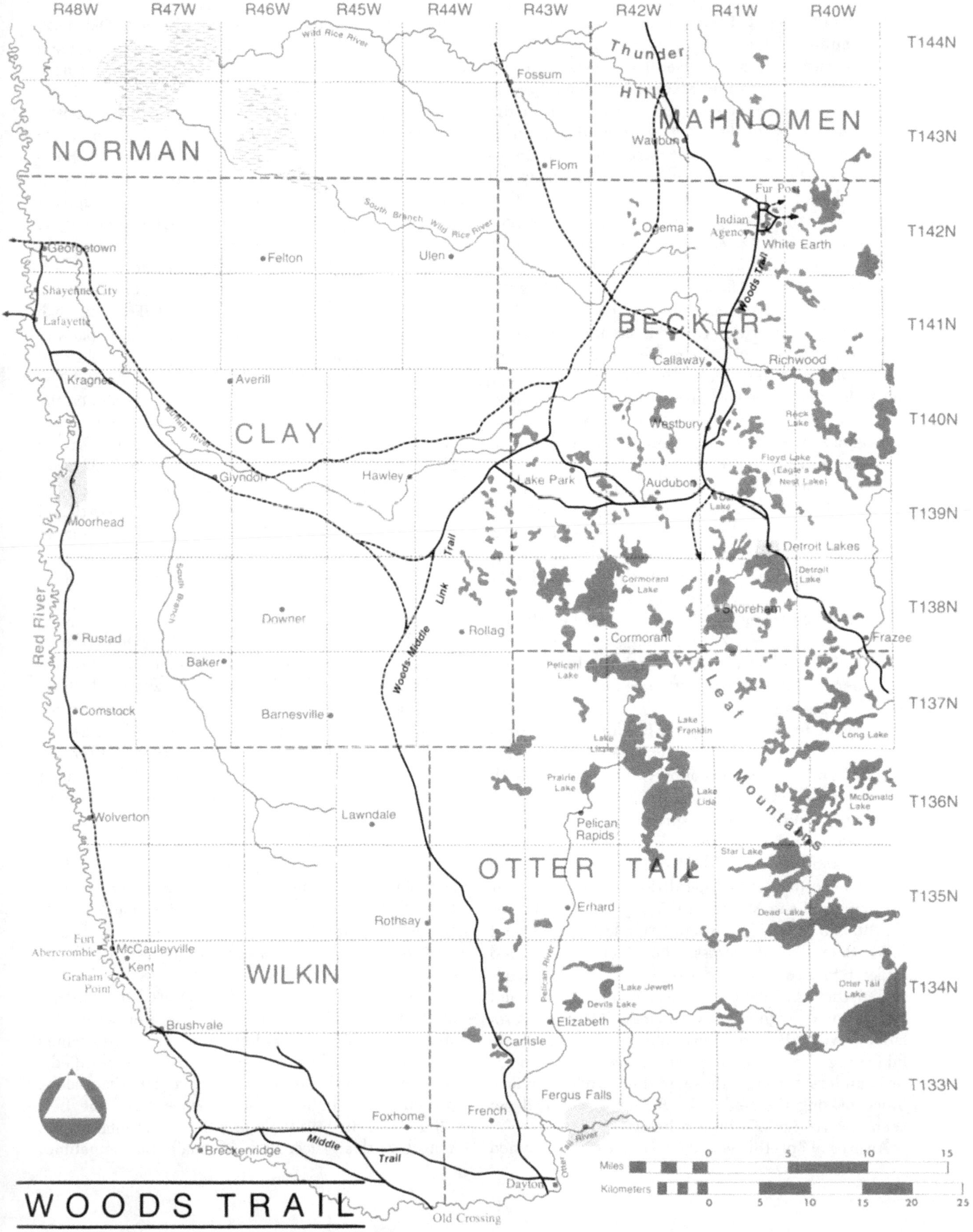

R48W   R47W   R46W   R45W   R44W   R43W   R42W   R41W   R40W

T144N
T143N
T142N
T141N
T140N
T139N
T138N
T137N
T136N
T135N
T134N
T133N

Wild Rice River
Thunder
HINA
MAHNOMEN
Fossum
Waubun
Flom
NORMAN
South Branch Wild Rice River
Georgetown
Felton
Ulen
Opema
Indian Agency
Fur Post
White Earth
Woods Trail
Shayenne City
Lafayette
BECKER
Callaway
Richwood
Kragnes
Averill
CLAY
Westbury
Rock Lake
Buffalo River
Floyd Lake (Eagle's Nest Lake)
Glyndon
Hawley
Lake Park
Audubon
Moorhead
Lake
Detroit Lakes
Red River
South Branch
Downer
Rollag
Cormorant Lake
Detroit Lake
Shoreham
Frazee
Woods-Middle Link Trail
Rustad
Baker
Barnesville
Cormorant
Pelican Lake
Leaf
Lake Franklin
Long Lake
Comstock
Lake Lizzie
Mountains
Prairie Lake
Lake Lida
McDonald Lake
Wolverton
Lawndale
Pelican Rapids
Star Lake
OTTER TAIL
Erhard
Dead Lake
Rothsay
Fort Abercrombie
McCauleyville
Kent
Graham Point
WILKIN
Pelican River
Lake Jewett
Devils Lake
Otter Tail Lake
Brushvale
Elizabeth
Carlisle
Fergus Falls
Foxhome
French
Breckenridge
Middle Trail
Dayton
Otter Tail River
Old Crossing

WOODS TRAIL

Miles   0   5   10   15
Kilometers   0   5   10   15   20   25

South of the Sand Hill River some uncertainty as to the evolution of the trail exists. By 1872, when the area was surveyed, a well-used trail swung east in a long, S-shaped curve into Mahnomen County, crossing the Wild Rice River a short distance from the County Road 5 bridge just west of the town of Mahnomen. It angled east through Waubun to present White Earth, where an Indian agency and store had been established in 1868. At White Earth it made a nearly 90-degree turn, heading straight southwest to Oak Lake. But another less circuitous route between the Sand Hill River and Oak Lake may also have existed farther to the west, avoiding the detour to White Earth and the hilly country south of Mahnomen. The written record is silent on this variation; only the logic of topography and a few obscure maps testify to its possible reality. In this stretch, near the Wild Rice River ford, also occurred a major fork, where travelers who wished to keep to the prairie instead of braving the woods could follow a Link Trail to the Middle Trail at Elbow Lake.[16]

Descriptions of the country from the Sand Hill to the Wild Rice River varied with the weather and the moods of the writers, but all agreed that the road was bad. In wet weather it was soft and in dry weather it was "rutty & rough." On a gloomy day in 1859 "Every brook was a river, every swamp a lake, the road a swamp. A cold steam rose from the soaked earth, our spirits were damped, the jaded horses plodded heavily on." So muddy was the ford of the Wild Rice that one rider had to leap from his horse into the water in order to extricate the animal.[17]

On went the trail through a line of rolling ridges called the Thunder Hills, which "rose in successive ranges" amid a scenic country interspersed with woods, meadows, and lakes. West of the hills "an apparently boundless plain spread out its wearisome sameness of surface before us." To the southeast appeared "another range of hills and the blue outline" of trees where the continental divide stood guard over the source of the Mississippi. The next obstacle was the Buffalo River, "an insignificant little stream not more than 3 yards across," but "very muddy and difficult to ford." Beyond the Buffalo, the trail continued through "verdant slopes, secluded vales and oak-crowned heights." Nevertheless, "All seems desolation," wrote Robert Clouston in 1846, "and a painful feeling of solitude casts a shade over one's mind as he wanders through those seldom trodden wilds: Since passing the Red Lake River . . . we had not seen one vestige of a human being."[18]

An area of "prettily wooded lakes," each one named and known by the cart drivers, followed. Oak Lake was an often-mentioned landmark, for a mile west of it was the junction of a popular connecting trail from Georgetown, Lafayette, and the mouth of the Sheyenne River. Its origins are uncertain, but it is known that in 1856 Colonel Charles F. Smith had to "cut a road through the timber" in order to reach the Woods Trail from the Link Trail in this area. The next year George H. Belden of the Corps of Topographical Engineers mapped a "New Trail to Cheyenne City & Lafayette," joining the Woods Trail at Oak Lake. In 1858 an expedition of commissioners to locate salt-spring lands for the new state of Minnesota seems to have gone this way to reach the Link Trail. In 1859 the party that transported the disassembled parts of the "Anson Northup" to Lafayette "left the old road about a mile west of Oak Lake . . . and traveled by compass in a northwesterly direction to a point on the Red River opposite the mouth of the Sheyenne." The settlers of the area in 1907 remembered it as having been a "well traveled road . . . by the Indians, half-breeds and fur traders." It seems to have been used in conjunction with the routes along both the north and south sides of the Buffalo River; when going to Georgetown via the former, travelers crossed the Buffalo at the old Link Trail ford in T140N, R43W.[19]

Passing along the south shore of Eagle's Nest (now Floyd) Lake, the Woods Trail reached Detroit Lake, or Lake Forty-Four — "so called from the date of the discovery of this route." This was the halfway point on the road to Crow Wing, and many parties camped here, feasting on the fish from the lake and the profusion of berries from the woods. After the long trek over the prairie, this body of "the clearest water, enlivened by the whiteness of a flock of swimming and wading pelicans," seemed "one of the finest . . . in the North West" to a weary traveler in 1859. The trail followed the northern and eastern lake shores for several miles, and on at least one occasion the Indian ponies "chose to walk in the shallow water to cool their unshod feet, sorely tired by our hasty crossing of many leagues of burnt prairie."[20]

At Detroit Lake the trail first entered thick forests of "Oak, Elm, Birch, pine, juniper, iron-wood . . . some of which were very large and must have attained a great age, as their moss-covered trunks testified." Advancing south through Frazee and Perham along present U.S. Highway 10, it soon entered the Leaf Mountains, the hills that mark the continental divide. Travel in this "succession of small, but sometimes steep hills" had its perils, especially for the oxen. One man could not decide "whether the toiling up, or rushing down hill, was most to be dreaded. During the ascent, the strain on the oxen was severe . . . but when we came to go down there was danger in every step. The utmost efforts of the drivers, in beating the oxen about the head and holding them back by main force, were requisite to prevent them gallopping down the declivity and upsetting the carts."[21]

The woods and hills that made oxcart travel troublesome nonetheless enhanced the scenery. To the west "the view was bounded by woods, in which numerous small lakes were visible; while eastwards stretched a magnificent section of rolling prairie" broken only by "the range of high wooded hills, which ran along its edge." Up and down wound the cart caravans, now disappearing from sight, now reappearing over the top of the next ridge. Three fords of the Otter Tail River (or the Little Red River, as some called it) occurred between Detroit and Otter Tail lakes, the first two where U.S. Highway 10 now crosses near Frazee and Luce, and the third where State Highway 78 crosses at Rush Lake. At the latter spot the trail, which had been progressing along the western beach of the lake for a few miles, ran straight through the water on a sand bar in 1859. The small lakes along this stretch were "alive with ducks [and] geese," reminding one passing Canadian of "the appearance of the ponds in Red River and the Assinniboine valleys."[22]

Otter Tail City, which from 1850 to 1860 was the site of an important trading post on the trail, stood on the northeastern shore of Otter Tail Lake adjoining the mouth of the river. Several fur posts had preceded it there. In 1859, when it was the seat of Otter Tail County, the city boasted seven buildings; two were occupied, and two others housed a United States land office and a post office. In 1862, after the stage road on the Middle Trail route had come into heavy use, the land office was moved to Alexandria, and by 1872 Otter Tail City was abandoned. In the 1860s several tracks linked the Middle Trail with the Woods Trail at this spot. One led nearly due south to Chippewa station on the Middle Trail stage road. Another, which went west to the Red River via Dayton near present-day Fergus Falls, was the route of a state road authorized in 1858. A historical plaque marks the site of this wilderness crossroads at the junction of State Highways 78 and 108 on the shore of Otter Tail Lake.[23]

From Otter Tail City the trail turned east to cross the continental divide into the Mississippi watershed.

"To call the apex a height of land is a misnomer, for it is one of the softest and apparently most low-lying parts of the route," said an 1860 account. Nevertheless, the character of the land changed markedly at this point, for the trail left behind the "rich deep black mould" of the Red River Valley and began to advance over a "light, sandy soil." Travelers were greeted by "grand old woods of oak, maple, ash, birch, and poplar" in which "very nice driving was requisite to avoid running against the trees or over the stumps." It was easy to snap an axle, which meant several hours of delay while the cart was unloaded and a tree was felled to make another. Between East and West Leaf lakes lay a townsite called Leaf City. "We marched through a city without being aware of the fact till some time afterward," a journalist wrote in 1860; "a solitary house passed by us rather unconcernedly, had been . . . designated Leaf City!" This house and acres of ambition are now commemorated by a marker on State Highway 108. East of the marker a country road follows the trail for several miles along the north shore of East Leaf Lake.[24]

Break time — cart repair along the trail

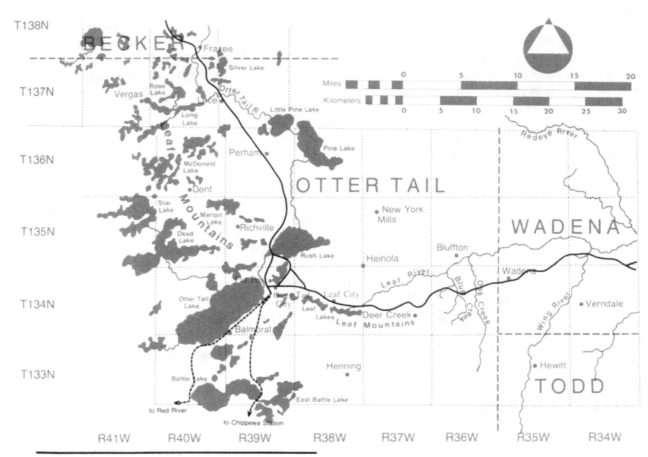

W O O D S   T R A I L

Along the south bank of the "narrow and shallow" Leaf River the trail made its way only a few miles from the stream itself. In 1846 a fire reduced the forest here to ashes; "the black and smoking ruins of many a noble oak lay around our path," wrote Clouston. Eleven years later, however, another traveler found that the Leaf River was "fringed with a magnificent forest." The stretch from Leaf City to the Crow Wing River was in 1860 the "most difficult part of the trail." A traveler that year advised that "many a worn-out axle and broken wheel attest the power of its stumps and coulees to make the spring and fall brigades of loaded carts look well to their gearing." The route passed through present Wadena, where it is marked in Sunnybrook Park on Wadena County Road 4. From there it angled northeast "through sloughs innumerable and fathomless" to the Wing River, crossing not far from its mouth, where a spring of clear water was much used by travelers. Though the Wing was "a shallow and narrow stream," this crossing, like so

many others, was not without its dangers. When Clouston and his crew of experienced cart drivers crossed in 1846, "one of the people stumbled and fell while taking a heavily laden cart down the bank and the wheel passed over his body: we tried to bleed him but the blood would not flow: it is horrible when people are dangerously ill and no medical assistance near."[23]

Old Wadena, 15 miles east of the modern city of that name, was the next key point on the trail. It stood on the western bluff overlooking the Crow Wing River between the mouths of the Leaf and Partridge rivers and numbered more than 100 inhabitants during its peak years from 1855 to 1860. Here in 1857 a party from the north found "a new store well-stocked with goods, which the enterprising owner said he had built and furnished for the benefit of the Red River people." Here also Peter Roy ran an inn with the ubiquitous name of Halfway House, in honor of its position between Otter Tail City and the village of

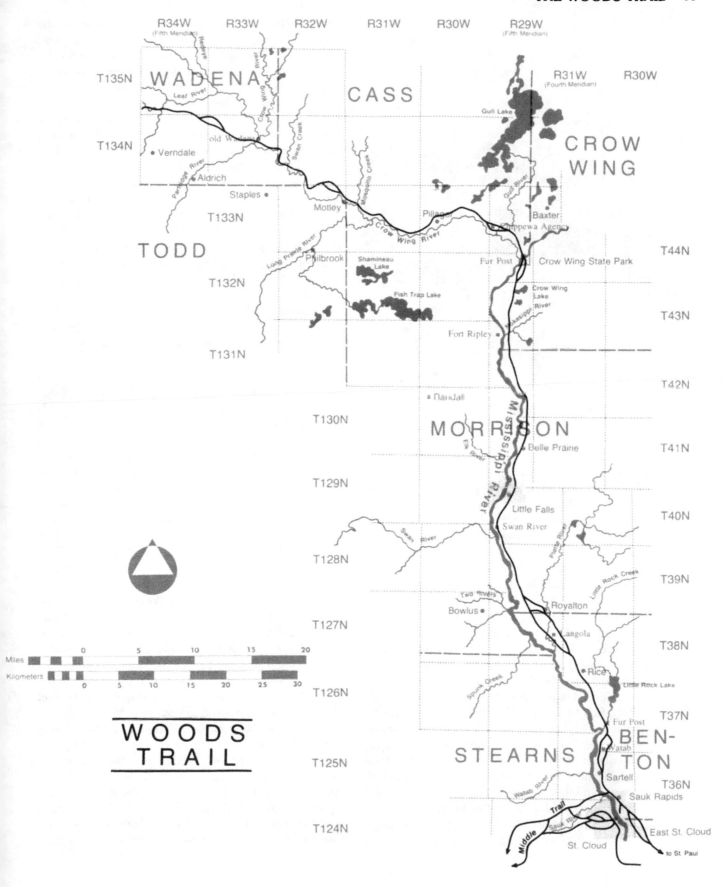

WOODS
TRAIL

En route to Crow Wing from Otter Tail City about 1859

Crow Wing. Though the Crow Wing River ford was usually shallow and sandy, a rope ferry, established in 1859, was welcomed by the cart brigades. The site of old Wadena is now a Wadena County park and campground, accessible from U.S. Highway 10.[26]

From the crossing the trail led along the northeastern bank of the Crow Wing, "heavily wooded with Norway and White Pine, interspersed with tamarac swamps." While passing through the pine forests "the road was all that could be desired, the straight stems of these northern palms looking like stately colonnades, through and between which your horses' hoofs were muffled in the leaves of last year, but where the tamarac grows, look out for trouble." Unless those areas were newly corduroyed "with the bark still on the tamarac poles, and these laid straight and close," a tamarack-corded stretch excelled at "smashing wheels [and] tripping up beasts of burden." When a heavy cart broke or displaced a tamarack pole, there was no problem if the driver relaid a new pole immediately, "but the driver of the first cart trusts that this will be done by the next, and the next, by the next, till all have passed and then all join in the hope that the next brigade will really take the matter in hand."[27]

Journeying on toward the Mississippi, the country grew "more hilly and rugged," with fir the most common tree and fallen timber a problem on the path. An 1859 group found this part of the trail exhausting. "Two or three of the party held each vehicle at the side to prevent its tipping over in the mire; others pushed behind, and some went before, to bring the oxen to a halt after every step. While those in the rear were stumbling along, in this fashion, the woods resounded with the shouts of the teamsters in the vanguard, who were endeavoring to urge their cattle through a tamarac spring swamp, situated on the brow of a steep hill." The very idea of a swamp on a hill was inconceivable to this inexperienced traveler: "There it lay, however, with an ox and cart imbedded in its midst." To get through this "villainous morass," the men cut pine boughs and spread them over the mud for a firmer footing. "Splash, splash went the unfortunate animals, lowing piteously, and sinking to the middle at every step, in the desperate attempt to haul through the heavily-laden waggons at their heels." The last 20 miles to Crow Wing were improved after 1858 when an "excellent road" was constructed by the United States Army.[28]

At the junction of the Gull and the Crow Wing rivers, the trail passed the buildings of a Chippewa Agency. Moved to the Gull River site from Sandy Lake in 1851, the agency was until 1869 the scene of annuity payments and efforts to adapt the Ojibway to an agricultural life-style. A passing journalist saw 2,000 or 3,000 Ojibway gathered at the agency for annuity payments in 1859. Only a few cellar depressions and a fragmentary trail can be seen today on land owned by a utility company. Between the Chippewa Agency and Crow Wing State Park other fragments of the trail still exist on private property.[29]

The crossing of the Mississippi River was a major problem in the years before a ferry was established in 1849 at the mouth of the Crow Wing. In 1846 Clouston managed to secure the help of a group of Ojibway Indians and their canoes. Even so, the banks were too steep for one "awkward brute of a horse," which somersaulted backward down the slope. In later years the Crow Wing ferry, located at the upper part of the town, "at a point where the river is quite narrow and deep," could be crossed for 25 cents.[30]

On the east bank of the Mississippi at the thriving Crow Wing settlement, southbound cart brigades often stopped to transfer their contents to wagons for the last leg of the trip to St. Paul. Going north, the village was also the point at which the goods brought by wagon from St. Paul were finally loaded onto carts and the money not spent by the drivers already was "generally got rid of." American Fur Company traders had inhabited the site of Crow Wing intermittently since 1826, although continuous occupation did not begin until 1837. In 1846 William Aitken's post there — "two or three wretched houses called 'the fort'" — was disparaged by Clouston as "an abominable hot-bed of bugs and fleas." However, the presence of the pretty métis daughter of the resident trader, Allan Morrison, seems to have reconciled Clouston to the other disadvantages of the place.[31]

Thirteen years later a visitor was more favorably impressed by the settlement. Its site, he said, "is somewhat elevated, near the bank of the Mississippi, affording a pleasant view over upon the western side, both above and below the two graceful mouths of the Crow Wing River." As the main depot for the Ojibway trade, Crow Wing at that time had a white population of about 100, augmented from time to time by "a caravan of Red Lake Indians" who came down to trade and camped around the settlement in tents or birch-bark lodges. In the 1860s Crow Wing reached the height of its prosperity, and its population soared to 600. Stores, warehouses, hotels, boardinghouses, saloons, and churches graced the streets of "this Paradise of trappers, traders, and lumbermen — this Babel of mixed races and tongues." One visitor ventured to predict a great future for the town, but he was wrong. After the railroad chose to cross the Mississippi at Brainerd instead of at Crow Wing, prosperity drained away, taking the people with it. Today Crow Wing State Park encompasses the site of trails and long-gone buildings as well as the old ford over the Mississippi.

Once past Crow Wing the most difficult parts of the

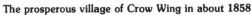

The prosperous village of Crow Wing in about 1858

Woods Trail were left behind, for from here on the improved military road superseded the old route after the mid-1850s. Southward along the east bank of the Mississippi, the carts followed a "fine level road" leading through "an arid waste of sandy hills, the soil of which is scarcely covered by the short, *scrubby* grass that seems hardly to take root in the ground." A later and more charitable view of the countryside described the prairie soil as "rather sandy but its deficiency in clay is said to be compensated for by its richness in organic sediments." An occasional "solitary farm house and barn . . . loom[ed] up in the distance" far from any town, "looking cheerless and unsociable in their isolation on those boundless and almost treeless savannahs."[32]

Closely following present State Highway 371, the trail ran through the portion of the Fort Ripley Military Reservation that then lay on the east bank of the river, bypassing the fort itself on the opposite bank. Founded in 1848–49 to maintain peace among the Winnebago, the Ojibway, and their Dakota neighbors to the south, Fort Ripley kept watch over this section of the Woods Trail for nine years before it was temporarily abandoned. Trouble arose among the Ojibway and the white settlers after the fort's evacuation, and the troops returned to monitor the peace until 1877, long after the Red River trade had ceased to flow along the road opposite the fort. From the trail little could be seen of Fort Ripley but a line of fieldpieces standing in "a warlike attitude" along the riverbank. A ferry at the mouth of the Nokasippi River connected with the fort. In the years when stages ran from Crow Wing to St. Paul, they crossed by ferry to pick up the mail at the fort, recrossing to head south again.[33]

About 10 miles below Fort Ripley the trail passed the establishment of missionary Frederick Ayer, who moved there from Red Lake in 1848 and opened a school for Indian and white children. Local lore has it that he borrowed oxen from the trader Henry M. Rice, who was freighting on the trail at that time, to plow his first fields. A small settlement of métis farms, which Ayer called Belle Prairie, grew up near the mission, about two miles north of the present town of the same name. From the site of old Belle Prairie the trail can now be followed along Morrison County Road 260 into Little Falls.[34]

Little Falls is one of the towns along the route that does not trace its beginnings to the Indian trade. A Canadian journalist on his way to Red River in 1859 paused to recount its history: "Some years ago, its site was purchased by a company, and as it commanded splendid water-power, grist and saw mills were speedily in process of erection, buildings went up, stores were opened," and land originally bought for $1.50 per acre increased in value to $50.00. The population increased accordingly, and the merchants grew bold, extending their business as far as Red River. Between 1858 and 1860, however, crop failures and other disasters led to a drastic decline in population, which dipped to 250. Not until the 1880s did the town recover its former prosperity.[35]

During the years of Red River traffic, Little Falls was of less importance than a trading settlement two miles to the south known variously as Swan River, Aitkins, or Aitkinsville, where travelers could lunch on wild ducks, potatoes, and apple pie at the hotel. The trading post at Swan River was opened in 1848 by William Aitken of the American Fur Company, who also operated a ferry over the Swan River in 1849. Little remains of either the village or the fur post today, but one can still follow the Woods Trail from Little Falls almost to Royalton on a county road along the riverbank.

During the stagecoach era a succession of stage stops and hotels sprinkled the trail south from Little Falls. Among them were James Lambert's Bellevue House west of present Royalton, Langola on the Platte River, and George Rice's tavern west of the present village of Rice. At Little Rock Creek was a ford where the energetic Aitken operated yet another post which was called Petites Rochers in 1846. Two miles farther south at the once-booming settlement of Watab, David Gilman ran a well-known hotel and trading post founded in 1848. Here a branch of the trail can be followed for a few miles along Benton County Road 55 next to the river. South of Sartell the trail coincides with Benton County Road 33 and U.S. Highway 10 into Sauk Rapids and East St. Cloud. [36]

Trading posts originated in the 1840s at the rapids where the Sauk River joins the Mississippi. That conducted by Henry Rice was taken over by Jeremiah Russell in 1849. The post was conveniently located where travelers bound south from Red River on the Middle Trail crossed the Mississippi. After 1857 the celebrated Hyperborean Hotel, later the Russell House (named for the trader), became a well-known stop on the stage routes between St. Paul and Fort Ripley and St. Paul and Breckenridge. At this bustling frontier crossroads, traffic from the Middle and Woods trails converged for the last stretch into St. Paul. Gone were the sloughs and forests of the Ojibway country. A fine sand track carried the wayfarers from Red River toward their journey's end.[37]

The Russell House in Sauk Rapids

6 ~ THE MIDDLE TRAIL

THE MIDDLE TRAIL, also known as the St. Cloud, Sauk River, Sauk Rapids, Plains, and East Plains trail, stretched from the Red River to St. Cloud, following the divide between the waters of the Minnesota and the upper Mississippi rivers. Probably the most used of the Red River routes over the years, the Middle Trail was also the most complex in evolution. It consisted of several tracks, each of which came into being at a different period. From the north a tangled network of links connected it with the Woods and North Dakota trails, and from Breckenridge east to St. Cloud the route was complicated as time passed by the development of frontier stage and wagon transportation, which overlapped with oxcart activity for more than 10 years.

The earliest Middle Trail traced a wide arc south from the Otter Tail River, following a succession of lakes — Lightning, Elbow, Elk, Pike, White Bear (now Minnewaska), George, and Henry. It left the prairie and entered the Sauk Valley at present Richmond, following the Sauk River northeast to St. Cloud on the Mississippi. It was not an easy route, for not only were long stretches "desperately destitute of wood," but it was also pockmarked by "innumerable sloughs and morasses" which made it "rather moist for ordinary travel," as one man wrote in classic understatement.[1]

While this trail was adequate for the use of Red River caravans and government expeditions throughout the 1840s and 1850s, frontier entrepreneurs found that it did not serve their purposes as settlement filtered westward up the Sauk Valley. Improved state roads from St. Cloud to Breckenridge and from Breckenridge to Georgetown were authorized by the new state legislature in 1858 as an impetus to immigration. That June a surveying party set out from St. Cloud to chart a new course north of the old Red River Trail which would link a number of potential townsites in the Sauk Valley. Following the present route of Interstate 94, it shortened the trip to Breckenridge by nearly 30 miles. "If the necessary exertion is made to cut out the roadway through the brush and timber, and to bridge a few of the bad sloughs . . . I have no doubt but the whole country along the line will be settled within two years," predicted a member of the surveying party.[2]

Despite valiant efforts on the part of the citizens of St. Cloud, Alexandria, and Breckenridge, the spring of 1859 saw the eastern part of the new road little nearer to completion than it had been the year before. In May, the United States Army stepped into the picture in the form of Major George W. Patten and a troop of luckless infantrymen from Fort Abercrombie. Patten had been in command at Fort Ripley in 1858

A long line of carts on the prairie

when orders came to abandon that post and proceed to Fort Abercrombie. After a difficult journey over the Woods Trail, the troops arrived at Fort Abercrombie, erected a sawmill, and were about to commence operations when they were ordered to proceed forthwith back to Fort Ripley. It was May, and the old Middle Trail was obstructed by impassable sloughs, so Patten and his men made their way east along the track of the newly surveyed state road. Having constructed much of the road as he went, Patten was within two days' reach of St. Cloud, "out at elbows, out of provisions, his carriage a wreck, his wagons badly broken, his mules worn out; and his men and himself in the same condition," when he was overtaken by an express carrying a letter ordering him back to Fort Abercrombie! The major's only satisfaction was that he had inadvertently succeeded in "doing the State some service by aiding to open this thoroughfare."[3]

It was left to a private company to improve the new road so that vehicles could use it in summer. During 1859 the path was "straitened out and bridged, and partially disentangled of the bad places" by James C. Burbank's Minnesota Stage Company, which had acquired a contract to carry mail to Fort Abercrombie and hoped to start weekly passenger service from St. Cloud to the Red River. A lucrative arrangement with

The Minnesota Stage Company was still running in 1877, when proprietors Blakeley and Carpenter issued this ticket to Mr. and Mrs. Charles Cavileer of Pembina

the Hudson's Bay Company to ship freight through Minnesota gave the stage firm an extra incentive to make the new road passable.

A great proportion of the oxcart trade chose to take advantage of the stage company's bridges and grade, and substantial parts of the new state road became *de facto* Red River trails after 1859. Nevertheless, the old trail farther south was not totally abandoned, and

the two parallel paths spawned a bewildering number of links and alternates that allowed traffic to bypass bad stretches.

The evolution of the Middle Trail was further complicated after 1864 by the superimposition upon part of its length of a government road and stage route leading to Fort Wadsworth (later Fort Sisseton, South Dakota). Supplies for the fort were shipped up the Mississippi to St. Cloud, hauled west along the stage road to Sauk Centre, and transported across Pope County on the route of present State Highway 28 to the site of Glenwood. There the Fort Wadsworth Trail crossed the old Middle Trail and continued southwest along Lake Minnewaska toward present Morris and Browns Valley. Parts of the Fort Wadsworth route were used by stagecoaches in the 1860s and may well have served as short cuts for Red River carts.[4]

The earliest approach to the Middle Trail from the north was via one or the other of the North Dakota routes. Travelers forded the Red as far north as Georgetown, as far south as the Bois de Sioux River, and at Graham's Point or Breckenridge in between, to reach the Middle Trail by a variety of connecting paths. How many trails from the north existed on the Minnesota side of the Red is difficult to ascertain. The topographic evidence argues against the existence of a track from Pembina on the east shore of the Red River. Unlike those on the west side, the tributaries from the east meandered into broad marshes for miles before falling into the Red, making travel close to the river almost impossible except in the driest seasons.

Nevertheless, as early as 1823, when Major Stephen H. Long passed down the east bank of the Red without any apparent difficulty, he noted the existence of a "blind road made by the people of Pembina." This early path north of the Red Lake River may have been obliterated by a severe flood three years later. At any rate, by 1832 the east side was "impassable owing to the succession of swamps," and traffic switched to the west side, which was "much drier and in every way better suited for travelling."[5]

By 1856 Colonel Charles F. Smith reported that there was no river trail on the east bank from Pembina to the Red Lake River, "owing to the marshy nature of the soil." South of the latter, however, he recorded three trails: the inland Woods Trail, a "middle road," and a river road "which keeps along the bank of the Red river at various short distances." Fifteen years later in 1871 a northbound immigrant found no road at all along the east bank below Georgetown. Thus the question of whether such a trail existed for any appreciable length of time remains unsolved. If one did exist, however, it seems clear that it was seldom used by the through traffic of Red River trains.

The "middle road" which Smith mentioned in 1856 was another of the approaches to the Middle Trail from the north. This Link Trail did not in reality extend as far north as the Red Lake River, but took off from the Woods Trail about five miles south of the ford at the Wild Rice River's north branch. From there it swept southwest past a group of salt lakes, crossed the upper Buffalo River, and continued south along the range of uplands known as the Leaf Mountains. Its advantages were that it enabled travelers to keep on the east side of the Red out of danger from roaming bands of Dakota, while it avoided the most troublesome terrain of the Woods Trail by staying on the edge of the prairie until it joined the main Middle Trail at Elbow Lake.

Despite these obvious benefits, little is known of this route. Kittson and Charles T. Cavileer used it in 1851 when traveling north to alert the Ojibway to the coming treaty negotiations at Pembina. They found it swampy but passable. When Colonel Smith stumbled on a stretch of it in Clay County more or less by accident in 1856, he reported that it ran over a "prairie high and rolling, with numerous marshes in the hollows." Army surveyors in the mid-1850s referred to it as "the Main Road leading to the Red River of the North" and as "the Sauk Rapid trail," suggesting that in those years it was often used in conjunction with the Middle Trail. Routes along the Buffalo River connected the Link Trail with Georgetown in Clay County, and when that settlement became a magnet for cart traffic after 1858 the southern half of the Link Trail and the Buffalo River paths saw heavy traffic from trains going to and from the Middle Trail.[6]

Georgetown was established near the site of an old crossing of the Red at the mouth of the Sheyenne River. Muddy banks made this ford "so horribly bad" that it was little used in early years. In the late 1850s, however, the two tiny settlements of Lafayette, Minnesota, and Dakota City, North Dakota, grew up at the crossing, hoping to attract cart traffic. When the Hudson's Bay Company decided to ship supplies to Fort Garry through the United States, James McKay, the firm's trusted field manager, was commissioned to choose a site for a depot and transfer point. He selected a spot about two miles northwest of the present Minnesota village of Georgetown, a point which marked the practical head of navigation on the Red. Here supplies carted north from St. Paul after 1858 were loaded onto steamboats for the journey to Canada.[7]

Although founded strictly as a company enterprise, Georgetown soon grew into a "little settlement . . . placed under cover of the belt of timber which clothes the banks of the river." Oxcart trains hauled goods to it for transfer to steamboats; other carts continued their journey after crossing the Red at the Lafayette ford or on the Georgetown ferry. At a later date the stage route to Pembina also crossed to the west bank here. The site of Georgetown is now marked in a wayside rest on Clay County Road 36.

A heavily used trail hugged the east bank of the Red River from Georgetown south to Breckenridge. One enthusiast proclaimed that "no better road can be found anywhere." Despite its proximity to the river, it was dry and "level as a floor." Through the sites of present Moorhead, Comstock, Wolverton, and McCauleyville, it followed the edge of the "dark bays and promontories of timber which cover the spiral involutions of the river bottoms." To the east rose the "perpetual mirage-like spectre of the Leaf or Pelican hills" and to the south and west was the "endless platitude of the wide sea of grass." At present Brushville, a trail branched off eastward, providing a short cut to the Otter Tail River fords. This was probably a late addition built by the Minnesota Stage Company to link Dayton on the Otter Tail with Graham's Point on the Red.[8]

Breckenridge, where Red River caravans sometimes paused at the halfway point on their long journey, was founded in 1857 in the optimistic tradition of townsite speculation. Not only was the site at the junction of the Otter Tail and Bois de Sioux rivers supposed (without much practical foundation) to be the head of navigation on the Red, it was also the proposed terminus of the Minnesota and Pacific Railroad. "Breckenridge must be a central point in the future settlement of the country," a sanguine journalist predicted in 1859, but fulfilling the prediction proved to be an uphill battle. By 1859 a sawmill and one house had been erected. The following year a group of travelers was accommodated in a "shanty, half log-house, half dug-out, which already sheltered ten men packed in rows." Devastated in the Dakota War of 1862, Breckenridge recovered slowly. Though many parties on the Middle Trail paused there, an equal number seem to have bypassed it to the north and south.[9]

The state-authorized stage road and the old trail parted about five miles east of Breckenridge, the road

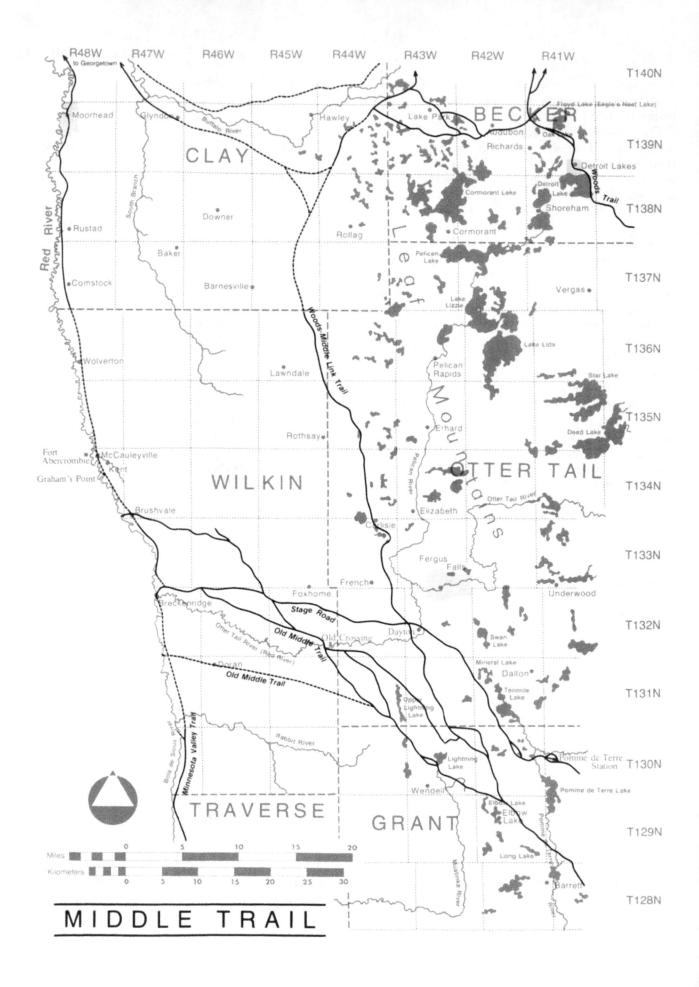

MIDDLE TRAIL

staying on a straight course for Dayton, where it crossed the Otter Tail River, and the trail angling south to the "Old Crossing," a ford near the border of Wilkin and Otter Tail counties five miles southeast of present Foxhome. Which path was followed depended largely upon personal preference; the stage road, as one traveler explained in 1859, had "the advantages of shortness, settlement and bridges, while the other or prairie route, is less hilly, and in summer would probably be more free from mosquitoes, and such like annoyances, and for about 90 miles is without a settler."[10]

From Breckenridge to the Otter Tail crossing the old or lower trail kept close to the river through an area later known as the Breckenridge or Dayton Flats. In 1849 it was described as "low and flat, and during periods of continuous heavy rains . . . covered to the depth of an inch or two with standing water." In a dry season the Old Crossing was only two or three feet deep with a rocky bottom and solid banks. But when the water was high, the Otter Tail was transformed into a "large, dark-looking stream, winding with rapid current through a deep channel some forty feet below the level of the prairie." At such times the ford could be dangerous.[11]

It was almost disastrous to an 1851 party that included Norman Kittson, Father Georges Belcourt, and Charles Cavileer. Riding their horses into the river, Belcourt and Cavileer went down "head first in ten or more feet of water." Cavileer wrote: "On looking around for his 'Reverence' I saw he . . . was off the horse and holding on in desperation to his saddle. I knew he could not swim, and feared he was taking his last baptism. I hollered to him to slide as far back as he could, and reach for the tail and then let go [of the saddle]. Being perfectly cool, he did as I told him. He got the tail, let go the saddle, and it was even then laughable to see the long coated gentleman scudding along with a one horse power as if sharks were after him." The site of this ford is one mile east of the bridge where present Wilkin County Road 19 crosses the Otter Tail.

South of the Old Crossing the trail split into several parallel branches, the most southwesterly being the oldest. Between the Otter Tail and the continental divide at Elbow Lake, the prairie was "high and undulating, and dotted over with lakes of various dimensions." To the north could be seen the blue outline of the wooded Leaf Mountains, appearing much taller at a distance than they actually were. To the west was an "immense rolling plain" stretching to the Bois de Sioux River.[12]

Over the latter plain ran another track linking the Middle Trail with the fords of the Bois de Sioux. Although this path was probably the most heavily used in the years before Breckenridge was established, little information concerning it has survived. In the dry summer of 1851 it was said to cross a "very uninteresting country, destitute of lakes, and the grass dry and in some places already burned off, with stagnant ponds and a sluggish creek." In wet years, however, the stretch metamorphosed into a vast swamp; a traveler in 1850 recorded a miserable ride over miles of flooded land where the water sometimes stood knee-deep to a man on horseback. No trees grew between the Bois de Sioux and Lightning Lake, so users of this route had to take care to bring firewood with them. Once they arrived at the Mustinka River, the traverse was over, and caravans often camped amid the sheltering woods where the Mustinka flows out of Lightning Lake.

At Elbow Lake the Link Trail joined the Middle Trail from the north. The main route then paralleled present State Highway 55 to Glenwood. Having passed the divide, it crossed the headwaters of the Pomme de Terre and the Chippewa, both of which flow into the Minnesota River. Beyond the Chippewa it pursued a circuitous course over "a prairie that was a succession of ups and downs" around deep ravines, streams, and lakes. In this stretch travelers were often forced to leave the trail in search of a more practical path, with the result that they sometimes rambled for 20 miles in order to advance 10. The halfway point between the Chippewa and Minnewaska Lake was heavily wooded Pike Lake at present Farwell. After passing it, the trail plunged into 12 successive miles of mud and mire.[13]

Sloughs were the greatest plague of the Middle

Getting out of a slough

Trail. Although they could be found along any of the Red River routes, the Middle Trail spawned them in such profusion that an itinerary reads like a catalog of esoteric bogs. One type was called the *terre-tremblante*. It was formed when spring water running over a bed of sand was covered with "vegetable mould" — algae, duckweed, and other organic slime — to a depth of about three feet. "The water running underneath keeps the superincumbent mass moist and unstable," one observer explained, "so much so that it can be sometimes shaken for ten or fifteen feet around." Other types of sloughs assumed a more "plausible appearance," the only indication of their miry nature being "a ranker growth of grass, perhaps of a different color, in the low ground."[14]

It was the duty of the wagon master to ride ahead of the train to spot and test the sloughs before the carts ventured into them and to seek out the best way of crossing them — if one existed. "The foremost cart approaches, and, at the first step, the mule sinks to his knees," a traveler related. "Some mules lie down at this point; but most of ours were sufficiently well broken to make one more spasmodic leap. . . . Belabored by oaths, kicks, whip-lashes, and rope-ends, the mule may rise and plunge . . . until the cart is on solid ground." More often, however, human intervention was needed. The animal was unhitched, and the men made a "grass bridge" to bring the cart or wagon to dry ground. To make it, the "long, heavy grass is cut and twisted into large knots, and by lifting

one wheel at a time and thrusting these underneath, the wagon is finally raised nearly to the surface. Then a thick platform of grass is placed in front of the wagon, a long rope is made fast to the heap, and a horse to the rope, and thus mind triumphs over matter."

The fine prairie ridge at Minnewaska Lake was a hospitable spot where the carts often paused before embarking upon the laborious stretches on either side of it. In 1849 the lake was accurately described as "a beautiful sheet of water, with heavy bodies of timber around it, alternating with prairie, which in many places descends in handsome slopes to the water's edge." East from Minnewaska the trail passed over more "rolling prairie, thickly interspersed with marshes and small, sluggish streams." Boulders and stones impeded progress along the hills, valleys, and basins. The east branch of the Chippewa River — a "swift, narrow, but deep stream" — had to be crossed before reaching Lightning Lake (present Grove and McCloud lakes on the border of Pope County).[15]

Lightning Lake was so named in 1849 by members of the Woods-Pope party when they camped there in a thunderstorm. A bolt of lightning struck one of their tents, "shivering the tent poles into splinters, and burnt [the] bedding and clothing as if a red-hot iron had passed over them." A lieutenant was injured, and the expedition was thereafter wary of setting up iron tent poles during a prairie storm.

The road from Lightning to Lake Henry was a cor-

Minnewaska Lake, then called White Bear Lake, in the days of cart traffic, about 1853

ridor of marshes and small streams. As far as the north fork of the Crow River it followed a ridge, passing oak groves and small, wooded lakes abounding in game. The Crow was "a bold little stream" only 20 feet wide but marshy for 100 feet on either side. This muddy crossing was succeeded by a long stretch over "bad roads, or rather, over a bad prairie." George Lake, called "Lake Henrie" by some passers-by, and Lake Henry, sometimes called Lake David, were the next landmarks. Gradually the land descended from the heights of the divide and began to resemble a "rolling prairie." The broken land disappeared, and the trail ran straight over "a flat, undiversified surface, with occasionally a gentle undulation" to the valley of the Sauk River.[16]

The Sauk ford at Richmond was deep and muddy. In spring carts had to be floated or rafted across, sometimes to the detriment of their contents. One traveler watched helplessly from the banks as he saw his party's fully loaded cart "gradually slide off the raft and the wheels being over the side begin to subside in the deep river. I shouted out as loud as I could 'Les Carabines,'; La Bonne sprung forward & caught the shafts of the sinking cart; being a man of immense strength he contrived to hold the cart [while] the whole affair was towed over to our side." The site of this accident can now be seen slightly upstream from the spot where State Highway 23 crosses the Sauk. Beyond this ford the stage road again joined the old Middle Trail, and the two continued together into the comparative civilization of the lower Sauk Valley.

"All the freshness had died out of the solitudes when Capt. Blakel[e]y had marked out stations and stables for a stage route," lamented a journalist who went to Red River in 1859, the year Burbank's service began. Offsetting the loss of wilderness romance, however, was an often-expressed hope that the stage route would be the first link in an imperial "chain of active commercial communication, which it is the ambition of the people of Minnesota to stretch across the Northwestern wilderness to the Pacific Ocean." The road carried more symbolic freight than it did traffic in that first year of 1859, and in subsequent seasons its fame (if not its commerce) was extended by a steady stream of journalists who traversed it in search of empire. Its popularity among newsmen made this state stage road the most thoroughly documented of all the Red River routes.[17]

The earliest stretch of the road to be opened was the part from Breckenridge to Alexandria, for it ran over a "vast and luxuriant prairie" with only two belts of timber to bar the passage. A group of Red River carts was among the first to go this way in September, 1858. The new road branched off from the old Middle Trail just five miles west of Breckenridge and continued nearly due east for another 20 miles over the wet prairie called the Breckenridge Flats.[18]

It approached the Otter Tail just at the spot where the river, leaving the hilly region of its source, turned due west into the Red River Valley and took on the characteristics of a prairie stream. The Otter Tail River appeared suddenly, for no timber or bushes grew nearby to signal its presence. Instead of the relatively easy ford at the Old Crossing, the traveler here confronted "a rapid current broken by rocky shoals, between tortuous bluff banks, not less than one hundred feet high." In the late 1850s the stage road's crossing was the site of the "nascent city" of Dayton, consisting of one log cabin. As early as 1859 a solid, log dam and bridge was constructed there, to be superseded by a ferry in the 1860s. The site of the crossing, now known as Dayton Hollow, is still visible near the Otter Tail Power Company's dam off Otter Tail County Road 1 three miles south of Fergus Falls.

The pleasant country from Dayton to Alexandria inspired columns of rapturous description in the newspapers of the 1850s. The road rose and fell over alternate ridges of woods and plain. To the south the prairie stretched away in "one unbroken level, unrelieved by a single object." To the north could still be seen the wooded Leaf Mountains, marking the continental divide. Some travelers were charmed by the grassy, parklike hills covered with wild flowers and oaks, which undulated before them like a "great green wave." Others praised the lakes, of which a multitude "glisten in the folds of the serpentine vales." None remained unaware that this region would be a prime lure for the farmers and immigrants pouring into the new state.[19]

Stage stops stood at intervals of 15 to 20 miles along the road. One of the first was Pomme de Terre station (later fortified against the Dakota and called Fort Pomme de Terre), followed by Chippewa station near Evansville. They were scarcely more than log shanties at which meals of "salt pork and raw bread with potatoes" could be obtained. Compensating for the roughness of this cuisine was the abundance of ducks, pelicans, and prairie chickens along the route. When sportsmen traveled aboard the stagecoaches, drivers routinely stopped at lakes for a round of shooting before going on; one rider remarked that "The inside of the stage looked like a poulterer's shop on the last Saturday before Christmas."[20]

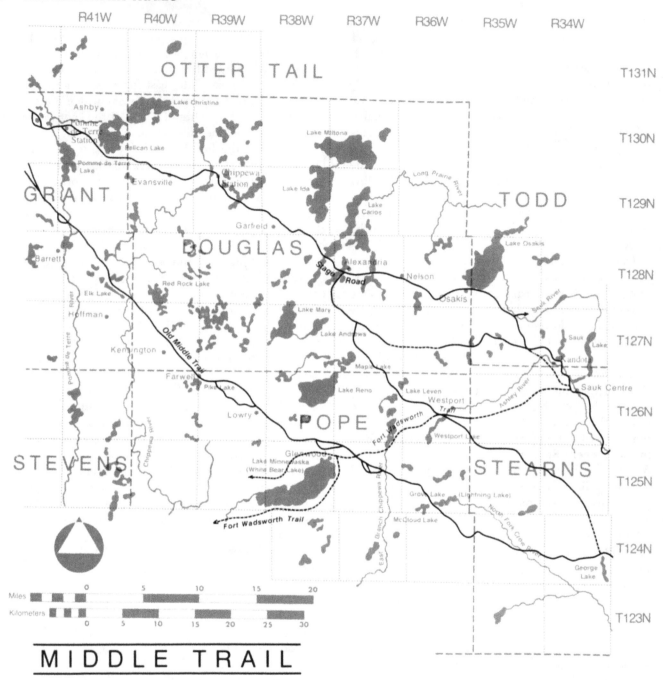

MIDDLE TRAIL

The road first crossed the Pomme de Terre, a rapid little stream with a stony bottom and precipitous banks. Then it passed Pelican Lake, so called because of the large flocks of these white birds which at times floated so thickly on the water that the lake seemed from a distance to be covered with whitecaps. Continuing on past Evansville, the road crossed the Chippewa River and entered a succession of swamps and sloughs where it was difficult to breathe without inhaling mosquitoes. From Garfield to Alexandria the old state stage route can be followed on present Douglas County Road 22.[21]

It was with great relief that most travelers arrived at the "place which, when it gets to be a place, is to be called Alexandria." Located between the two worst stretches of the road, the village was a little island of civilization. Although in 1859 it consisted of exactly two houses, Alexandria's convenient location halfway between Breckenridge and St. Cloud, as well as its abundance of wood and water for camping, attracted to it "as complete a Congress of parties traveling to and from Red River . . . as if this had been deliberately appointed as the rendezvous for all the vagabonds and renegades in the country." The settlement, situated in the midst of "A cluster of beautiful lakes, cold and marvelously clear, and connected together by little rivulets . . . like a chain of diamonds," became the seat of Douglas County in 1858, when the entire newly created county contained exactly six votes. Its strategic location on the stage road assured its success as a commercial center, and by the late 1860s its streets saw upward of 2,000 carts in a season.[22]

At Alexandria the road branched. While the main stage route continued to Osakis through a belt of forest and swamp, another parallel trail veered southeast over the prairie. A pleasant early path, it was used before 1859 to cross the grasslands of southern Douglas and Todd counties. From it an offshoot continued south through "a succession of verdant undulating prairies and stately groves" past Maple and Leven lakes to present Westport. There a stage road from Sauk Centre to Glenwood, which doubled as the Fort Wadsworth Trail in the 1860s, intersected the trail.[23]

Two choices were available at Westport to eastbound drivers. One road followed the Ashley River Valley to rejoin the main state road at Sauk

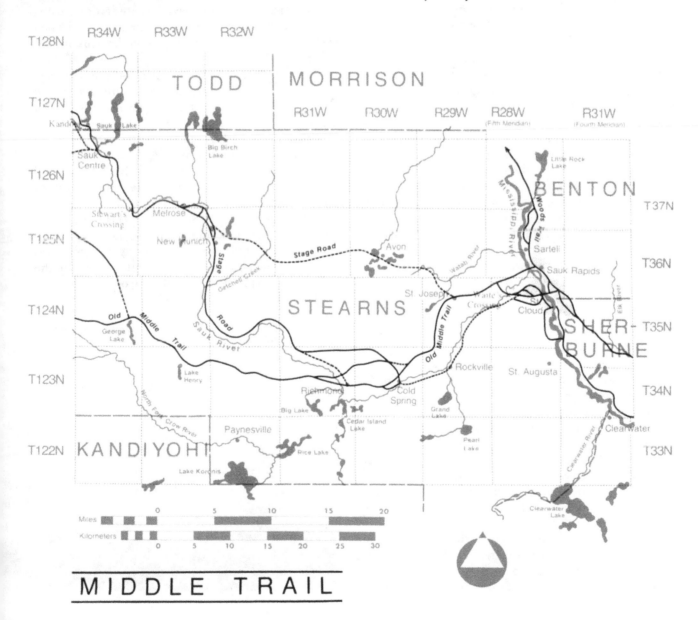

MIDDLE TRAIL

Centre, another favorite rendezvous of the Red River carts in the 1860s. The other stretched south along the divide between the Sauk and Crow rivers through Stearns County, to meet the old Middle Trail at Lake George. Of these two branches, the latter was certainly followed by the Red River carts as early as 1858 and as late as 1869, for it was shorter than the state stage road, had more grass to feed the teams, and possessed a more level roadbed. The Ashley River route between Sauk Centre and Alexandria was used by the stages (and probably by the cart trains) as an alternative when the main trail through Osakis was impassable.[24]

The state stage road from Alexandria was the most northern alternative. "I thought I knew what bad roads were but never saw them until I came here," lamented a traveler between Alexandria and Osakis, where State Highway 27 now runs. This wooded segment was "the terror of this route." Though it was only 12 miles long, it could take a day and a half to accomplish its passage. The road, according to one journalist, "writhes in the agonies of the million-barbed venom of mosquitoes, through the intestines of a deep wood." At each turn "your horse was balking at a labyrinth of stumps, where there was no place to put his foot: this extending for ten rods, and there terminating in a slough aggravated by the floating débris of a corduroy bridge, and this ending in a mud-hole . . . with one stump upright to prevent your wading comfortably through it, to transfix your horse or upset the cart." Throughout the 1860s the main road continued to be intermittently impassable, forcing traffic to use the more southerly routes.[25]

When travelers reached the one-house city on the pebbly beaches of Osakis Lake, they achieved a merited rest from bogs. The "town" of Osakis was in 1860 "a charming little place — everything so neat about it, that if you were inclined you might use the housemaids' test and eat your dinner off the floor." Here a marker on State Highway 27 now commemorates the early stage road.[26]

Past this outpost was a stretch over "a hump-backed knobby prairie, but generally free from bogs and sloughs," leading to the settlement of Kandota. Founded by artist Edwin Whitefield amid a flurry of speculation in 1858, this abortive townsite was situated at the southernmost end of Fairy Lake, "the great ornament of this wild country." By 1860 it consisted of "a single house on a high ridge, at the foot of which flows the Ashley River. . . . In front of the house stands a tall flag pole, and the whole place has a romantic aspect." Here the road crossed the Ashley

River and continued to Sauk Centre, where it entered the Sauk Valley proper.

From Sauk Centre, the track wound "spirally like a grape-vine round the twisted stem of the Sauk River — over it and *under* it, and on both sides of it." The left (northeast) bank of the Sauk was heavily timbered with poplar, while the right was almost continuous prairie. Nevertheless, the road followed the left bank, taking advantage of a thin aisle of sand beside the stream. For this reason it was called the "Old Sand Road." It can be followed nearly the entire way from Sauk Centre to Richmond on Stearns County roads 186, 237, 12, 177, and 23, all of which run along the old right of way.[27]

The first ford south of Sauk Centre was called Winnebago Crossing in early days and Stewart's Crossing in later years. It was an easy one, made to avoid a belt of timber that obstructed passage on the Sauk River's left bank. The next crossing, just north of New Munich, was too deep to ford. All the carts and wagons had to be unhitched and the entire load pulled over by means of a rope stretched across the river. By the late 1860s, when regular coaches replaced the wagons that served as stages in the early years, a bridge may have existed here.[28]

On the other side of the Sauk River, the road branched. The state stage route dived straight through 25 miles of intervening timber where Interstate 94 now runs to St. Joseph. This was the last part of the stage road to be opened, and it advanced over hilly, forested country with heavy clay soil. Thus it was not much used except as a winter road until the railroad was built along it in the 1870s.

The easier way followed the long curve of the Sauk

Travelers approaching one of the many crossings of the Sauk River about 1853

River through New Munich to Richmond. This was the route of a state road from St. Cloud to Long Prairie, which was surveyed in 1858 and probably in use before then. Those who traveled it agreed on the beauty of the Sauk Valley. "Lakes and streams are met successively, and pleasant groves of oak diversify the undulating prairie which stretches away in graceful curves, till in the dim distance it meets the horizon." Only one tributary of the Sauk gave any trouble — Getchell Creek south of New Munich. Here misfortune struck at least one group of unlucky travelers when their wagon caught on a snag while fording the flooded creek. "The wagon, borne down by the impetuous current, careened like a ship in a storm, and in one moment all the valuable outfit of the expedition . . . went swimming down with the current, or sank suddenly to the bottom." Fortunately, nearby German settlers could always be counted on to help a traveler in need — if the language barrier could be broken, for few of them spoke English.[29]

At Richmond the old Middle Trail joined the stage road, and the two routes continued northeast along the Sauk River to the Mississippi. From the ford at Richmond the united trail traversed a region of both woods and prairies. In 1857 the road was rough and circuitous because it wound around settlers' fences which had been built without regard to the right of way. Several parallel branches of the trail grew up between Richmond and Cold Spring, all of which were probably used by the carts. At Cold Spring, a place known from the earliest times for its spring "as clear and cold as the most thirsty could wish," there was a bad marsh to cross. Although the stream of spring water itself was only 10 feet wide and a foot deep, it was bordered on both sides by a slough 200 feet wide, aggravated by a steep hill, and in later years further impaired by a "shocking bad bridge." A better crossing was usually made by building a thick bridge of grass, over which the oxen and carts passed more easily.[30]

Beyond Cold Spring the trail again branched. One route led to St. Cloud along the top of a low ridge near the southeast side of the Sauk, now the route of State Highway 23. This road was, however, a late addition, probably little used by the carts. The other more heavily traveled branch on the north side of the river was reputed in 1851 to be the worst part of the trail between Sauk Rapids and Pembina. Leaving Cold Spring along present Stearns County Road 2, it passed over Jacob's Prairie, an opening five miles long flanked with timber on both sides. Veering north to St. Joseph, the trail encountered wooded swamps "which would to an Eastern[er] seem impassable." One group recorded that they were "mired down over the most of the way, going only five miles in two days." After passing the German village of St. Joseph, the trail emerged onto a narrow strip of prairie separating the waters of the Sauk and Watab rivers. At this point early travelers continued on the north side of the Sauk to the town of Sauk Rapids on the Mississippi. After 1855, however, most traffic turned east to the mushrooming town of St. Cloud, crossing the Sauk at what later became known as Waite's Crossing.[31]

During the later years of cart traffic, St. Cloud served the same purpose on the Middle Trail that Traverse des Sioux did on the Minnesota Valley Trail. It was the place where cargo could be transferred to boats for shipment to St. Paul and where many caravans of Red River carts ended their journey. The townsite was first linked to the Red River Trail in 1855, when a road was built from St. Cloud north to the main trail. At Waite's Crossing a bridge, constructed in 1858 and washed out shortly thereafter, was replaced by a "lunatic ferry." In 1860 another bridge was completed which lasted almost to the end of the Red River trade. Waite's Crossing is now marked where Stearns County Road 4 bridges the Sauk River west of the St. Cloud Veterans' Hospital.[32]

St. Cloud grew so fast during the heyday of the Red River trails that the carters from Canada must have regarded it with amazement. In 1854 it did not exist; by 1858 there were two schools, a district land office, a post office, three churches, a sash factory, a sawmill, a planing mill, a flour mill, a newspaper, a library, and five steamboat arrivals weekly. As might be expected from its position as a shipping center, hotels and warehouses were among the first businesses to thrive — the former to accommodate travelers and immigrants to Red River, the latter to accommodate trade goods.

The drivers of most of the larger cart trains did not put up in hotels, however, but camped on the prairie just west of what is now downtown St. Cloud, for reasons one exasperated Hudson's Bay Company official learned too late. In charge of a train of carts and their Indian and Scottish métis drivers "who have never before seen a railroad nor a town of this size," this man was called back from St. Paul, where he had gone to dispose of the company's furs, by the news that "pandemonium reigns" in the streets of St. Cloud.

"The citizens . . . are not used to as much horse-racing as takes place around Fort Garry," he wrote apologetically. "While our men raced their horses through the streets . . . the usual traffic suffered, but far worse was the discovery that the long bridge across

A traders' camp in the woods near St. Cloud, about 1868

the Mississippi, only recently built, was a wonderful racetrack. The large CAUTION and NO FASTER THAN A WALK means nothing to those who enjoy the bliss of ignorance in the form of illiteracy. They galloped under these conspicuous signs at either end and when the long span swayed with their motion their delight was all the more. The Chief of Police attempted to stop them, but not knowing any law but that of the Hudson's Bay Company they took him prisoner!" When the brigade leader returned, he ordered the camp moved farther out of town and peace was restored.

In the years before the Mississippi bridge was built, the brigades crossed the river at three ferries, located where the State Highway 152 bridge, the St. Germain Street bridge, and the Tenth Street bridge now stand. Many a traveler on the Middle Trail may have felt the same relief Major Woods expressed when at last he arrived at the Mississippi: "right glad we were . . . once more to see this magnificent river. We have been wading, swimming, and plunging through dirty little streams dignified with the titles of rivers, until we began to lose the true conception of what a real river was."

Once over the Mississippi the Middle Trail joined the Woods Trail and both continued along the well-used road to St. Paul. For travelers having that destination, the journey was not yet over. But the notorious sloughs of the Middle Trail were past, and as Major Woods hopefully put it, "Here our troubles end."

7 ~ THE METROPOLITAN TRAIL

THE EXTENSION of the Woods and Middle trails leading down the east side of the Mississippi to St. Paul wandered through wilderness for only a few years of its history. From the time the area was opened to settlement in 1837, homesteads, inns, and townsites began to spring up along the route, a trend that reached a crescendo in the late 1850s. "The great cities are marching with rapid stride up the Mississippi — Manhattan, Monticello, St. Cloud, Sauk Rapids," the *St. Anthony Express* announced in 1855. To a Canadian traveling along this stretch, many of these spawn of speculators' imaginations seemed like "burlesque towns." He noted that "The rapidity with which these communities spring up, is only equalled by the remarkable speed with which they are duplicated." At many of them everything requisite for a thriving metropolis existed — "except the people."[1]

Like the Middle and Woods trails, the Metropolitan Trail was complicated by the construction of a military road overlapping the route of the old Red River Trail. Surveyed in 1851 and begun in 1852, the military road was intended to link Point Douglas at the mouth of the St. Croix River and Fort Ripley on the Mississippi by the shortest and easiest route. From St. Cloud south, the army engineers found that the west bank of the Mississippi was hilly and covered with timber, making passage difficult. The east bank, which was the route of the old trail, was an open

prairie with scattered oak groves. It was intersected by numerous small tributaries of the Mississippi, but these were easily forded, ferried, or bridged. Only in four places did the surveyors find it necessary to deviate from the old Red River Trail — a stretch in Sherburne County, at Elk River, at Anoka, and from St. Anthony to St. Paul. The new trail, "excepting a few places where it is exceedingly sandy," was "an uncommonly superior road," open in all seasons of the year and supplied with bridges and grading. After 1852 the Red River traffic followed this "military and commercial thoroughfare" instead of the old meandering track over the prairie.[2]

Coming from the Middle Trail, travelers joined the Metropolitan Trail by crossing the Mississippi at one of a number of fords and ferries that spanned the river from Sauk Rapids on the north to Clearwater on the south. The ford at Sauk Rapids, the oldest crossing, was 500 feet wide. Here a ferry was established as early as 1849. Farther downriver, at least one of the three St. Cloud ferries was operating every year after 1855. At St. Augusta a ferry existed at least as early, and some carts went as far down the west bank as Clearwater, the low-water head of navigation on this section of the upper Mississippi, where the Min-

Destination achieved — enjoying a pipe in camp about 1858, probably in St. Paul

nesota Stage Company tried fruitlessly for a time to promote a major crossing. Coming from the Woods Trail, river crossings were not a problem, for the carts simply continued down the east side of the river from Sauk Rapids.[3]

In East St. Cloud, the first man-made feature on the trail was a tavern which stood opposite the Lower Town ferry near the present Tenth Street bridge. Opened by John Emerson in 1857, the Emerson House was a stage stop at which "the table is plentifully provided with excellent food" — if it was possible to reach the table through the crowds of Red River cart drivers who swarmed into the place. It was wise to stop at the Emerson House when traveling south; throughout the 1850s it was the last good inn for many miles. The country from St. Cloud to Big Lake was sparsely populated, for the land was almost entirely held by speculators who wished to develop their investments as townsites rather than as homesteads, and so asked higher prices than farmers were willing to pay.[4]

South from St. Cloud, the route of the military road diverged from that of the earlier Red River Trail as far as Big Lake, where they rejoined. In this area the Elk River runs parallel to the Mississippi, and the old trail followed the Elk. Through present Cable and Becker it advanced "over the fine smooth prairie and through occasional strips of woodland" predominantly composed of oak, ash, elm, and birch. On a bend of the Elk River a tavern for passing Red River cart drivers was operated as early as 1846 by Canadian Joseph Jerome. In 1848 Jerome sold his claim to another Canadian, William Sturgis, who cleared it as a farm which was named "The Big Meadows" for "its vast meadows of fine hay." The tavern then passed into the hands of Joseph Thompson, who continued to operate it until the military road bypassed the spot and deprived the little settlement of the traffic that had created it.[5]

The military road followed the route of what may have been an even older Red River Trail close to "the wooded banks of the silent Mississippi" where Sherburne County Road 8 now runs. During the 1850s it linked many of the hopeful townsites that mushroomed along the stage road and at each possible steamboat landing. Clear Lake was the first of these abortive cities, situated about two miles southwest of the present town of the same name. Marseilles, a few miles farther on, shared the ignominious fate of its upstream neighbor.[6]

Along the river the stages "rattled away through oak groves [and] through a prairie with scarcely a tree to be seen," wrote a passenger. "Beautiful groves of oak . . . nestled here and there like island gems in a peaceful sea." Unlike the meandering track of the old trail, the military road pushed straight and businesslike over the rolling, sandy plain. "Everybody who travels it seems conscious that it is a *government* road," remarked a traveler in 1856.

Big Lake was heralded from afar by "the welcome outline of a belt of timber on the horizon." It was a favorite stopping place even before a settlement grew up on its shores. "The lake is anything but a big lake, being the size of a common New England pond," commented one American. But compensating for its lack of size were an abundance of "fine large fish" (especially lake bass) and the carnelians on its "beautiful sloping, sandy and gravelly shores." There settler Joseph Brown opened a tavern in 1849. As late as 1857 it was still the only visible building in the budding town of Humboldt, then the seat of Sherburne County. This versatile structure doubled as courthouse and coroner's office until it burned to the ground in December, 1857. Humboldt soon after lost its distinction as the county seat and changed its name to Big Lake, which it retains today.[7]

Past Big Lake the united trail and military road ran southeast to Elk River, more or less on the route of present U.S. Highway 10. Through "a fine country" of "rolling prairies diversified with trees," the trail continued on the south side of the Elk to a ford at its mouth, but the military road crossed above Orono Lake and skirted the north bank of the river. On the banks of this "little stream of beautifully clear water" a number of inns flourished, including the Elk River House founded in 1850 by Pierre Bottineau, the famed Red River guide. Bottineau had opened a trading post on the trail at Elk River in 1848, and he stayed long enough to help found the town of Orono, now within the limits of Elk River. This townsite was pronounced "quite a smart little place" by a passing traveler in 1857.[8]

South of Elk River the road bumped over a sandy stretch which displayed "very little of that fertility that Minnesota boasts of." Here the Red River Trail looped to the east away from the Mississippi, but the military road ran straight south as does the present highway. It passed the homestead of Oliver H. Kelley, founder of the National Grange, who moved to the area in 1850 to promote the hopeful village of Itasca. In 1851 it was a "town in miniature, one of the embryos, that bids fair to become something in course of time." Despite high hopes that it would become a thriving river port, a passing journalist in 1856 dismissed Itasca as "an unassuming place, and not so pretty as its name." The townsite has long since disappeared, but a wayside rest marks its location. Kelley's farm is preserved as a historic site.

In 1851 the road from Itasca to the Rum River at Anoka proceeded over "as fine a prairie as the sun ever shone upon, extending N. & E. as far as the eye could reach with a farm just opened here and there." Three different crossings of the Rum figured in the history of the Red River trails. All of them were located within the present city of Anoka. The earliest was near the present Anoka State Hospital, where low banks and a broad but shallow bed provided a perfect natural ford. The detour which had to be made to reach it also conveniently bypassed some deep gullies on the east edge of the town. The construction of a mill dam on the Rum River in 1854 obliterated the ford. Another old crossing was at the very mouth of the Rum, where a ferry operated during the 1850s. The third crossing came into being when the military road was constructed through Anoka. A bridge, built in 1853, spanned the river where the present Main Street bridge stands. There is also evidence that some carts may have taken advantage of the ferry over the Mississippi at Anoka and continued their journey along the west side of the river.[9]

The town of Anoka, founded in 1853, was by 1857 "quite a large thriving place, with a number of mills, manufactories, &c." From there the Red River carts had to battle a succession of "severe sand hills" along the general course of present Anoka County Road 1. In 1851 the route to the south was "uninhabited, flat, marshy and very uninteresting, no prairies, but a thick undergrowth of bushes and 'oak opening[s].'" After passing Coon Creek within present Coon Rapids, the carts arrived at Rice Creek, on the south side of which stood John Banfill's well-known house and tavern. From 1848 to 1853 Banfill presided over this bit of the trail as ferryman, postmaster, storekeeper, miller, and hotel owner. In 1851 he laid out the townsite of Manomin around his establishment, and by 1856 the place had grown into "a tidy settlement." Manomin is now part of the city of Fridley, and Banfill's tavern is preserved by the Anoka County Historical Society.[10]

From Fridley the road straggled across "an almost unbroken plain" to the village of St. Anthony, now encompassed by the city of Minneapolis. South of the present city limits it kept fairly close to Marshall Street Northeast, along which a driver in the 1850s might have seen "fine farms at times on either hand and numerous new and very comfortable houses, of log and frame." Near Lowry Avenue Northeast the trail meandered off to the east, returning again to Marshall at its junction with Main Street Southeast. The military road, however, continued along Marshall to its intersection with Northeast Broadway; then it cut diagonally to University Avenue at East Hennepin. Through St. Anthony the military road followed University Avenue Southeast (then Third Street), while the trail ran down the center of Main Street.[11]

"The Red River carts used to be all day passing our house," one early resident of Main Street recalled. "Whenever the Red River carts came by, I used to tie the dog to the doorlatch," another woman wrote. "I did not want any calls from such rough looking men as

Carts creaking through Main Street in St. Anthony about 1855, with the Mississippi River on the left

they were." The brigades made their way to the very center of town, in spite of the normal traffic in the little milling city. But if the residents of St. Anthony were inconvenienced by the cart trains, the caravans from Canada were sometimes equally disoriented by the close quarters of the city. One "wild Indian horse" was so unused to the sight of domestic pigs and sheep that it nearly carried its rider into the Mississippi.

A deep ravine between 13th and 14th avenues Southeast made it necessary for the trail to loop away from the river to the first practical crossing at University Avenue. When the military road came through, a

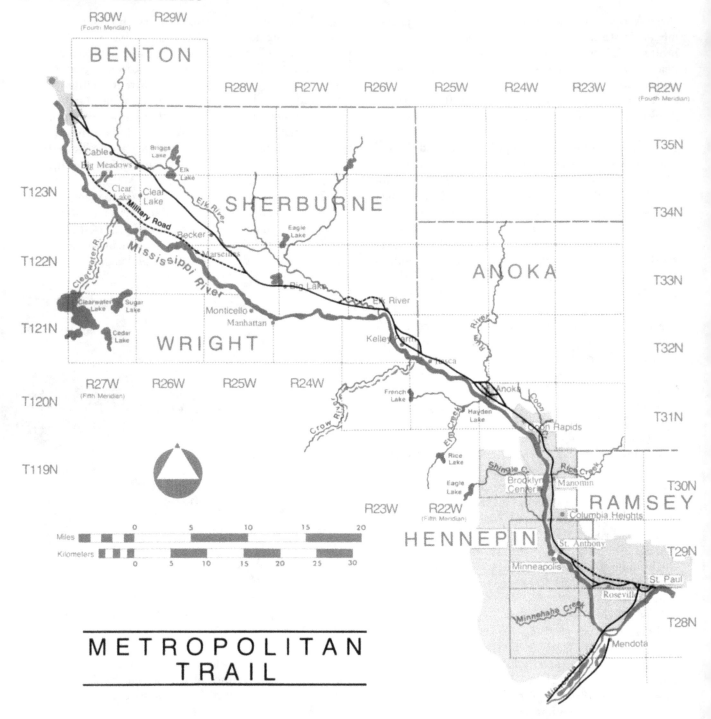

METROPOLITAN TRAIL

substantial bridge was constructed at this spot. Past the ravine, the road and trail again parted. The road cut straight across to what is now Territorial Road, south of the Burlington Northern railroad yards, continuing from there on a diagonal to Robert Street in St. Paul. The trail tended southeast through the University of Minnesota's Minneapolis campus and Prospect Park to the intersection of present Interstate 94 and State Highway 280 near the boundary with St. Paul. From there to Lexington Avenue in St. Paul the trail followed the present course of the freeway, deviating to the north and south to avoid some of the hills along the way.[12]

Opinions varied over the years on the condition of the road between St. Anthony and St. Paul. One traveler in 1851 remarked that "a few bad places only

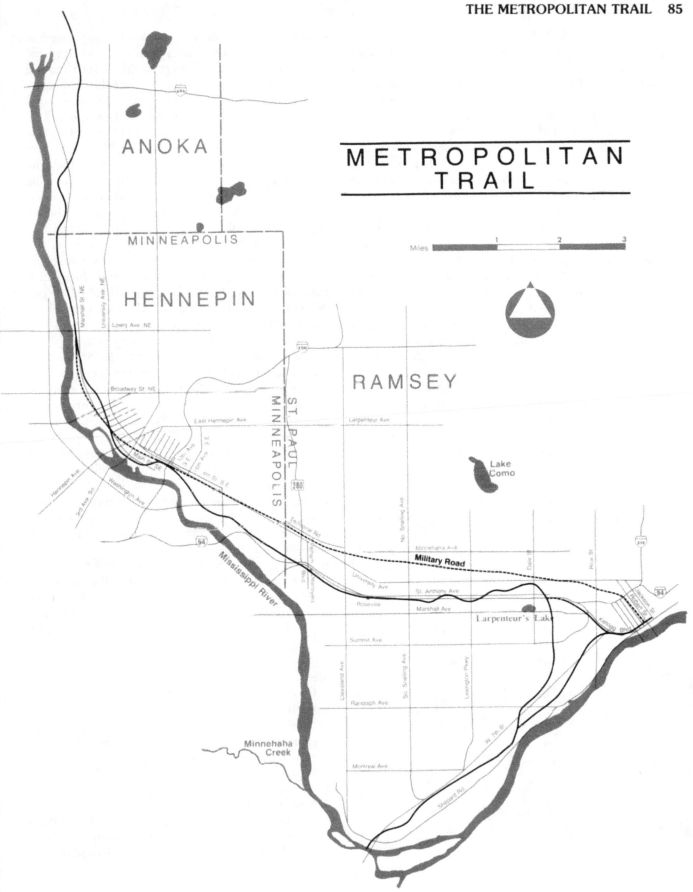

need to be planked and graded and we have at once a fine natural thoroughfare over the smooth hard prairie." By 1857 the road seems to have deteriorated, for in that year a traveler from St. Cloud maintained that it was "the worst nine miles of the whole journey." It ran over a hilly prairie, with "some fine clear valleys through which fine springs of water are scattered." Along this stretch fields of ripening wheat and oats could be seen on either side. Though by 1849 there was almost continuous settlement along the road, it was many years before the farmers were forced out by the expanding cities.

Near the intersection of St. Anthony Avenue and Pelham Boulevard in present St. Paul stood the main landmark on the road between St. Anthony and St. Paul. This was Stephen Desnoyer's tavern, known in later years as the Halfway House. Built in 1843, the inn served all passers-by for years, and its owner also did a thriving business trading in furs. A mile east of the tavern a townsite named "Roseville" was laid out on the trail in 1856, only to be absorbed by the city of St. Paul. At present Lexington Avenue in St. Paul the trail wandered off north of the freeway route to avoid a slough. After touching University briefly near Dale Street it headed south again, crossed the freeway, and skirted Summit Hill just below the Cathedral of St. Paul. Here it joined Kellogg Boulevard, then known as Third Street, and followed it down the hill and along the river to Jackson Street, where the steamboat landing and the fur warehouses marked the end of the long trek from the Red River.[13]

To the citizens of St. Paul, the annual arrival of the Red River carts was a sight as "novel and original [as] has ever appeared since Noah's Ark was evacuated." One journalist, who witnessed the spectacle in 1847, wrote, "Into St. Paul they came, on the 10th of July, a caravan of one hundred and twenty carts in single file,

wearily moving along by moonlight. Long after the head of the caravan had reached the village, the lengthened train of followers could be seen moving over the undulating prairie, partly visible and partly hidden, between the billowy ridges of the extended plain, crawling onward like some huge serpent."[14]

The drivers also attracted attention with their "swarthy complexions, straight long black hair, and wild, devil-may-care look." Their costume, which one early St. Paulite described as "a curious commingling of civilized garments and barbaric adornments," was as strange as the "unintelligible French and Indian jargon" they spoke. Overcoming any prejudice that existed among St. Paul's shopkeepers, however, was the "abundance of specie" the drivers spent in the stores and taverns, as well as the choice furs which they sold by the lot to the highest bidder. As one newspaper reminded its readers in 1855, "these French Half Breeds are our 'fellow citizens' who help make and are subject to the same laws as ourselves."

If the meeting of cultures in frontier St. Paul required broad-mindedness, the effort was certainly not one-sided. Some of the Canadians were convinced that the land grew progressively more barbarous as they went south, and that St. Paul constituted the very nadir of civilization. Robert Clouston, who arrived with a Hudson's Bay Company train in 1846, wrote that St. Paul "is a wretched little village consisting of [a] few scattered houses stuck here and there on the top of a steep bank almost *overhanging* the Mississippi: almost every house is either a shop or a 'grocery' (i.e. tavern) . . . and certainly, a grocery keeper cannot complain that he had no patronage, for, drinking whisky seems to occupy at least half the time of the worth[y] *citizens* of St. Paul's while the 'balance' of their time is employed in cheating each other or imposing upon strangers." His summation of the character of St. Paulites was succinct: "They seem an indolent, lazy, worthless class of men, so the miserable and dirty appearance of their houses may be imagined."[15]

Given the opinions entertained on both sides, it is not surprising that the Red River trains chose to camp outside the city while they rested their oxen, repaired their carts, sold their goods, and bought the supplies they needed for the ensuing year. Their customary rendezvous was Larpenteur's Lake, a "fine body of clear water" that once lay between present Dale, St. Albans, Carroll, and Marshall streets. "It was no uncommon sight to see from a thousand to fifteen hundred carts encamped around 'Larpenteur's lake,' . . . loaded with buffalo robes, furs of all descriptions,

Desnoyer House, its busy days ended, about 1894

dressed skins, moccasins, buffalo tongues and pemican," one early businessman recalled. From this outpost on the top of Summit Hill they awaited the arrival of steamboats carrying the goods they required — scythes, cradles, pitchforks, rakes, hoes, spades, corn shellers, horse-powered gristmills, flour, blankets, chains, chairs, tables, bureaus, clocks, harnesses, saddles, tubs, pails, and tinware, according to one early list. A disabled ox could be replaced for $40 or $50, but ready-made Red River carts were hard to come by and cost $15 apiece when they could be found.[16]

After a rest of about three weeks the Red River caravans were again loaded and ready to start the long trip back over the trails. It may be that there were many men like Clouston who "bade adieu with much pleasure to the villainous den of blackguards" that was St. Paul and struck out eagerly for the wholesome north. But there were probably others in the brigades like young Hyacinthe Villeneuve who looked forward to the annual trek to the bustling city as long as the carts and oxen made the journey.[17]

As for the people of St. Paul, the departure of the last cart train of the year must have signaled the end of summer. There is a tone of regret in the reflections of one journalist who watched the exodus in 1847. "They are now again on their way back to the frozen wilds of the north," he wrote, "many of them, probably never again to commune with the great world." He might have been surprised had he foreseen the resilience of the people who braved the long journey for more than 20 years thereafter to claim their share in the goods of the "great world."

During the years of cart traffic the people from Red River saw St. Paul mature from a squalid frontier "nest of Satan" into a busy river town, graced with cultural aspirations and visions of a metropolitan future. A Hudson's Bay Company clerk who brought a brigade down in 1870 admitted in his diary that he was "thoroughly enjoying this lively city after years of comparative isolation" in the north. The Merchants Hotel, a rambling, conglomerate building of logs, lumber, brick, and stone on the corner of what is now Kellogg Boulevard and Jackson Street served throughout the 1860s as "the headquarters for all the Red River traders and travellers who come in largest numbers during [June] and again in the early fall." In those months it was "alive with Red River freighters and Hudson's Bay Company's officers. Old friends of both sides of the border meet here on their travels and the old families of St. Paul are as hospitable as ever."[18]

They had good reason to be. The business generated by the Red River people had grown steadily. Between the years 1855 and 1863 alone, according to one estimate, this international trade brought $1,466,766 worth of furs and robes into St. Paul, accounting for four-fifths of the fur business handled there. In these years the struggling capital of Minnesota had almost no agricultural hinterland and was bypassed by the territory's prosperous lumber industry. It could and did, however, claim to be one of the largest fur markets in America — second only to St. Louis. When grain from the Red River Valley and the plains of Manitoba and Saskatchewan began to replace buffalo robes, the lines of communication that had already been established in response to the fur trade helped St. Paul and its growing twin, Minneapolis, to draw commerce southward despite the attractions of water transportation on the Great Lakes.[19]

Carts at Third Street (now Kellogg Boulevard) and Washington Street in St. Paul, where the St. Paul Public Library now stands, about 1858

REFERENCE NOTES AND SOURCES FOR THE MAPS

CHAPTER ONE / *The History of the Trails* / pages 1 to 26

[1]John P. Pritchett, ed., "A Letter by Lord Selkirk on Trade Between Red River and the United States," in *Canadian Historical Review*, 17:418–423 (December, 1936).

[2]Rhoda R. Gilman, "The Fur Trade in the Upper Mississippi Valley, 1630–1850," in *Wisconsin Magazine of History*, 58:8–13 (Autumn, 1974).

[3]For the main facts of Dickson's career, as outlined here and below, see Louis A. Tohill, *Robert Dickson, British Fur Trader on the Upper Mississippi: A Story of Trade, War, and Diplomacy* (Ann Arbor, 1927).

[4]For general accounts of Selkirk and the Red River Colony, see John M. Gray, *Lord Selkirk of Red River* (London, 1963); John P. Pritchett, *The Red River Valley 1811–1849: A Regional Study* (New Haven and Toronto, 1942).

[5]Thomas Clark to Dickson, April, 1814, in the Selkirk Papers, Public Archives of Canada, Ottawa, microfilm copy in the Minnesota Historical Society (hereafter abbreviated MHS); Jacob Van der Zee, "Episodes in the Early History of the Des Moines Valley," in *Iowa Journal of History and Politics*, 14:338–340 (July, 1916).

[6]Tohill, *Robert Dickson*, 93, 94; Duncan Graham to Selkirk, October 11, December 7, 1816; Graham to Michael McDonnell, November 5, 1816; Dickson to Selkirk, November 1, 1816 — all in Selkirk Papers; Thomas Forsyth to William Clark, October 3, 1819, in the William Clark Papers, Missouri Historical Society, St. Louis, photostatic copy in MHS.

[7]Selkirk to Alexander MacDonell, September 14, 1817; Selkirk to James Bird, September 28, 1817; Selkirk to Dickson, October 18, November 3, 1817; Dickson to Selkirk, December 1, 1817 — all in Selkirk Papers; Jacob Franks to John Lawe, March 11, 1818, in *Wisconsin Historical Collections*, 20:34–36 (1911).

[8]Selkirk to MacDonell, September 28, 1817, Selkirk Papers; Benjamin O'Fallon to William Clark, May 20, 1818, in Clarence Carter, ed., *Territorial Papers of the United States — Louisiana-Missouri Territory*, 15:407–409, 412 (Washington, D.C., 1951); Tohill, *Robert Dickson*, 91–95.

[9]Ramsay Crooks to James H. Lockwood, August 21, 1819, in Mackinac Letterbook, 1816–20, Missouri Historical Society, St. Louis, copy in MHS; Bernard Brisbois, "Traditions and Recollections of Prairie du Chien," and Dickson to John Lawe, April 18, 1820 — both in *Wisconsin Historical Collections*, 9:299 (1882), 20:164; Alexander Ross, *The Red River Settlement: Its Rise, Progress, and Present State*, 50 (London, 1856). See also typewritten extracts from Hudson's Bay Company Records in MHS, including reports and correspondence on the Dakota trade, 1819, 1820, and a journal kept by Bourke in 1819–21. The originals are in the Hudson's Bay Company Archives, Winnipeg.

[10]Henry H. Sibley, "Reminiscences: Historical and Personal," in *Minnesota Historical Collections*, 1:384 (1902); Brisbois, in *Wisconsin Historical Collections*, 9:299.

[11]Forsyth to Clark, October 3, 1819, in Clark Papers; Crooks to Joseph Rolette, March 28, 1822, Mackinac Letterbook, 1820–25, Stuart House, Mackinac Island, Mich., copy in MHS; George Simpson to Andrew Colvile, May 20, 1822, Selkirk Papers.

[12]Sibley, in *Minnesota Historical Collections*, 1:383; Ross, *Red River Settlement*, 73; Crooks to Rolette, March 28, 1822, Mackinac Letterbook; Van der Zee, in *Iowa Journal of History and Politics*, 14:340; "Extract from [William] Kempt's Journal," in E. H. Oliver, ed., *The Canadian North-West: Its Early Development and Legislative Records*, 1:248 (Canadian Archives, *Publications*, no. 9 — Ottawa, 1914).

[13]Alvin C. Gluek, *Minnesota and the Manifest Destiny of the Canadian Northwest: A Study in Canadian-American Relations*, 33 (Toronto, 1965); David Lavender, *The Fist in the Wilderness*, 335 (New York, 1964).

[14]Lavender, *Fist in the Wilderness*, 336; Tohill, *Robert Dickson*, 98–100; Lawrence Taliaferro Journal, January 12, 1822, Taliaferro Papers, MHS; Dickson passport signed by Calhoun, April 27, 1822, in *Wisconsin Historical Collections*, 20:254.

[15]Lavender, *Fist in the Wilderness*, 347, 367–370, 378–380.

[16]Joseph R. Brown to Henry H. Sibley, January 3, 1855, Henry H. Sibley Papers, MHS; *Minnesota Pioneer* (St. Paul), April 7, 1853.

[17]E. Neil Mattson, *Red River Carts Trek Historic Pembina Trail*, 3–7 (Warren, Minn., 1958); Elliott Coues, ed., *New Light on the Early History of the Greater Northwest: The Manuscript Journals of Alexander Henry . . . and of David Thompson*, 1:191, 205, 211 (Reprint ed., Minneapolis, 1965).

[18]William H. Keating, comp., *Narrative of an Expedition to the Source of St. Peter's River, Lake Winnepeek, Lake of the Woods, &c. Performed in the Year 1823*, 2:38–40 (Reprint ed., Minneapolis, 1959).

[19]Keating, *Narrative*, 2:38; Gluek, *Minnesota and Manifest Destiny*, 32.

[20]Gluek, *Minnesota and Manifest Destiny*, 33; Samuel Woods, *Report . . . Relative to his Expedition to Pembina Settlement*, 26–29, 40–52 (31 Congress, 1 session, *House Executive Documents*, no. 51 — serial 577), hereafter cited as Woods, *Report*.

[21]Keating, *Narrative*, 1:386, 444–447, 2:2; Augustus L. Chetlain, *The Red River Colony*, 21 (Chicago, 1893).

[22]Chetlain, *Red River Colony*, 20–24; Ann Adams, "Early Days at Red River Settlement and Fort Snelling," in *Minnesota Historical Collections*, 6:88–93 (1894).

[23]Chetlain, *Red River Colony*, 26; Pritchett, *Red River Valley*, 229.

[24]Chetlain, *Red River Colony*, 27; Pritchett, *Red River Valley*, 229, 232.

[25]E[dward] D. Neill, "Occurrences in and Around Fort Snelling, From 1819 to 1840," in *Minnesota Historical Collections*, 2:124, 127 (1860–67); Charles van Ravenswaay, ed., "Voyage from the Red River in Hudson's Bay Territory to St. Louis, Missouri, in the Year 1827: The Diary of John Corcoran," in *Bulletin of the Missouri Historical Society*, 13:268–273 (April, 1957).

[26]Ross, *Red River Settlement*, 82; Gluek, *Minnesota and Manifest Destiny*, 21; Robert Campbell, "A Journey to Kentucky for Sheep," in *North Dakota Historical Quarterly*, 1:35–42 (October, 1926).

[27]Campbell, in *North Dakota Historical Quarterly*, 1:42–45.

[28]Pritchett, *Red River Valley*, 231–236; Robert Campbell Journal, 1808–1851, p. 27, in Bancroft Library, University of California — Berkeley, microfilm copy in MHS.

[29]Gluek, *Minnesota and Manifest Destiny*, 19–21; W. L. Morton, *Manitoba: A History*, 73–75 (Toronto, 1957); George W. Featherstonhaugh, *A Canoe Voyage up the Minnay Sotor*, 1:216 (Reprint ed., St. Paul, 1970); "Captain Marryat in Minnesota, 1838," in *Minnesota History*, 6:177 (June, 1925).

[30]Gluek, *Minnesota and Manifest Destiny*, 33, 37–43, 46; Morton, *Manitoba*, 74; D. Geneva Lent, *West of the Mountains: James Sinclair and the Hudson's Bay Company*, 64–73, 85–90 (Seattle, 1963).

[31]Neill, in *Minnesota Historical Collections*, 2:127; Rhoda R. Gilman, "Last Days of the Upper Mississippi Fur Trade," in *Minnesota History*, 42:124–129 (Winter, 1970).

[32]Pritchett, *Red River Valley*, 253; Gluek, *Minnesota and Manifest Destiny*, 46.

[33]Neill, in *Minnesota Historical Collections*, 2:138; Gilman, in *Minnesota History*, 42:129. The first reference found to the new route as "the road made by the northern people" is in a letter from Norman W. Kittson to Sibley, August 22, 1844, Sibley Papers.

[34]Stephen R. Riggs, *Mary and I: Forty Years With the Sioux*, 115 (Boston, 1887); Riggs to Sibley, August 22, 1844; Kittson to Sibley, August 22, 1844 — both in Sibley Papers; Peter Garrioch Journal, 1843–47, pp. 21–23, typescript in Provincial Archives of Manitoba, Winnipeg.

[35]George H. Gunn, "Peter Garrioch at St. Peter's," in *Minnesota History*, 20:119, 128 (June, 1939); Garrioch Journal, 1843–47, pp. 16, 24, 25.

[36]Garrioch Journal, 1843–47, pp. 23–25.

[37]Garrioch Journal, 1843–47, pp. 25, 27.

[38]Garrioch Journal, 1843–47, pp. 28–37.

[39]Robert Clouston, "Sketch of Journey between R.R.S. and St. Peter's in United States — 1846," p. 52, typescript in MHS.

[40]Gilman, in *Minnesota History*, 42:129–131.

[41]Gilman, in *Minnesota History*, 42:131; Clarence W. Rife, "Norman W. Kittson, A Fur-Trader at Pembina," in *Minnesota History*, 6:225–229 (September, 1925); Andrew McDermot to Sibley, June 3, 1844; Kittson to Sibley, July 16, August 28, 1844, February 6, 1845 — all in Sibley Papers.

[42]Lent, *West of the Mountains*, 96–99, 167–172.

[43]McDermot to Sibley, June 3, 1844; Kittson to Sibley, August 22, 1844, February 6, 1845; Martin McLeod to Sibley, September 28, 1844; Joseph Rolette, Jr., to William H. Forbes, November 7, 1844 — all in Sibley Papers; Garrioch Journal, 1843–47, p. 37.

[44]Kittson to Sibley, February 6, September 10, 1845, Sibley Papers; Gluek, *Minnesota and Manifest Destiny*, 50.

[45]Kittson to Sibley, September 10, 1845, Sibley Papers; Augustin Grignon, "Seventy-Two Years' Recollections of Wisconsin," in *Wisconsin Historical Collections*, 3:238n (1857).

[46]Receipt for steamboat passage, Prairie du Chien to St. Peters, September 1, 1843; copy of license issued by James P. Hays at La

Pointe, August 7, 1845; Alexander Christie to Fisher, September 17, 1845, January 10, 1846 — all in Henry M. Fisher Papers, Archepiscopal Archives, St. Boniface, Man., microfilm copies in MHS; Kittson to Sibley, February 6, 1845, Sibley Papers; Gluek, *Minnesota and Manifest Destiny*, 51.

[47]Kittson to Sibley, March 2, 1846, Sibley Papers; Gluek, *Minnesota and Manifest Destiny*, 51.

[48]Kittson to Sibley, March 2, 1846, Sibley Papers.

[49]Kittson's pattern of operations described here and in the two paragraphs below is based upon his correspondence and that of his associates in the Sibley Papers. See also Rife, in *Minnesota History*, 6:225–252.

[50]See, for example, Christie to Sibley, May 15, 21, 1845, Sibley Papers.

[51]Gluek, *Minnesota and Manifest Destiny*, 57–59; Lent, *West of the Mountains*, 188–194, 207, 214.

[52]Gluek, *Minnesota and Manifest Destiny*, 60–67; Morton, *Manitoba*, 76.

[53]Lent, *West of the Mountains*, 195–203, 228–286; Gluek, *Minnesota and Manifest Destiny*, 87.

[54]Gluek, *Minnesota and Manifest Destiny*, 68–70; Donald Gunn and Charles R. Tuttle, *History of Manitoba*, 302 (Ottawa, 1880).

[55]Elaine A. Mitchell, "International Buying Trip: Fort Garry to St. Louis in 1846," in *Minnesota History*, 36:37–53 (June, 1958); Christie to Sibley, September 10, 1846; Clouston to Sibley, October 3, 1846 — both in Sibley Papers.

[56]Gluek, *Minnesota and Manifest Destiny*, 57–59, 73.

[57]Gluek, *Minnesota and Manifest Destiny*, 73–77; Gunn and Tuttle, *History of Manitoba*, 303–305; Lent, *West of the Mountains*, 207–214.

[58]Gluek, *Minnesota and Manifest Destiny*, 86–92; Mattson, *Red River Carts*, 13; St. Paul Financial, Real Estate, and Railroad Advertiser, December 12, 1857; J. Fletcher Williams, *A History of the City of Saint Paul and of the County of Ramsey, Minnesota*, 304–307 (Minnesota Historical Collections, vol. 4, 1876); Isaac I. Stevens, *Narrative and Final Report of Explorations for a Route for a Pacific Railroad*, 55 (36 Congress, 1 session, *House Executive Documents*, no. 56, part 1 — serial 1054).

[59]*The Nor'-Wester* (Winnipeg), March 28, 1860.

[60]Edward S. Wortley, Earl of Wharncliffe, Diary, 1850, p. 50, in Wharncliffe Papers, MHS; James Carnegie, Earl of Southesk, *Saskatchewan and the Rocky Mountains*, 9 (Edinburgh, 1875); [Manton Marble], "To Red River & Beyond," in *Harper's New Monthly Magazine*, 21:305 (August, 1860); Lucy L. W. Morris, ed., *Old Rail Fence Corners: Frontier Tales Told by Minnesota Pioneers*, 102 (Reprint ed., St. Paul, 1976); *Nor'-Wester*, March 28, 1860.

[61]*St. Cloud Visiter*, June 24, 1858.

[62][Samuel H. Scudder], *The Winnipeg Country or Roughing it with an Eclipse Party*, 116 (Boston, 1886). Details of cart construction here and in the paragraph below are from John C. Schultz, *The Old Crow Wing Trail*, 14, and W[illiam] G. Fonseca, *On the St. Paul Trail in the Sixties*, 1–8 (Historical and Scientific Society of Manitoba [hereafter HSSM], *Transactions*, no. 45, 56 — Winnipeg, 1894, 1900). For another discussion of cart construction which includes many variations, see Harry B. Brehaut, "The Red River Cart and Trails," in HSSM, *Papers*, series 3, no. 28, pp. 8–15 (Winnipeg, 1971–72).

[63]Schultz, *Old Crow Wing Trail*, 18; Fonseca, *On the St. Paul Trail*, 7.

[64]Schultz, *Old Crow Wing Trail*, 13, 25; Morris, ed., *Old Rail Fence Corners*, 34.

[65][Charles Hallock], "The Red River Trail," in *Harper's New*

Monthly Magazine, 18:615 (April, 1859); *Nor'-Wester*, March 28, 1860.

⁶⁶Schultz, *Old Crow Wing Trail*, 16; W[illiam] J. Healy, *Women of Red River*, 15–28 (Winnipeg, 1923); George F. G. Stanley, *Louis Riel*, 17, 22 (Toronto, 1963); *St. Paul Daily Pioneer and Democrat*, July 2, 1856.

⁶⁷Schultz, *Old Crow Wing Trail*, 15.

⁶⁸Joseph J. Hargrave, *Red River*, 452 (Montreal, 1871); Morris, ed., *Old Rail Fence Corners*, 68, 115; Schultz, *Old Crow Wing Trail*, 15; *Wharncliffe Diary*, 43; *Nor'-Wester*, March 28, 1860.

⁶⁹Arthur J. Larsen, "The Development of the Minnesota Road System," 161, Ph.D. thesis, University of Minnesota, 1938, copy in MHS; *Henderson Democrat*, April 3, June 12, 1856, August 13, 1857.

⁷⁰Schultz, *Old Crow Wing Trail*, 12; *St. Paul Daily Pioneer and Democrat*, September 10, 1859.

⁷¹Keating, *Narrative*, 2:13; Garrioch Journal, 1837, p. 66, typescript in Provincial Archives of Manitoba, Winnipeg; John Warkentin and Richard I. Ruggles, *Manitoba Historical Atlas*, 123, 125, 129, 132, 147 (Winnipeg, 1970).

⁷²Marble, in *Harper's New Monthly Magazine*, 21:296.

⁷³Woods, *Report*, 1–36; John Pope, *The report of an exploration of the Territory of Minnesota*, 1–56 (31 Congress, 1 session, *Senate Executive Documents*, no. 42 — serial 558); C[harles] F. Smith, "Report of an expedition of Companies B and F, 10th regiment of infantry, to the Red River of the North, in 1856," in 35 Congress, 2 session, *House Executive Documents*, no. 2, 426–434 (serial 998); Gluek, *Minnesota and Manifest Destiny*, 111; Charles T. Cavileer, "The Red River Valley in 1851," December 10, 1891, p. 8, Cavileer Papers, MHS. Pope's work is hereafter cited as Pope, *Report*; Smith's is cited Smith, "Report."

⁷⁴Rife, in *Minnesota History*, 6:244; Willoughby M. Babcock, "With Ramsey to Pembina: A Treaty-Making Trip in 1851," in *Minnesota History*, 38:1–10 (March, 1962).

⁷⁵Rife, in *Minnesota History*, 6:248; Marble, in *Harper's New Monthly Magazine*, 21:582 (October, 1860); Gluek, *Minnesota and Manifest Destiny*, 111.

⁷⁶Williams, *History of Saint Paul*, 47–49. Nearly every letter in Kittson's correspondence with Sibley reveals his love of horses. After retirement, he built a famous race track in St. Paul.

⁷⁷[Charles E. Flandrau], "An Old French Trader of Romantic Memory," in *Magazine of Western History*, 12:583–591 (October, 1890); Robert Watson, *Notes on the Early Settlement of Cottage Grove and Vicinity, Washington Co., Minn.*, 18 (Northfield, 1924). Through his mother's mother, Madeline De Verville, Rolette was descended from one of the oldest and most distinguished French-Indian families in the Northwest. His father, however, was a native of Quebec and his mother's father, Henry M. Fisher, was of British ancestry.

⁷⁸Williams, *History of Saint Paul*, 160, 370; Marble, in *Harper's New Monthly Magazine*, 21:582.

⁷⁹Williams, *History of Saint Paul*, 322; Cavileer, "Red River Valley in 1851," p. 9.

⁸⁰Biographical information here and below is from Margareth Jorgensen, "Life of Pierre Bottineau," an unpublished research paper written in 1925, microfilm copy in MHS. See also Martha C. Bray, "Pierre Bottineau: Professional Guide," in *North Dakota Quarterly*, 32:29–37 (Spring, 1964); Garrioch Journal, 1843–47, p. 22.

⁸¹McLeod's account here and in the following two paragraphs is from Grace Lee Nute, ed., "The Diary of Martin McLeod," in *Minnesota History Bulletin*, 4:408–415 (August–November, 1922).

⁸²*Dictionary of Canadian Biography*, 10:473 (Toronto, 1972); Schultz, *Old Crow Wing Trail*, 12; Hariot G. Hamilton-Temple-Blackwood, Marchioness of Dufferin and Ava, *My Canadian Journal 1872–1878*, 258 (Reprint ed., Don Mills, Ont., 1969).

⁸³Schultz, *Old Crow Wing Trail*, 12.

⁸⁴Southesk, *Saskatchewan*, 8, 9, 14.

⁸⁵Lent, *West of the Mountains*, 220.

⁸⁶Stanley, *Louis Riel*, 21, 32–34.

⁸⁷Dousman to Fisher, August 20, 1847, August 6, 1853, Fisher Papers.

⁸⁸Gluek, *Minnesota and Manifest Destiny*, 87–91, 100–103.

⁸⁹Russell Blakeley, "Opening of the Red River of the North to Commerce and Civilization," in *Minnesota Historical Collections*, 8:46 (1898); Gluek, *Minnesota and Manifest Destiny*, 137, 140–144.

⁹⁰Gluek, *Minnesota and Manifest Destiny*, 129–131.

⁹¹Gluek, *Minnesota and Manifest Destiny*, 133–136.

⁹²Willoughby M. Babcock, "Gateway to the Northwest: St. Paul and the Nobles Expedition of 1859," in *Minnesota History*, 35:249–262 (June, 1957).

⁹³Blakeley, in *Minnesota Historical Collections*, 8:48; Marion H. Herriot, "Steamboat Transportation on the Red River," in *Minnesota History*, 21:249 (September, 1940).

⁹⁴Blakeley, in *Minnesota Historical Collections*, 8:50; Gluek, *Minnesota and Manifest Destiny*, 143.

⁹⁵Blakeley, in *Minnesota Historical Collections*, 8:50–52; Gluek, *Minnesota and Manifest Destiny*, 144.

⁹⁶Gluek, *Minnesota and Manifest Destiny*, 144. Until the records of the Hudson's Bay Company were opened to historians in the 1950s, its share in ownership of the "Anson Northup" was only guessed at. See Herriot, in *Minnesota History*, 21:251n.

⁹⁷Gluek, *Minnesota and Manifest Destiny*, 145–148.

⁹⁸Blakeley, in *Minnesota Historical Collections*, 8:59; Herriot, in *Minnesota History*, 21:250.

⁹⁹Gluek, *Minnesota and Manifest Destiny*, 146, 155.

¹⁰⁰Grover Singley, *Tracing Minnesota's Old Government Roads*, 25–35 (St. Paul, 1974).

¹⁰¹Blakeley, in *Minnesota Historical Collections*, 8:61.

¹⁰²Blakeley, in *Minnesota Historical Collections*, 8:59.

¹⁰³Kenneth Carley, *The Sioux Uprising of 1862*, 53–58 (2nd ed., St. Paul, 1976).

¹⁰⁴Blakeley, in *Minnesota Historical Collections*, 8:60.

¹⁰⁵Material here and in the paragraph below is from Ella Hawkinson, "The Old Crossing Chippewa Treaty and Its Sequel," in *Minnesota History*, 15:282–300 (September, 1934).

¹⁰⁶Gluek, *Minnesota and Manifest Destiny*, 162–164; Arthur J. Larsen, "The Northwestern Express and Transportation Company," in *North Dakota Historical Quarterly*, 6:50 (October, 1931).

¹⁰⁷Blakeley, in *Minnesota Historical Collections*, 8:61; Gluek, *Minnesota and Manifest Destiny*, 164–167; Larsen, in *North Dakota Historical Quarterly*, 6:54; *McClung's St. Paul Directory, and Statistical Record for 1866*, 213 (St. Paul, 1866); *Alexandria Post*, August 7, 1869.

¹⁰⁸Larsen, in *North Dakota Historical Quarterly*, 6:54; Grace C. Hall, *The Wadsworth Trail*, 5–7 (Morris, Minn., 1938).

¹⁰⁹Gluek, *Minnesota and Manifest Destiny*, 165.

¹¹⁰Richard S. Prosser, *Rails to the North Star*, 11, 17 (Minneapolis, 1966); Larsen, "Minnesota Road System," 190.

¹¹¹Gluek, *Minnesota and Manifest Destiny*, 193; *St. Paul Daily Press*, September 12, 1863; *St. Cloud Democrat*, June 14, 1866.

¹¹²Stanley, *Louis Riel*, 49–58.

¹¹³Stanley, *Louis Riel*, 59–65.

¹¹⁴Morton, *Manitoba*, 121–144.

[115]Gluek, *Minnesota and Manifest Destiny*, 262–294; Stanley, *Louis Riel*, 169–176.

[116]The material on Hill in this and the following paragraphs is from Albro Martin, *James J. Hill and the Opening of the Northwest*, 69–83 (New York, 1976).

CHAPTER TWO / *The Manitoba Trails* / pages 27 to 33

SOURCES FOR THE MAPS

Most of the information shown on the accompanying map was derived from 1871 township survey maps as reproduced in J. Johnston, "Map of the Province of Manitoba," in *New Standard Atlas of the Dominion of Canada*, map 92–93 (Montreal, 1875), supplemented by Henry Y. Hind, "Map of Part of the Valley of Red River North of the 49th Parallel," in [George Gladman], *Report on the Exploration of the Country Between Lake Superior and the Red River Settlement* (Toronto, 1858); and "Map to Illustrate a Narrative of the Canadian Red River Exploring Expedition of 1857," in Hind, *Narrative of the Canadian Red River Exploring Expedition of 1857*, vol. 1 (Reprint ed., New York, 1969).

Dotted lines have been used to indicate portions of the trails not shown on the 1871 survey maps, except in the case of the trail between Ste. Agathe and St. Norbert on the west side of the Red River. The route nearest the river follows Hind; that farther from the river represents the survey version. The dotted line running through Letellier is also based on Hind. These are the only two places where Hind and the surveys disagree to any extent. A trail may also have existed on the west side of the river from the settlements near Headingley on the Assiniboine to St. Joseph. See Morton, *Manitoba*, 157.

[1]For this and the paragraph below, see Gladman, *Report*, 268; William Douglas, "'The Forks' Becomes a City," in HSSM, *Papers*, series 3, no. 1, p. 66 (Winnipeg, 1945).

[2]Southesk, *Saskatchewan*, 32.

[3]C[hristopher] C. Andrews, *Minnesota and Dacotah: In letters descriptive of a Tour through the North-West, in the Autumn of 1856*, 109 (Washington, D.C., 1857); Douglas, in HSSM, *Papers*, series 3, no. 1, p. 72; Morton, *Manitoba*, 73.

[4]For this and the paragraphs below, see Morton, *Manitoba*, 60–68, 159; George Bryce, *Worthies of Old Red River*, 1 (HSSM, *Transactions*, no. 48 — Winnipeg, 1896).

[5]Morton, *Manitoba*, 64; Healy, *Women of Red River*, 55; Andrews, *Minnesota and Dacotah*, 109; J. Wesley Bond, *Minnesota and Its Resources*, 290, 291 (Chicago and Philadelphia, 1856).

[6]Gladman, *Report*, 268; Andrews, *Minnesota and Dacotah*, 109, 110; M. S. Osborne, "The Architectural Heritage of Manitoba," in R. C. Lodge, ed., *Manitoba Essays*, 54, 65–70 (Toronto, 1937); Bond, *Minnesota*, 288.

[7]Charles N. Bell, *The Old Forts of Winnipeg*, 30–32 (HSSM, *Transactions*, new series no. 3 — Winnipeg, 1927); Keating, *Narrative*, 2:68; Alexander Ross, *The Fur Hunters of the Far West*, 2:261 (London, 1855); Douglas, in HSSM, *Papers*, series 3, no. 1, p. 66.

[8]Bell, *Old Forts of Winnipeg*, 32, 36; Scudder, *Winnipeg Country*, 119; George Reynolds, "The Man Who Created The Corner of Portage and Main," in HSSM, *Papers (Transactions)*, series 3, no. 26, p. 10 (Winnipeg, 1969–70).

[9]Gladman, *Report*, 343; Scudder, *Winnipeg Country*, 131. See also p. 14, above.

[10]Hargrave, *Red River*, 183–185.

[11]Hargrave, *Red River*, 375, 386; Gladman, *Report*, 268; Scudder, *Winnipeg Country*, 132; J[ames] C. Hamilton, *The Prairie Province; Sketches of Travel from Lake Ontario to Lake Winnipeg*, 227 (Toronto, 1876).

[12]Schultz, *Old Crow Wing Trail*, 18; Hargrave, *Red River*, 375, 386; Hind, "Map of Part of the Valley of Red River"; Gladman, *Report*, 267; Morton, *Manitoba*, 122, 158; Bond, *Minnesota*, 320.

[13]Scudder, *Winnipeg Country*, 133.

[14]Coues, ed., *New Light*, 1:63n; Wharncliffe Diary, 75; Hind, "Map of Part of the Valley of Red River"; Scudder, *Winnipeg Country*, 134.

[15]Southesk, *Saskatchewan*, 28. Kittson refers to the Hudson's Bay Company fort as Burke's post (probably meaning John P. Bourke), in letters to Sibley dated September 10, 1845, March 2, 1846, and April 20, 1847, in Sibley Papers. See also Woods, *Report*, 19; *St. Paul Daily Pioneer and Democrat*, October 4, 1859; Schultz, *Old Crow Wing Trail*, 18; Hamilton, *Prairie Province*, 231.

[16]For this and the next two paragraphs, see Schultz, *Old Crow Wing Trail*, 12; Clouston, "Sketch of Journey," 1.

[17]Morton, *Manitoba*, 175; Edwin C. Guillet, *The Story of Canadian Roads*, 168 (Toronto, 1966).

CHAPTER THREE / *The North Dakota Trails* / pages 34 to 42

SOURCES FOR THE MAPS

The major part of the information represented on the accompanying map by solid red lines was derived from the original surveys of the state of North Dakota; manuscript township maps are preserved in the Office of the State Water Commission, State Office Building, Bismarck. Since those surveys were taken in 1867–78, they show the trails at a somewhat later date than when they were in use by Red River carts. In particular, they represent a time after Georgetown was a main crossing point of the Red. It has therefore been necessary to fill in details from other maps and accounts. Where this information is uncertain, a dotted line has been used.

The course of the trail from Pembina to St. Joseph (Walhalla) and from St. Joseph to the Tongue River is from a fragmentary, undated manuscript map (ca. 1868) by Moses K. Armstrong, in the MHS. This same map shows the trail through Grafton (T157N, R53W) and in Traill County (T145N, R52–53W).

The possibility that a trail may have gone through Park River is suggested in "Trails of the Old Cart," an unidentified clipping in Masonic Grand Lodge File, North Dakota Institute for Regional Studies, North Dakota State University — Fargo.

The trails in Grand Forks County have been confirmed and elaborated from an undated map entitled "Grand Forks County," in Miscellaneous Folder, Orin G. Libby Papers, State Historical Society of North Dakota, Bismarck. This map was especially helpful in T153N, R50–51W and T152N, R50W near Grand Forks, T154N, R54W near Inkster, and T149N, R54W near Northwood.

The trails in T146N, R53W are from Traill County Folder, Dana Wright Papers, State Historical Society of North Dakota. The trail shown crossing the Goose River east of Hillsboro and continuing north through T146–148N, R50–51W is discussed in Bertha M. Kuhn, "The History of Traill County, North Dakota," 22. Master's thesis, University of North Dakota, 1917. It was not a major route.

The route of the trail south of Clifford and the more easterly route south of Rush River are largely compiled from "Field Notes of

Capt. Pope's expedition from Fort Snelling to Pembina, made in 1849," copied by Alfred J. Hill, November, 1860, in Hill Papers, MHS. Both the track of the Woods-Pope expedition and an "Old Road" from which the party diverged are shown on these manuscript maps; the "Old Road" is the one we attempted to reconstruct here. The Woods-Pope expedition, to avoid a second crossing of the Rush near Erie, left the trail and continued on east of the Rush through Cass County. They seem to have joined the trail once again near Clifford.

There are a number of reasons for believing that Woods and Pope crossed the Maple and Sheyenne rivers farther east in their journey north than on their return, when they probably used the Watson and Nolan crossings. Their description of the land, the distances and directions traveled, the few landmarks laid down on Pope's manuscript maps, and his route as drawn on his published map, all indicate that the two officers throught they were traversing country considerably east of the route of the later well-used trail via the Nolan and Watson crossings. The more easterly dotted line on the accompanying map shows a hypothetical reconstruction of their route going north; the more westerly dotted line represents the probable route of travelers using the Watson crossing of the Maple, a route which Ramsey's party described as a "new road" in 1851. See p. 40, above. The southern half of this latter trail in T138–139N, R52W is from Dana Wright, "Military Trails in Dakota: The Fort Totten-Abercrombie Trail," in *North Dakota History*, 13:map facing p. 110 (July, 1946). The northern half in T140–141N, R52W is conjectural.

The configuration of the trails at the Nolan crossing of the Sheyenne in T136N, R51W is from a sketch drawn by Dana Wright in 1946, enclosed in a letter from Mrs. Glennis Eckre to Ann Rathke, State Historical Society of North Dakota, September 20, 1976, copy in MHS.

The trail shown by a dotted line in T132–133N, R47–49W is deduced from Stevens, *Narrative*, 54.

United States Geological Survey maps and geologic maps in Gordon L. Bell, *The Red River Valley of North Dakota* (Bismarck, 1963) have been used extensively in compiling this map. Other gaps in the state survey records were filled in with dotted lines where reasonable deductions as to the trails' routes were possible.

[1] *St. Paul Daily Pioneer and Democrat*, September 11, 1859.

[2] Coues, ed., *New Light*, 1:xxiv, 79–81, 181; Pritchett, *Red River Valley*, 83–86; H. V. Arnold, *The History of Old Pembina 1780–1872*, 98 (Larimore, N. Dak., 1917).

[3] Keating, *Narrative*, 2:39, 40; Woods, *Report*, 28. For a detailed account of the buffalo hunts, see Ross, *Red River Settlement*, 241–274.

[4] Gluek, *Minnesota and Manifest Destiny*, 31, 48; Keating, *Narrative*, 2:39, 41; Woods, *Report*, 27; p. 5, above.

[5] For this and the paragraph below, see Woods, *Report*, 19; Wharncliffe Diary, 49; Bond, *Minnesota*, 275.

[6] Gluek, *Minnesota and Manifest Destiny*, 57, 104; Bond, *Minnesota*, 277; Woods, *Report*, 19, 36–43; Rife, in *Minnesota History*, 6:239; Francis P. Prucha, *A Guide to the Military Posts of the United States 1789–1895*, 96 (Madison, 1964).

[7] Rife, in *Minnesota History*, 6:248, 249; Arnold, *History of Old Pembina*, 119; *St. Paul Daily Pioneer and Democrat*, October 4, 1859; Smith, "Report," 444.

[8] Smith, "Report," 427n; Bond, *Minnesota*, 276; Coues, ed., *New Light*, 1:189; Gluek, *Minnesota and Manifest Destiny*, 114; Harvey and Myrtle Dalzell *et al.*, comps., *Walhalla Quasquicentennial An-niversary*, 3 ([Walhalla, N. Dak.?], 1973); Stanley, *Louis Riel*, 157, 161, 184.

[9] Bond, *Minnesota*, 276; Dalzell *et al.*, *Walhalla*, 3, 29.

[10] Moses Armstrong, undated map, in MHS; Smith, "Report," 443.

[11] Bond, *Minnesota*, 272. The poplar islands are shown on Pope, "Map of the Territory of Minnesota," in *Report*, facing p. 56.

[12] Kuhn, "History of Traill County," 22; *St. Paul Daily Pioneer and Democrat*, September 11, 1859. On prairie travel, see, for example, Clouston, "Sketch of Journey," 6, 7.

[13] Featherstonhaugh, *Canoe Voyage*, 1:382; Martin McLeod, "Minnesota River," undated manuscript in McLeod Papers, MHS; Nute, ed., in *Minnesota History*, 4:411.

[14] Edmund C. and Martha C. Bray, eds., *Joseph N. Nicollet on the Plains and Prairies*, 36 (St. Paul, 1976); Marble, in *Harper's New Monthly Magazine*, 21:305.

[15] For this and the paragraph below, see *Nor'-Wester*, March 14, 1860; Clouston, "Sketch of Journey," 2, 16; Woods, *Report*, 12. Clouston was on the east side of the Red River in the passage quoted.

[16] Pope, "Map of the Territory of Minnesota"; *St. Paul Daily Pioneer and Democrat*, September 11, 1859; Marble, in *Harper's New Monthly Magazine*, 21:310.

[17] Bond, *Minnesota*, 271; "Field Notes of Capt. Pope's expedition," 27, in Hill Papers.

[18] For this and the paragraph below, see Nute, ed., in *Minnesota History*, 4:410; Woods, *Report*, 17, 18.

[19] Wright, in *North Dakota History*, 13:86n (January–April, 1946); *St. Paul Daily Pioneer and Democrat*, September 10, 11, 1859. Fort Totten was founded in 1867; see Prucha, *Guide to the Military Posts*, 112.

[20] The spot described may have been somewhere east of Galesburg; however, attempts to identify Woods's "cluster of hills" have been unsuccessful. See Woods, *Report*, 17; Wharncliffe Diary, 35; Nute, ed., in *Minnesota History*, 4:411. For an explanation of the route of the trail here, see "Sources for the Maps," above.

[21] Wharncliffe Diary, 35; Woods, *Report*, 16; Wright, in *North Dakota History*, 13:106; *Minnesota Pioneer*, October 30, 1851. This paragraph is based on the assumption that Woods and Pope followed a route that took them east of the Nolan and Watson fords; see "Sources for the Maps," above.

[22] Woods, *Report*, 16, 21; Wright, in *North Dakota History*, 13:106n, 108; Alexander Ramsey Diary, August 31, 1851, in Ramsey Papers, MHS; "Anthony Nolan History," 1975, anonymous typescript enclosed in Eckre to Rathke, September 20, 1976, copy in MHS; Bond, *Minnesota*, 262; Stevens, *Narrative*, 55, plate 9. Another ford of the Sheyenne existed near Kindred; see *Fargo Forum*, July 27, 1958, sec. C, p. 2.

[23] On the name of Graham's Point, see Garrioch Journal, 1837, p. 80; Graham to Selkirk, December 7, 1816, Selkirk Papers. On Fort Abercrombie, see Woods, *Report*, 15, 16; Roy P. Johnson, "The Siege at Fort Abercrombie," in *North Dakota History*, 24:11 (January, 1957); Hallock and Marble, in *Harper's New Monthly Magazine*, 19:44 (June, 1859), 21:306; *St. Paul Daily Pioneer and Democrat*, September 9, 1859.

[24] H. V. Arnold, "Local Sketches — No. 3. The Old Trails," an unidentified clipping in Masonic Grand Lodge File, North Dakota Institute for Regional Studies; *St. Paul Daily Pioneer and Democrat*, September 11, 1859.

[25] Campbell, in *North Dakota Historical Quarterly*, 1:36; Nute, ed., in *Minnesota History*, 4:397; Garrioch Journal, 1837, pp. 58, 60, 63, 69, 72.

[26]Campbell, in *North Dakota Historical Quarterly*, 1:37; Garrioch Journal, 1837, pp. 62, 64, 66; Charlotte O. Van Cleve, *"Three Score Years and Ten," Life-Long Memories of Fort Snelling, Minnesota*, 49–52 (Minneapolis, 1888).

[27]Garrioch Journal, 1837, p. 66; Campbell, in *North Dakota Historical Quarterly*, 1:36, 37; Clouston, "Sketch of Journey," 7. The latter was actually traveling on the opposite side of the river.

[28]Blakeley and George N. Lamphere, "History of Wheat Raising in the Red River Valley," in *Minnesota Historical Collections*, 8:48, 50, 62–64, 10:9 (Part 1, 1905); undated interview of Joe Colosky by Orin G. Libby, in Libby Papers.

CHAPTER FOUR / *The Minnesota Valley Trail* / pages 43 to 54

SOURCES FOR THE MAPS

The major sources for the maps of the Minnesota Valley Trail were the original U.S. land survey plats, 1853–70, in the Minnesota Secretary of State's office, St. Paul. As this was the earliest of the Red River trails in Minnesota, the survey maps are vague about its route. In many cases the surveyors marked the trail "Government Road" or "Military Road." Where the survey maps had gaps, the guesses of the U.S. Works Projects Administration (hereafter abbreviated WPA), Minnesota, Red River Trails Maps, in Division of Archives and Manuscripts, MHS, were followed. Where both of the sources had gaps, dotted lines were used.

Information on the branch of the trail north of Wheaton was obtained in an interview of the authors with Fred Trende of Rosholt, S. Dak., May, 1976. Also helpful in the Big Stone-Lake Traverse area were a map enclosed in Stephen R. Riggs to David Greene, May 16, 1839, in American Board of Commissioners for Foreign Missions Papers, MHS; and "A Rough Sketch of Lt. Col. J. J. Abercrombie's route . . . in July & August 1858," copy in Hill Papers. Southeast from Big Stone Lake, a helpful source was B. M. Smith and A. J. Hill, "Map of the Ceded Part of Dakota Territory" (St. Paul, 1861), which showed the more southerly branch of the trail through T120–122N, R42–45W, and the route appearing as a dotted line on the south side of the river in T116–120N, R40–45W. The former probably represents an earlier route than the more northerly branch laid down on the survey maps; since none of the early travelers on this section of the trail mentioned passing Artichoke Lake, it is probable that the earliest trail ran some distance south of it. The branch of the trail in T119N, R42W, near Milan, and the dotted link in T118N, R41W, were documented in *Watson Voice*, April 22, 1937, p. 5. Confirmation and details on the trails in Lac qui Parle County were provided by Mrs. Charles (Micki) Buer of Canby, Minn.

In Renville County, the dotted line shown running along the riverbank is assumed from the fact that the bluff trail-river trail pattern existed both north and south of Renville County, and there is no reason to think it did not continue in this area. Featherstonhaugh, *Canoe Voyage*, 1: 328, also mentioned a cart trail along the river in this stretch. A. A. Davidson, "Historic Trail Renville County," in Historical Markers and Monuments: Historic Trails, Renville County, WPA Papers, MHS, offered another reconstruction of the bluff trail in this county, compiled from the reminiscences of old settlers in the 1930s. This version varied substantially from the original surveys.

In Nicollet County, the most southerly loop of the trail to the ford near Judson has been shown because this was apparently the route mentioned by a member of Joseph N. Nicollet's 1838 expedition. He noted that they joined "the road of the Red-river people" at what was probably the Judson crossing. Bray and Bray, eds., *Nicollet on the Plains*, 119.

[1]Adams, in *Minnesota Historical Collections*, 6:92; Featherstonhaugh, *Canoe Voyage*, 1:328; *Minnesota Democrat* (St. Paul), July 20, 1853.

[2]The Minnesota Valley was used by Kittson's brigades from 1844 to 1855, the latter date being the last recorded trip by this route. See Kittson to Sibley, July 16, 1844, March 30, 1845, August 7, 1846, Sibley Papers; *Weekly Minnesotian* (St. Paul), July 24, 1852; *Minnesota Democrat*, July 20, 1853, June 27, 1855; Thomas Hughes, *Old Traverse des Sioux*, 41, 104 (St. Peter, 1929). For instances of Dakota friendliness to the cart trains, see p. 7, above.

[3]Larsen, "Minnesota Road System," 142; Lydia S. Wulff, ed., *Big Stone County History*, 7 (Chokio, Minn., 1959); Franklyn Curtiss-Wedge, *The History of Redwood County Minnesota*, 1:219 (Chicago, 1916). In "Rough Sketch of Lt. Col. J. J. Abercrombie's route," in Hill Papers, it was noted that "The road now travelled differs somewhat from original trail," but no indication was made of how much or where.

[4]The winter and summer roads are mentioned by Stephen R. Riggs, *Taĥ-Koo Wah-Kaṅ; or, The Gospel Among the Dakotas*, 119 (Boston, 1869); and by Martin McLeod in *St. Anthony Express*, November 1, 1851. Riggs's son remembered the brigades on the north side only; see Thomas L. Riggs, "Sunset to Sunset: A Lifetime With My Brothers, the Dakotas," in *South Dakota Historical Collections*, 29:109 (Pierre, 1958).

[5]Keating, *Narrative*, 2:3; Smith, "Report," 440; "Rough Sketch of Lt. Col. J. J. Abercrombie's route," Hill Papers; Warren Upham, *Minnesota Geographic Names: Their Origin and Historic Significance*, 554 (Reprint ed., St. Paul, 1969); Garrioch Journal, 1837, p. 89; Campbell, in *North Dakota Historical Quarterly*, 1:37, called the stretch from the Otter Tail River to Lake Traverse the "Traverse de Sioux," a name that did not persist.

[6]Upham, *Minnesota Geographic Names*, 217; Garrioch Journal, 1837, pp. 83, 85.

[7]Keating, *Narrative*, 2:1,3,5; Van Ravenswaay, ed., in *Bulletin of the Missouri Historical Society*, 13:270.

[8]The post was in T125N, R49W, sec. 2. See Grace Lee Nute, "Posts in the Minnesota Fur-Trading Area, 1660–1855," in *Minnesota History*, 11:379 (December, 1930); Campbell, in *North Dakota Historical Quarterly*, 1:37; Lucile M. Kane, June D. Holmquist, and Carolyn Gilman, eds., *The Northern Expeditions of Stephen H. Long: The Journals of 1817 and 1823 and Related Documents*, 170, 307 (St. Paul, 1978); Featherstonhaugh, *Canoe Voyage*, 1:385.

[9]Van Ravenswaay, ed., in *Bulletin of the Missouri Historical Society*, 13:271; Garrioch Journal, 1837, p. 89.

[10]Featherstonhaugh, *Canoe Voyage*, 1:398.

[11]The post was in T122N, R49W, Sec. 4. Charles W. De Greef to MHS, March 15, 1931, in Publications Miscellaneous Files, MHS Archives; Featherstonhaugh, *Canoe Voyage*, 1:399; Keating, *Narrative*, 1:384–386; Nute, in *Minnesota History*, 11:379.

[12]Featherstonhaugh, *Canoe Voyage*, 1:374–377; Garrioch Journal, 1837, p. 86.

[13]Garrioch Journal, 1837, p. 89; Keating, *Narrative*, 1:374, 375; Kane, Holmquist, and Gilman, eds., *Long Expeditions*, 296.

[14]June D. Holmquist and Jean A. Brookins, *Minnesota's Major Historic Sites: A Guide*, 113–116 (2nd ed., St. Paul, 1972); Bray and Bray, eds., *Nicollet on the Plains*, 107; Riggs, *Mary and I*, 63; Mary

H. Kerlinger, "Reminiscences of missionary effort among the Dakota Indians," 76, photostat in Alexander G. Huggins and Family Papers, MHS.

[15] For this and the paragraph below, see Holmquist and Brookins, *Major Historic Sites*, 113–116; Garrioch Journal, 1837, p. 91; Stephen R. Riggs, "Your Fathers, where are they?" address dated November 9, 1871, in Riggs Family Papers, MHS; Michael J. Smith, "Historic Sites in the Minnesota River Valley: A Compilation," 45, typescript in MHS. McLeod's irreligious views are apparent in Nute, ed., in *Minnesota History*, 4:417, 419.

[16] For this and the paragraph below, see Garrioch Journal, 1837, p. 91; Campbell, in *North Dakota Historical Quarterly*, 1:37; Featherstonhaugh, *Canoe Voyage*, 1:349; Keating, *Narrative*, 1:373; Upham, *Minnesota Geographic Names*, 292.

[17] Martin McLeod to "Mr. Editor," August, 1851, McLeod Papers; Morris, ed., *Old Rail Fence Corners*, 14; Francis J. Marschner, comp., "The Original Vegetation of Minnesota," map (St. Paul, 1974); Warren Upham, *The Geology of Central and Western Minnesota: A Preliminary Report*, 28 (St. Paul, 1880); Bray and Bray, eds., *Nicollet on the Plains*, 113.

[18] Keating, *Narrative*, 1:360; Woods, *Report*, 16, 18; Bond, *Minnesota*, 263; Marble, in *Harper's New Monthly Magazine*, 21:308.

[19] The three later Minnesota River fords were in T117N, R41W, sec. 13, 16, and T118N, R41W, sec. 32, according to Mrs. Buer to the authors, April 3, 1978. See also *Watson Voice*, April 29, 1937, p. 4; Bray and Bray, eds., *Nicollet on the Plains*, 111, 112; Nute, ed., in *Minnesota History*, 4:428; Davidson, "Historic Trail Renville County," WPA Papers.

[20] Holmquist and Brookins, *Major Historic Sites*, 121–130.

[21] Featherstonhaugh, *Canoe Voyage*, 1:328; Sibley to McLeod, October 6, 1846, McLeod Papers; Charles E. Flandrau, "The Inkpa-du-ta Massacre of 1857," in *Minnesota Historical Collections*, 3:403 (1880); Wallace F. Simpson, "Tchanshaypi Redwood County 100th Anniversary," n.p., mimeographed pamphlet in MHS.

[22] For this and the paragraph below, see Keating, *Narrative*, 1:362, 363; Holmquist and Brookins, *Major Historic Sites*, 121–130; Upham, *Minnesota Geographic Names*, 69.

[23] Willoughby M. Babcock, ed., "Up the Minnesota Valley to Fort Ridgely in 1853," in *Minnesota History*, 11:176, 177 (June, 1930); Riggs, *Tah-Koo Wah-Kan*, 114; Holmquist and Brookins, *Major Historic Sites*, 133.

[24] Featherstonhaugh, *Canoe Voyage*, 1:318; Garrioch Journal, 1837, p. 99; Babcock, ed., in *Minnesota History*, 11:175.

[25] For this and the paragraph below, see Upham, *Geology of Central Minnesota*, 23; Bray and Bray, eds., *Nicollet on the Plains*, 53, 54, 115; interview of the authors with Paul Klammer and Leota Kellett, Brown County Historical Society, June, 1976; Kane, Holmquist, and Gilman, eds., *Long Expeditions*, 292.

[26] Joseph N. Nicollet recorded both routes on his sketch map of June 18, 1838; the northern one was marked "Route au Lac qui Parle." Nicollet himself traveled by the southern one to the ford at the Cottonwood. See Bray and Bray, eds., *Nicollet on the Plains*, 50–53; Hughes, *Old Traverse des Sioux*, 18; Eli L. Huggins to Charles and Amos Huggins, March 20, 1918, in Huggins Papers; Riggs, *Mary and I*, 50; *Weekly Minnesotian*, August 6, 1853.

[27] Bray and Bray, eds., *Nicollet on the Plains*, 50; Mary W. Berthel, *Horns of Thunder: The Life and Times of James M. Goodhue*, 190 (St. Paul, 1948); Hughes, *Old Traverse des Sioux*, 1, 102; W. C. Brown, "Address before Minn. Historical Society, Jan. 9, 1928," p. 2, Huggins Papers; Willoughby M. Babcock, "Louis Provençalle, Fur Trader," in *Minnesota History*, 20:259–268 (September, 1939). The name "Traverse des Sioux" refers to the path

across the prairie and not to the river crossing, as is often stated. See John C. Frémont, *Memoirs of My Life*, 1:34 (Chicago and New York, 1887). One early traveler calls the village "Port[age] Des Sioux," a name which does refer to the ford. See Van Ravenswaay, ed., in *Bulletin of the Missouri Historical Society*, 13:273.

[28] Holmquist and Brookins, *Major Historic Sites*, 121; *Minnesota Pioneer*, April 7, 1853; *Weekly Minnesotian*, August 6, 1853.

[29] Bray and Bray, eds., *Nicollet on the Plains*, 48; Mary B. Aiton, "Dr. Williamson — His Ancestry & life work," 7, Thomas S. Williamson and Family Papers, MHS; Neill, in *Minnesota Historical Collections*, 2:127; Garrioch Journal, 1837, p. 96; Frémont, *Memoirs*, 1:34; Riggs, *Mary and I*, 82.

[30] McLeod to "Mr. Editor," August, 1851, McLeod Papers; Arthur J. Larsen, "Roads and Trails in the Minnesota Triangle, 1849–60," in *Minnesota History*, 11:391 (December, 1930); *New York Daily Tribune*, July 20, 1854.

[31] Kane, Holmquist, and Gilman, eds., *Long Expeditions*, 289, 290; Bray and Bray, eds., *Nicollet on the Plains*, 48; Keating, *Narrative*, 351.

[32] For this and the paragraph below, see *Minnesota Democrat*, June 7, 1854; McLeod to "Mr. Editor," August, 1851, McLeod Papers; Morris, ed., *Old Rail Fence Corners*, 60.

[33] For this and the paragraph below, see McLeod to "Mr. Editor," August, 1851, McLeod Papers; *Minnesota Democrat*, June 7, 1854; Featherstonhaugh, *Canoe Voyage*, 1:294.

[34] *Minnesota Democrat*, June 7, 1854; Featherstonhaugh, *Canoe Voyage*, 1:291; Keating, *Narrative*, 1:345; Smith, "Historic Sites," 11; Invoice Book, 63:11, May 28, 1838, Sibley Papers.

[35] Kane, Holmquist, and Gilman, eds., *Long Expeditions*, 287; McLeod to "Mr. Editor," August, 1851, McLeod Papers; Smith, "Historic Sites," 6–8; Julius A. Coller, *The Shakopee Story*, 35 (Shakopee, 1960); *New York Daily Tribune*, July 20, 1854; Berthel, *Horns of Thunder*, 184–186.

CHAPTER FIVE / *The Woods Trail* / pages 55 to 68

SOURCES FOR THE MAPS

The Woods Trail was the most thoroughly mapped of the Red River trails; not only did the U.S. land surveys show it in great detail, but two army road surveys and a railroad survey overlapped large portions of it.

At its northernmost end, the trail was thoroughly surveyed in 1872. Information can be found on the Minnesota survey maps and on two manuscript maps entitled "Sheet No. 2 of Location Showing St. Vincent Extension of the St. Paul & Pacific R.R." and "Map of Located Line St. Paul & Pacific R.R. from Junction with N.P.R.R. in T. 140 R. 42W. 5th Mer. to St. Vincent," both in Great Northern Railway Company Records, Burlington Northern Building, St. Paul, copies in MHS. However, for T154–155N, R45W, the township survey maps do not show the trail; this section has been reconstructed by the authors from N[ewton] H. Winchell, *Geology of Minnesota*, 4:plates 62, 63 (Geological and Natural History Survey of Minnesota, Final Report — St. Paul, 1899).

The variant route indicated by a dotted line in T141–146N, R41–44W is one possible resolution of much contradictory testimony about the route of the trail in this area. The more easterly route through White Earth is the only one positively identifiable as a Red River Trail, since it was labeled as such on the state survey maps of 1872. Why it should have taken a detour via White Earth in an era before the Indian agency was established in 1868 is difficult to explain. The other route is shown in two sources: an anonymous manuscript, "Map of Minnesota," ca. 1870?, in Lake Superior and Puget Sound Company Records: Maps, Northern Pacific Railway Company Records, MHS; and J.B. Power, "McClung's Map of Minnesota Prepared expressly to accompany his Work 'Minnesota As It Is in 1870'" (St. Paul, 1870). These two maps substantially agree on the course of the Woods and Link trails and disagree with the state survey maps only in the area in question (T141–146N, R41–44W).

[J. S. Sewall and Charles W. Iddings], "Sectional Map of the Surveyed Portion of Minnesota and the North Western Part of Wisconsin" ([St. Paul, 1860]) has the persuasive testimony of Alfred J. Hill for its accuracy in this area; see Hill, "The Old Red River Trails — A Memorandum," August 28, 1894, in Hill Papers. Although it shows the Woods Trail taking a course almost exactly between the two shown here, the Sewall and Iddings map is probably an attempt to represent the eastern or White Earth route. See Iddings, "Continuation of Reconnoissance of Fort Ripley & Red River Road via Crow Wing River," in George H. Belden, "Field Notes of Explorations & Reconnoissances Made in Connection with the Survey of the Above Road," 1857, copy in Hill Papers, which records Iddings' survey of the Woods Trail. A close reading of his notes shows that he must have been on the more easterly trail and merely did not note the sharp turn at White Earth.

Evidence for the route of the Link Trail, which branched off from the Woods Trail in this area, is also complex. Two sources pinpoint the place at which it left the Woods Trail, often called "the forks": George H. Belden, "Map of Survey and Location of Road, Fort Ripley via Crow Wing River to the Main Road Leading to the Red River of the North," 1857, in Secretary of State Records, Minnesota State Archives, MHS; "Copy of Col. Nobles' Field Notes between Pembina & Otter Tail Lake," in Hill Papers. The location of both the Link and Woods trails in this section is complicated by the records of a commission to locate salt-spring lands for the state of Minnesota in 1858. One of the sections of salt land claimed contained a portion of what the commissioners believed to be the Link Trail in unsurveyed country along the Wild Rice River. See N[ewton] H. Winchell, Report . . . Concerning the Salt Spring Lands, 11–14 (Geological and Natural History Survey of Minnesota, Miscellaneous Publications, no. 3 — St. Paul, 1874); J.D. Skinner, "Portion of Map Accompanying the Report of the Commission to Locate the Capitol & Salt Lands," copied by Alfred Hill, in Hill Papers; "Map of Western Minnesota from Town 117 North to Sandhill River Showing the Salt Spring and Public Building Lands," 1858, in Minnesota State Auditor, State Land Office Records, Minnesota State Archives. The question of exactly where the claimed salt land was becomes important to any sorting out of the trail routes in this area. Data in the margin of Hill's "Sketch of Country from Otter Tail Lake to Detroit Lake, Reduced from Map Drawn by the Indians for C.W. Iddings," in Hill Papers, imply that Hill thought the salt lands were in T141–142N, R42W, west of present Ogema. If this is true, it contradicts Power's version of the Woods Trail's route on "McClung's Map of Minnesota." Power, however, located the salt lands in T143–144N, R43–44W, on the Woods rather than the Link Trail. For the lower Link and Buffalo River trails, see "Sources for the Maps," Chapter 6.

The route of the Oak Lake Trail joining the Woods and Link trails and Lafayette is taken from the state surveys, but since so many settlers' roads existed in this area when the survey was made, there is some doubt whether the road depicted is actually the route the old Red River Trail followed. The two branches shown are the ones that cut through the least woods and therefore were most likely to have been used by the carts.

South of Detroit Lake the state surveys are supplemented by two U.S. Army maps: Belden, "Map of Survey and Location of Road," in Minnesota State Archives; E.A. Holmes, "Map of Reconnaisance of Road from Fort Ripley via Crow Wing River to the Main Road Leading to the Red River of the North," June, 1855, in Records of the Office of the Chief of Engineers, Record Group 77, National Archives, Washington, D.C. These maps corroborate the survey maps at most places; where they disagreed, preference was given to the oldest map.

No attempt has been made to show the military road which was built along the route of the Woods Trail from near Motley to Sauk Rapids, since its route is discussed in detail in Singley, Old Government Roads, 32–35.

[1] On Garrioch, see pp. 9–11, above. Kittson to J. H. Simpson, July 16, 1855, in 34 Congress, 1 session, House Executive Documents, no. 1, p. 491 (serial 841); William B. Mitchell, History of Stearns County Minnesota, 1:418 (Chicago, 1915).

[2] Schultz, Old Crow Wing Trail, 20, 21.

[3] Garrioch Journal, 1843–47, pp. 31, 37; Clouston, "Sketch of Journey," 1. Garrioch mentioned many of his companions, but Hallett was not among them. The latter was mentioned in Schultz, Old Crow Wing Trail, 4, and in many later sources.

There is a persistent tradition that an earlier trail existed along the approximate present route of the Burlington Northern railway, west of the well-defined beach-ridge trail. According to this tradition, early fords were located at Beltrami and Fisher. No primary sources have been found to confirm such a route. Township survey maps from the 1870s show a fragmentary, unidentified trail along the line of the railroad, with fords at Beltrami and Crookston (not Fisher), but it does not join the lower portions of the Woods Trail. A search of the Great Northern Railway Company Records in the Burlington Northern Building, St. Paul, and the MHS failed to turn up evidence that the railroad was built along a pre-existing trail, raising the possibility that the trail may have come into being in conjunction with settlement along the railroad. The earliest source which makes a case for the existence of two trails, R[eturn] I. Holcombe and William H. Bingham, eds., Compendium of History and Biography of Polk County, Minnesota, 46–52 (Minneapolis, 1916), hopelessly confuses the Woods, Middle, and North Dakota trails; for instance, Major Woods's description of the North Dakota ridge trail is quoted as evidence of a trail through Fisher and Beltrami. Other information on the tradition of an earlier trail may be found in Thomas M. McCall, Centennial History of Polk County, chapters 7, 14 (Crookston, 1961); McCall, "Red River Valley Trails," in Polk County Historian, May, 1960, p. [2]; Historical Markers and Monuments: Historic Trails, Polk County, WPA Papers. On the possibility of a trail along the east bank of the river, see Chapter 6.

[4] For this and the paragraph below, see Singley, Old Government Roads, 34, 35; Simpson to J.J. Abert, July 21, 1855, in 34 Congress, 1 session, House Executive Documents, no. 1, p. 488; Belden, "Map of Survey and Location of Road," 1857, in Secretary of State Records, Minnesota State Archives. The "Main Road Leading to the Red River of the North," to which the Woods Trail was supposed to be improved, was the Link Trail discussed in Chapter 6, below. It met the Woods Trail about five miles south of the ford of the Wild Rice River.

[5]Singley, *Old Government Roads*, 25, 32, 33.

[6]Warren Upham, *The Glacial Lake Agassiz*, 463 (United States Geological Survey, *Monographs*, vol. 25 — Washington, D.C., 1896); Historical Markers and Monuments: Historic Trails, Kittson County, WPA Papers.

[7]Hind, *Narrative*, 1:255, 256; Schultz, *Old Crow Wing Trail*, 19, 20; *Nor'-Wester*, March 14, 1860; Hallock Business and Professional Men's Association, *Community Fact Survey: Hallock, Gateway to Northwestern Minnesota*, 15 ([Hallock, 1971?]); interview of the authors with Keith Rosengren, Kittson County Historical Society, May, 1978.

[8]Southesk, *Saskatchewan*, 265; Hind, *Narrative*, 1:256; Clouston, "Sketch of Journey," 4; "Nobles' Field Notes," in Hill Papers.

[9]Upham, *Glacial Lake Agassiz*, 413, 432, 433; Schultz, *Old Crow Wing Trail*, 20; Clouston, "Sketch of Journey," 5.

[10]Upham, *Minnesota Geographic Names*, 331; Clouston, "Sketch of Journey," 4, 5; Hind, *Narrative*, 1:256, 257.

[11]Clouston, "Sketch of Journey," 6; Hind, *Narrative*, 1:258; interview of the authors with J.H. Sylvestre, Crookston, May, 1977; *St. Paul Daily Press*, October 2, 1863; Minnesota, *Special Laws*, 1857–58, p. 183; *Nor'-Wester*, March 14, 1860.

[12]Holmquist and Brookins, *Major Historic Sites*, 164–166.

[13]Clouston, "Sketch of Journey," 6; Southesk, *Saskatchewan*, 24.

[14]Hind, *Narrative*, 1:258; Marble, in *Harper's New Monthly Magazine*, 22:320 (February, 1861); Schultz, *Old Crow Wing Trail*, 25, 26; *Nor'-Wester*, March 14, 1860.

[15]Clouston, "Sketch of Journey," 7, 9; Hind, *Narrative*, 1:258, 259.

[16]On the Link Trail, see Chapter 6. On the White Earth establishment, see Gerald R. Vizenor, comp., *Escorts to White Earth 1868 to 1968: 100 Year Reservation*, 133–144 (Minneapolis, 1968). For the route of the trails, see "Sources for the Maps," above.

[17]Southesk, *Saskatchewan*, 23; "Nobles' Field Notes," in Hill Papers; Clouston, "Sketch of Journey," 10.

[18]Clouston, "Sketch of Journey," 11, 12.

[19]Smith, "Report," 449; Belden, "Map of Survey and Location of Road" and "Map of Western Minnesota From Town 117 North to Sandhill River" — both in Minnesota State Archives; Alvin H. Wilcox, *A Pioneer History of Becker County Minnesota*, 219 (St. Paul, 1907). On the Link Trail, see Chapter 6, below.

[20]Southesk, *Saskatchewan*, 20; Clouston, "Sketch of Journey," 12, 13; "Nobles' Field Notes," in Hill Papers; Schultz, *Old Crow Wing Trail*, 21.

[21]Clouston, "Sketch of Journey," 12; *Nor'Wester*, March 14, 1860.

[22]*Nor'-Wester*, March 14, 1860; Hind, *Narrative*, 1:261, 262.

[23]Upham, *Minnesota Geographic Names*, 390; Nute, in *Minnesota History*. 11:373; *Nor'-Wester*, March 14, 1860; Larsen, "Minnesota Road System," 180. The Fisk Montana Expedition of 1863, which had traveled via Fort Ripley and the Woods Trail, went west from here through Dayton and Fort Abercrombie. For descriptions of the road, see Helen M. White, ed., *Ho! for the Gold Fields: Northern Overland Wagon Trains of the 1860s*, 86 (St. Paul, 1966); William H. Clandening, "Across the Plains in 1863–1865," in *North Dakota Historical Quarterly*, 2:251 (July, 1928).

[24]*Nor'-Wester*, March 14, 1860; Schultz, *Old Crow Wing Trail*, 22.

[25]Clouston, "Sketch of Journey," 14, 50; Hind, *Narrative*, 1:262; Schultz, *Old Crow Wing Trail*, 22; Marble, in *Harper's New Monthly Magazine*, 22:322; *Wadena Pioneer Journal*, December 15, 1927, Fiftieth Anniversary Number, Supplement, p. 2.

[26]Upham, *Minnesota Geographic Names*, 560; Hind, *Narrative*,

1:262; Benno Watrin, "Old Pembina Trail," undated memorandum in Publications Miscellaneous Files, in MHS Archives; Clouston, "Sketch of Journey," 16; Marble, in *Harper's New Monthly Magazine*, 22:322.

[27]Schultz, *Old Crow Wing Trail*, 22.

[28]Clouston, "Sketch of Journey," 17; *Nor'-Wester*, February 14, March 14, 1860. A private landowner near Motley has marked the trail where it crosses the access road to his house. The trail on his land is kept open by animals. Interview of the authors with Peter Card, Jr., Staples Historical Society, September, 1976.

[29]Douglas A. Birk, "A Revised Preliminary Report on the Chippewa Agency Sites, Cass County, Minnesota," November 8, 1972, Archaeology Department, MHS; Marble, in *Harper's New Monthly Magazine*, 22:322; interview of the authors with Carl Zapffe, October, 1976.

[30]*Minnesota Register* (St. Paul), April 27, 1849; Clouston, "Sketch of Journey," 17; Andrews, *Minnesota and Dacotah*, 67.

[31]For this and the paragraph below, see Schultz, *Old Crow Wing Trail*, 24; Upham, *Minnesota Geographic Names*, 155; Clouston, "Sketch of Journey," 17, 18; Andrews, *Minnesota and Dacotah*, 65–68; Holmquist and Brookins, *Major Historic Sites*, 71; Hallock, in *Harper's New Monthly Magazine*, 19:54.

[32]Clouston, "Sketch of Journey," 18; *Nor'-Wester*, February 14, 1860.

[33]Holmquist and Brookins, *Major Historic Sites*, 68–70; Andrews, *Minnesota and Dacotah*, 63, 64; Singley, *Old Government Roads*, 34.

[34]Singley, *Old Government Roads*, 33; Edward D. Neill *et al.*, *History of the Upper Mississippi Valley*, 587 (Minneapolis, 1881); Andrews, *Minnesota and Dacotah*, 83.

[35]For this and the paragraph below, see *Nor'-Wester*, February 14, 1860; Neill *et al.*, *Upper Mississippi Valley*, 587, 589; Andrews, *Minnesota and Dacotah*, 63, 140; Harold L. Fisher, *The Land Called Morrison*, 52 (2nd ed., St. Cloud, 1976); *Minnesota Register*, April 27, 1849; Singley, *Old Government Roads*, 33.

[36]Fisher, *Land Called Morrison*, 52; Singley, *Old Government Roads*, 32; Clouston, "Sketch of Journey," 18; Neill *et al.*, *Upper Mississippi Valley*, 368.

[37]Neill *et al.*, *Upper Mississippi Valley*, 343; Willard F. McCrea, *Sauk Rapids Centennial Celebration 1854–1954*, n.p. ([Sauk Rapids], 1954).

CHAPTER SIX / *The Middle Trail* / pages 69 to 80

SOURCES FOR THE MAPS

The U.S. land surveys of the section of Minnesota through which the Middle Trail ran were made over a 20-year period. The eastern sections near St. Cloud were surveyed as early as 1856, the western ones near Moorhead as late as the 1870s. The fact that the surveyors moved into the Sauk Valley so early meant that they recorded the old trail in great detail, but they went through before the stage road was established. Therefore, the eastern portions of this later route have been reconstructed here from other sources.

The surveyors' records of the Middle Trail are also haphazard; its route across an entire township is frequently not shown. The interpretation of such missing links is often crucial. Where similar gaps occurred in other chapters, the WPA Papers in the MHS were followed, but these maps were found to be inaccurate for the Middle Trail and they have not been relied upon here. Gaps were reconstructed from documentary or local sources where these existed. Where no sources could be found, the authors' conjectures are indicated by a dotted line.

The surveyors recorded only one complete trail running through Clay County, the river road to Georgetown, and a tiny section in the upper corner of T139N, R44W, of the Woods-Middle-Link Trail. This small, labeled section was extended by recourse to the extremely detailed but fragmentary maps of the Special Commissioners' Land Examination Books, 1871–78, in Great Northern Railway Company Records, MHS. The rest of the route through Clay County was reconstructed from "Map of Minnesota," Lake Superior and Puget Sound Company Records, in Northern Pacific Railway Company Records. Also consulted were Power, "McClung's Map of Minnesota"; Taintor Bros. & Merrill, "Map of the State of Minnesota" (New York, [1874]); Sewall and Iddings, "Sectional Map of the Surveyed Portion of Minnesota."

The section of the Link Trail through Becker and Mahnomen counties was complicated by an uncertainty in the route of the Woods Trail; see "Sources for the Maps," Chapter 5. Through Wilkin and Otter Tail counties the Link Trail was mapped by the state surveyors.

The trails along the Buffalo River have been filled in from the Special Commissioners' Land Examination Books, in Great Northern Railway Company Records. A. T. Andreas' *An Illustrated Historical Atlas of the State of Minnesota*, 181 (Chicago, 1874) has been used with care, for it is frequently misleading as to the routes of roads.

The trail through southern Wilkin County from the Bois de Sioux to Lightning Lake is not shown on the survey maps, but it was recorded in Isaac I. Stevens, "Sketch of the progress of the Northern Pacific Railroad Exploration up to the crossing of the Shayen River, July 4th 1853," in 33 Congress, 1 session, *Senate Executive Documents*, no. 29, map (serial 695). In Grant County, T130N, R43W, there is a gap in the surveys which has been resolved with the help of William M. Goetzinger of Elbow Lake. For the Fort Wadsworth Trail route through Pope County and the trail through T126N, R36–37W, see Gustave C. Torguson's reports, in Historical Markers and Monuments: Historic Trails, Pope County, WPA Papers; anonymous interview conducted by Edson Lundquist, August 31, 1938, in Pope County Historical Society. In Todd County the stage road was reconstructed by Irene Delsing of Osakis.

The route of the Fort Wadsworth Trail in Stearns County is conjectural. The stage road and the trail in T125N, R34–35W, were clarified by Glanville Smith of Cold Spring. The course of the stage road from New Munich to St. Joseph is from Helen M. Latterell, Enoch E. Bjuge, and Glanville Smith, "The St. Cloud Daily Times' Centennial Year History Map of Stearns, Benton, and Sherburne Counties" (St. Cloud, 1949). On Stearns County trails, see also Roy D. Fentress, "Red River Trail," February 28, 1936, in Historical Markers and Monuments: Historic Trails, Stearns County, WPA Papers; Glanville Smith, "St. Cloud As It Was In 1856," in Gertrude B. Gove, ed., *St. Cloud Centennial Souvenir Album* ([St. Cloud], 1956).

[1] *St. Paul Daily Pioneer and Democrat*, July 6, 1859.

[2] Larsen, "Minnesota Road System," 180; *St. Cloud Visiter*, July 22, 1858.

[3] For this and the paragraph below, see *St. Cloud Democrat*, October 21, 1858, June 2, 1859 (quotations on Patten); Blakeley and George C. Tanner, "History of Fort Ripley, 1849 to 1859," in *Minnesota Historical Collections*, 8:54, 10:199; *St. Paul Daily Pioneer and Democrat*, July 6, 9, 1859.

[4] Hall, *Wadsworth Trail*, 5–7. On the routes, see "Sources for the Maps," above. The future route of the Fort Wadsworth Trail from Glenwood to Sauk Centre was followed in August, 1863, by a company of soldiers traveling east via the old trail. At the time this short cut was not considered a branch of the Red River Trail. See L. W. Collins, "The Expedition Against the Sioux Indians in 1863, Under General Henry H. Sibley," in Edward D. Neill, ed., *Glimpses of the Nation's Struggle*, second series, 202 (St. Paul, 1890). On the use of the Fort Wadsworth Trail as a stage road, see p. 77.

[5] The term "blind road" refers to a track so faint it can only be seen from a distance. For this and the paragraph below, see Kane, Holmquist, and Gilman, eds., *Long Expeditions*, 180; Campbell, in *North Dakota Historical Quarterly*, 1:36; Smith, "Report," 428; "Knute Steenerson's Recollections: The Story of a Pioneer," in *Minnesota History*, 4:150 (August–November, 1921). The U.S. township surveyors, going through the area in 1872, noted the existence of a trail along the east bank of the Red from the mouth of the Wild Rice to within 12 miles of the Red Lake River's mouth, but did not mark it as "Pembina Trail."

[6] On the route of the Link Trail, see "Sources for the Maps," above. Its northern portion is shown in Chapter 5. See also Cavileer, "Red River Valley in 1851," pp. 1, 2, 5; Smith, "Report," 448; Holmes, "Map of Reconnaisance of Road," National Archives Record Group 77; Iddings, "Continuation of Reconnoissance," in Belden, "Field notes," 85, Hill Papers; *St. Cloud Democrat*, July 28, 1859; Morris, ed., *Old Rail Fence Corners*, map.

A detachment of Major Edwin A. C. Hatch's battalion started for Georgetown on the route of the Link Trail in 1863; see C. W. Nash, "Narrative of Hatch's Independent Battalion of Cavalry," in *Minnesota in the Civil and Indian Wars 1861–1865*, 1:596 (St. Paul, 1890). Another link with the Woods Trail may have existed; Major Woods mentioned a route which he thought joined the Woods Trail near Otter Tail Lake. See Woods, *Report*, 14. On Pope's manuscript maps, however, this link is shown taking off from the main trail at Elbow Lake, which suggests it may have been the same Link Trail that Smith and Cavileer followed. See "Field Notes of Capt. Pope's Expedition," in Hill Papers. On the rumor of a "middle road" through Beltrami and Fisher, see Chapter 5, note 3.

[7] For this and the paragraph below, see *St. Paul Daily Pioneer and Democrat*, September 10, 1859; *Clay Sunday Press* (Moorhead), January 10, p. 6, January 17, p. 2, January 24, p. 2, 1948; Blakeley, in *Minnesota Historical Collections*, 8:54; Viscount Milton and W. B. Cheadle, *The North-West Passage by Land*, 18 (London, 1865).

[8] *Alexandria Post*, July 24, 1869; *St. Paul Daily Pioneer and Democrat*, September 10, 1859.

[9] Mrs. L. E. Jones, "Our Town in Early Days: A History of Breckenridge," n.p., typescript in MHS; *St. Cloud Visiter*, July 22, 1858; *Nor'-Wester*, February 28, 1860; Scudder, *Winnipeg Country*, 15.

[10] *St. Paul Weekly Pioneer and Democrat*, March 3, 1859. The Old Crossing here mentioned should not be confused with the better-known Woods Trail ford of the Red Lake River described in Chapter 5.

[11] For this and the paragraph below, see Pope, *Report*, 23; Woods, *Report*, 15; Hallock, in *Harper's New Monthly Magazine*, 19:44; Cavileer, "Red River Valley in 1851," 4.

[12] For this and the paragraph below, see Woods, *Report*, 15; *St. Paul Daily Pioneer and Democrat*, July 6, 1859; Pope, *Report*, 23;

Bond, *Minnesota*, 260; Wharncliffe Diary, 27; interview of the authors with William M. Goetzinger, August, 1976. Other expeditions that followed the trail to the Bois de Sioux were led by Isaac I. Stevens and C. F. Smith.

[13]Smith, "Report," 440; Woods, *Report*, 14; Stevens, *Narrative*, 49, 51; Willoughby M. Babcock, ed., "A Dragoon on the March to Pembina in 1849," in *Minnesota History*, 8:68 (March, 1927).

[14]For this and the paragraph below, see Woods, *Report*, 10; Hallock and Marble, in *Harper's New Monthly Magazine*, 19:42, 21:298.

[15]For this and the paragraph below, see Woods, *Report*, 12, 13; Bond, *Minnesota*, 257; Stevens, *Narrative*, 47, 48.

[16]Woods, *Report*, 12; Pope, *Report*, 19; Andrews, *Minnesota and Dacotah*, 150; Stevens, *Narrative*, 46, 48. For this and the paragraph below, see Wharncliffe Diary, 19–22.

[17]*St. Paul Daily Pioneer and Democrat*, September 9, 1859.

[18]For this and the paragraph below, see *St. Cloud Democrat*, September 30, October 7, 28, 1858; J. H. Bond, "A Journey to the Forks of the Red River of the North in 1860," in *North Dakota Historical Quarterly*, 6:235 (April, 1932); *St. Paul Daily Pioneer and Democrat*, September 8, 1859; Samuel R. Bond Journal, 14, in Ipswich (Mass.) Historical Society, typescript in MHS.

[19]*St. Paul Daily Pioneer and Democrat*, September 6, 1859; Hallock and Marble, in *Harper's New Monthly Magazine*, 19:42, 21:303.

[20]William M. Goetzinger, "Pomme de Terre: A Frontier Outpost in Grant County," in *Minnesota History*, 38:63 (June, 1962); *Daily Minnesotian* (St. Paul), July 6, 1860; Milton and Cheadle, *North-West Passage*, 17; *Nor'-Wester*, February 28, 1860. Chippewa station was in T129N, R39W, sec. 5.

[21]Bond, in *North Dakota Historical Quarterly*, 6:234; Hallock and Marble, in *Harper's New Monthly Magazine*, 19:42, 21:303.

[22]Hallock and Marble, in *Harper's New Monthly Magazine*, 19:42, 21:300, 302; *St. Paul Daily Pioneer and Democrat*, July 8, 1859; *Alexandria Post*, August 7, 1869.

[23]The early road through the southern corners of Douglas and Todd counties was described by Christopher C. Andrews in *St. Cloud Democrat*, September 16, 1858. On the route via Maple and Leven lakes, see *Alexandria Post*, May 5, 1869; *St. Cloud Democrat*, September 23, 1858. On the Pope County trails, see Daisy E. Hughes, *Builders of Pope County*, 16 ([Glenwood, 1930]).

[24]*Sauk Centre Herald*, November 5, 1868; *Alexandria Post*, June 26, 1869; Marion H. Herriot, ed., "Through Minnesota to the Canadian West in 1869," in *Minnesota History*, 24:333 (December, 1943). In 1858 the township surveyors labeled the section in T125N, R34–35W, "Red River trail," indicating it was already in use by oxcarts at that time.

[25]*St. Paul Daily Pioneer and Democrat*, July 7, 1859; Howard S. Brode, ed., "Diary of Dr. Augustus J. Thibodo of the Northwest Exploring Expedition, 1859," in *Pacific Northwest Quarterly*, 31:295 (July, 1940); White, ed., *Ho! for the Gold Fields*, 52; Marble, in *Harper's New Monthly Magazine*, 21:300; *Alexandria Post*, October 14, 1868, May 5, 1869.

[26]For this and the paragraph below, see *Nor'-Wester*, February 28, 1860; *St. Paul Daily Pioneer and Democrat*, July 6, 1859; Bertha L. Heilbron, "Edwin Whitefield: Settlers' Artist," in *Minnesota History*, 40:69–71 (Summer, 1966); Bond, in *North Dakota Historical Quarterly*, 6:234; *Daily Minnesotian*, June 22, 1860. Two facts confuse this stretch: some travelers called the Ashley River the Sauk, and the early townsite of Sauk Centre was on the east side of the river, not the west as it is now.

[27]*St. Paul Daily Pioneer and Democrat*, July 6, 1859; Glanville Smith to the authors, August 27, 1976.

[28]Both Marble and Joseph A. Wheelock, who traveled the stage road in 1859, omitted any mention of the Winnebago Crossing, claiming that they forded the river three times, not four. This may have been an oversight; not only did later travelers invariably cross the river at this point, but Russell Blakeley, who traveled just ahead of Marble and Wheelock in 1859, mentioned the crossing. For this and the paragraph below, see Blakeley, in *Minnesota Historical Collections*, 8:50; White, ed., *Ho! for the Gold Fields*, 51; Marble, in *Harper's New Monthly Magazine*, 21:299; *Alexandria Post*, September 4, 1869; Mitchell, *History of Stearns County*, 1:443; *St. Cloud Democrat*, January 6, 1859; Glanville Smith to the authors, August 27, 1976; *St. Paul Daily Pioneer and Democrat*, July 6, 1859. The belt of timber that obstructed traffic is visible on the state survey maps.

[29]*St. Cloud Democrat*, September 9, 1858; Hallock, in *Harper's New Monthly Magazine*, 18:617, 19:38; *St. Paul Daily Pioneer and Democrat*, July 6, 1859.

[30]*Weekly Minnesotian*, November 7, 1857; Woods, *Report*, 10; Stevens, *Narrative*, 41, 45. That both branches of the trail between Richmond and Cold Spring were used in the early days is indicated by the fact that Governor Ramsey's party seems to have followed the more northerly route in 1851, according to Glanville Smith to the authors, August 27, 1976, while Edwin Whitefield wrote in the *Minnesotian*, cited above, of following the route closer to the river in 1857.

[31]*St. Cloud Democrat*, August 19, 1858; Bond, *Minnesota*, 256; Hallock, in *Harper's New Monthly Magazine*, 18:616; Bond, in *North Dakota Historical Quarterly*, 6:233; Woods, *Report*, 11; Pope, *Report*, 18. Examples of early travelers who bypassed St. Cloud included the Woods-Pope expedition and Wharncliffe.

[32]For this and the paragraphs below, see *The Red River Trail: Souvenir of the dedication of a monument marking the trail at Waite's Crossing, Saturday, November 11, 1950*, n.p., pamphlet in MHS; *St. Paul Daily Pioneer and Democrat*, July 6, 1859; *St. Cloud Visiter*, June 17, 1858; Hallock, in *Harper's New Monthly Magazine*, 18:613; Mae Atwood, ed., *In Rupert's Land: Memoirs of Walter Traill*, 190, 192 (Toronto and Montreal, 1970); Woods, *Report*, 21.

CHAPTER SEVEN / *The Metropolitan Trail* / pages 81 to 87

SOURCES FOR THE MAPS

The land between St. Paul and Sauk Rapids was surveyed in the years 1847–50, when the Red River Trail was a well-traveled route but before the military road was built. The Metropolitan Trail shown on the accompanying maps is thus based entirely on the U.S. land surveys in the Minnesota Secretary of State's office, but the military road (shown by a dotted line) is based on the maps in Singley, *Old Government Roads*, 29–31.

[1]*St. Anthony Express*, July 14, 1855; *Nor'-Wester*, February 14, 1860; *Minnesota Democrat*, August 26, 1851.

[2]Singley, *Old Government Roads*, 25, 30, 31; "Field Notes of Capt. Pope's expedition," 2–5, in Hill Papers; *Anoka County Union*

(Anoka), July 8, 1931, p. 1; Andrews, *Minnesota and Dacotah*, 59; Bond, *Minnesota*, 223.

[3]*The Red River Trail: Souvenir of the dedication of a monument marking the trail at Waite's Crossing*, n.p.; F. W. Lander to Isaac I. Stevens, May 22, 1853, in 33 Congress, 1 session, *Senate Executive Documents*, no. 29, p. 25; *Minnesota Register*, April 27, 1849; *St. Cloud Daily Journal-Press*, November 26, 1927, sec. 2, p. 1. The route that the stage company tried to promote via Clearwater ran through Maine Prairie to Cold Spring on the Middle Trail, bypassing St. Cloud. For its route, see Silas Chapman, "Chapman's New Sectional Map of Minnesota" (Milwaukee, 1856). On the St. Cloud ferries, see Chapter 6.

[4]William B. Mitchell, "St. Cloud in the Territorial Period," in *Minnesota Historical Collections*, 12:646 (1908); *Weekly Minnesotian*, November 14, 1857; *St. Cloud Visiter*, December 24, 1857.

[5]*Minnesota Democrat*, August 26, 1851; Pope, *Report*, 16; Neill et al., *Upper Mississippi Valley*, 325.

[6]For this and the paragraph below, see Hallock, in *Harper's New Monthly Magazine*, 18:609; Singley, *Old Government Roads*, 30, 31; *Weekly Minnesotian*, November 14, 1857; Andrews, *Minnesota and Dacotah*, 59. The earlier variant of the Red River Trail which kept close to the Mississippi was brought to the authors' attention by Elaine Anderson of the Sherburne County Historical Society. This seems to be the route Robert Clouston followed in 1846. Pope in 1849 followed the more inland trail, but he marked an "Old Road" taking off from it at Big Lake and joining it again a few miles south of Sauk Rapids. See Clouston, "Sketch of Journey," 19, 20; "Field Notes of Capt. Pope's expedition," 4, 5, in Hill Papers.

[7]Hallock, in *Harper's New Monthly Magazine*, 18:610; Andrews, *Minnesota and Dacotah*, 60; *Minnesota Democrat*, August 26, 1851; Neill et al., *Upper Mississippi Valley*, 295, 315; *Weekly Minnesotian*, November 14, 1857; *St. Cloud Visiter*, December 24, 1857.

[8]For this and the paragraph below, see Clouston, "Sketch of Journey," 20; Singley, *Old Government Roads*, 30, 31; Neill et al., *Upper Mississippi Valley*, 296; *Weekly Minnesotian*, November 14, 1857; Bond, in *North Dakota Historical Quarterly*, 6:233; Holmquist and Brookins, *Major Historic Sites*, 59; *Minnesota Democrat*, August 26, 1851; Andrews, *Minnesota and Dacotah*, 60.

[9]*Anoka County Union*, July 8, 1931, p. 1, June 25, 1976, Bicentennial sec. 6, p. [4]; *Minnesota Democrat*, August 26, 1851; *Minnesota Register*, April 27, 1849; Singley, *Old Government Roads*, 30. Samuel R. Bond, traveling with the Fisk expedition of 1862, went north from Minneapolis to Anoka on the west side of the Mississippi; there are also numerous sources indicating that Red River carts could be seen on the approximate route of Lyndale Avenue North in Minneapolis. See Bond Journal, 4, typescript in MHS; Morris, ed., *Old Rail Fence Corners*, 50, 67.

[10]Upham, *Minnesota Geographic Names*, 22; *Weekly Minnesotian*, November 14, 1857; Smith, "Report," 439; *Minnesota Democrat*, August 26, 1851; Gen Rasmussen, "History of Fridley, Minnesota," 14, 17–19, typescript in MHS; Historic Sites Survey, Anoka County, in WPA Papers; Andrews, *Minnesota and Dacotah*, 59.

[11]For this and the paragraph below, see Andrews, *Minnesota and Dacotah*, 59; *Minnesota Democrat*, August 26, 1851; Singley, *Old Government Roads*, 28–30; Morris, ed., *Old Rail Fence Corners*, 37, 89; Clouston, "Sketch of Journey," 20.

[12]For this and the paragraph below, see Singley, *Old Government Roads*, 28; *Minnesota Democrat*, August 26, 1851; *Weekly Minnesotian*, November 14, 1857; Clouston, "Sketch of Journey," 20; Pope, *Report*, 16.

[13]*St. Paul Dispatch*, October 30, 1945, p. 13, December 12, 1956, p. 69; Edward D. Neill and J. Fletcher Williams, *History of Ramsey County and the City of St. Paul*, 259, 262, 268 (Minneapolis, 1881). The Roseville along the trail must have been the one mentioned by Joseph A. Wheelock in *St. Paul Daily Pioneer and Democrat*, June 23, 1859, as the first camping place of the Nobles expedition. It may also have given rise to persistent rumors that a Red River Trail ran through present Roseville, some distance to the north. A road from St. Paul through present Roseville was not in fact constructed all the way to Anoka until at least 1861; see *St. Paul Daily Press*, April 5, 1861.

[14]For this and the paragraph below, see *Wisconsin Herald* (Lancaster), July 31, 1847; Williams, *History of St. Paul*, 305; *St. Anthony Express*, July 14, 1855.

[15]Clouston, "Sketch of Journey," 21.

[16]August[e] L. Larpenteur, "Recollections of the City and People of St. Paul, 1843–1898," and Josiah B. Chaney, "Early Bridges and Changes of the Land and Water Surface in the City of St. Paul," in *Minnesota Historical Collections*, 9:385 (1901), 12:145 (1908); *St. Anthony Express*, July 14, 1855; *Nor'-Wester*, January 14, 1860.

[17]For this and the paragraph below, see Clouston, "Sketch of Journey," 48; interview of Hyacinthe Villeneuve by Mrs. John Mahon, typescript in biographies file, Libby Papers; *Wisconsin Herald*, July 31, 1847.

[18]Garrioch Journal, 1843–47, p. 79; Atwood, ed., *In Rupert's Land*, 29, 189.

[19]Williams, *History of St. Paul*, 307, 308.

INDEX

Picture Credits

We wish to thank the institutions in the list below for graciously granting permission to use pictures in their collections.

pages 1, 27, 30, 35 — Public Archives of Canada, Ottawa

pages 3, 19 bottom, 34 — Manitoba Provincial Archives, Winnipeg

page 8 — British Columbia Provincial Archives, Victoria

pages 10, 11, 13, 19 top, 25 (B. F. Upton, photographer), 39, 41, 43, 49 (Whitney's Gallery, St. Paul), 58, 63, 69 (Whitney's Gallery), 80, 81 (B. F. Upton, photographer), 86 (B. J. Sturtevant, photographer), 87, 70 (Charles T. Cavileer Papers) — Minnesota Historical Society

page 15 — James Carnegie, Earl of Southesk, *Saskatchewan and the Rocky Mountains*, 23 (Edinburgh, 1875)

pages 21, 28, 31, 38, 59, 66, 73 — [Manton Marble], "To Red River & Beyond," in *Harper's New Monthly Magazine*, 21:298, 307, 587 (August, October, 1860), 22:208, 309, 319, 321 (February, 1861)

pages 44, 74, 78 — Drawings by John Mix Stanley, in Isaac I. Stevens, *Narrative . . . of Explorations for a Route for a Pacific Railroad . . . from St. Paul to Puget Sound*, plates 3, 5, 7, in 36 Congress, 1 session, *House Executive Documents*, no. 56 (serial 1054)

page 46 — Drawing by Samuel Seymour engraved by J. Hill, in William H. Keating, *Narrative of an Expedition to the Source of St. Peter's River . . . under the Command of Stephen H. Long*, 2:frontispiece (Philadelphia, 1824)

page 51 — Newberry Library, Chicago

page 55 — Blue Earth County Historical Society, Mankato

page 67 — [Charles Hallock], "The Red River Trail," in *Harper's New Monthly Magazine*, 19:47 (June, 1859)

page 68 — [Willard F. McCrea], *Sauk Rapids Centennial Celebration 1854–1954*, n.p. ([Sauk Rapids, 1954])

page 83 — Minneapolis Historical Collection, Minneapolis Public Library

Printed in the USA
CPSIA information can be obtained
at www.ICGtesting.com
JSHW060239160824
68134JS00058BA/2659